# Video Production for School Library Media Specialists:

## Communication and Production Techniques

By Terry McConnell & Harry W. Sprouse

A Publication of THE BOOK REPORT & LIBRARY TALK
Professional Growth Series

Linworth Publishing, Inc.
Worthington, Ohio

**Library of Congress Cataloging-in-Publication Data**

McConnell, Terry, 1947-
    Great communication with video production in school libraries / by Terry McConnell and Harry W. Sprouse
        p. cm. – (Professional growth series)
    Includes bibliographical references (p. ).
    ISBN 0-938865-95-1
    1. School libraries--Activity programs--United States. 2. Media programs (Education)--United States. 3. Video recordings--Production and direction. 4. Television in education. I. Sprouse, Harry W., 1946-  II. Title.  III. Series.

Z675.S3 M325 2000
027.8--dc21                                                                                          00-044819

Published by Linworth Publishing, Inc.
480 East Wilson Bridge Road, Suite L
Worthington, Ohio 43085

Copyright © 2000 by Linworth Publishing, Inc.

Series Information:
    From The Professional Growth Series

All rights reserved. Reproduction of this book in whole or in part is prohibited without permission of the publisher.

ISBN 0-938865-95-1

5 4 3 2 1

# About the Authors

Terry McConnell

Harry W. Sprouse

A library media specialist at Mt. Vernon High School in Fairfax County, Virginia, Terry McConnell uses student video and multimedia production and desktop publishing to promote reading, writing, and research. He has also worked as a social studies teacher and school librarian in middle schools.

Terry has contributed numerous articles to THE BOOK REPORT, TECHNOLOGY CONNECTION, *Media and Methods, Cable in the Classroom,* and other journals. He graduated with a B.A. from DePauw University and an M.E. from Temple University and lives in Alexandria, Virginia.

According to Harry Sprouse, "Everyone has a great story to tell." Stories have been told and recorded since the beginning of time, and people have always used stories to teach and deliver messages. This is what great communication is all about.

Harry has worked as an elementary, middle and secondary library media specialist for 26 years in Virginia's public schools. He served as assistant director at the Washington Office of the American Library Association in Washington, D.C., and spent six months as a special librarian for the Department of Defense library in the Nuclear Defense Agency in Virginia.

Harry has contributed articles to the Virginia Education Association, Virginia Educational Media Association, Linworth Publishing, and Fairfax County Public Schools publications. This is his first book published by Linworth Publishing.

A member of Phi Delta Kappa educational fraternity, Harry graduated with a B.S. from James Madison University and an M.L.S. from the University of South Carolina. He lives in Springfield, Virginia, and is a library media specialist with his co-author, Terry McConnell, at Mt. Vernon High School in Fairfax County, Virginia.

# Acknowledgements

Terry McConnell dedicates this book to his wife, Marla McConnell, who turned his life from black and white into color. Many thanks go to his son, Daniel Reisch, for helping with this book's glossary.

Grateful appreciation goes to:

His sons Matt McConnell and Jason Reisch and his daughter Melissa McConnell for their support.

His family—Ruth Anne McConnell, H. John McConnell, Theresa G. McConnell, Henry and Marce Damm, Dorothy Rudolph, Albert and Estelle Kahn, Linda Kahn, Chris Gordon, Beth, Michael, Na'ama, Alon and Na'or Malichi and Mary Culhane.

His friends Jeff and Diane Salton, Karl Johnson, Floyd and Angie Godfrey, Howard and Mindy Bain, Dana van Bever, Judith A. Green, Jim Fitzgerald and Paul and Melissa Winkel.

The school librarians he's been lucky enough to work with over the years—Edith Ashworth, Linda Hunt, Pam Spencer and Janet Smith. The school librarian he works with every day, Harry Sprouse.

Harry has helped Terry define what a partnership between school librarians is all about. We have a unique working relationship with no agenda other than educating our students. Harry says, "We expect the best from our students; when our students are successful, we're successful."

His secretaries who for the last 27 years have done their best to keep him organized, Maureen McGuire, Helen Tipa, Barbara Griffith and Barbara Stecher.

The people who helped edit this book—Lainge Bailey, Marlene Woo-Lun, Carol Simpson, Judi Repman, Betty Morris, Lesley S.J. Farmer, and Wendy Medvetz.

The members of the Mt. Vernon High School Video Production Hall of Fame: Tony Perkins, Eric Cannavaro, Joe Pattisall, Darnley Hodge, Mike Guidotti, Frank Jackson, and Shawn Brayboy. These former students inspired him. A man who taught him a lot about video production, Augie Beasley.

Recent students who have taught him so much about TV production in the digital age, Wes Hunt and Brandon Roberts.

His colleagues at Mt. Vernon High School who have supported him over the years, including Dave Petruzzi, Scott Saylor, Debbie Berzins, Paul Shalonis, Jan Mosher, Dr. Calanthia Tucker, Dr. Roni Washington, Helena Bratten, Cindy Preito, Dana Bedden, John Gretz, Kathleen Pablo, and Dr. Cathy Crocker.

Harry Sprouse would like to thank his mother, Mrs. Rosa Mae Skinner, who instilled in him the desire to get an education and graduate from high school, even though she did not attend school beyond the sixth grade. Mrs. Skinner would say, "Get an education and no one will ever be able to take it away from you." Harry remembers the times when their furniture was repossessed and the lean years when his parents had trouble paying their bills and raising seven children. Mrs. Skinner also told her son, "Getting an education is the way to becoming anything you want to be." She believed that an education was the only thing standing in the way of improving his standard of living.

Today, Harry has a high school degree, a master's degree, including advanced graduate studies, and will, in five years, complete a 30-year career as a library media specialist.

# Table of Contents

| | | |
|---|---|---|
| ABOUT THE AUTHORS | | i |
| ACKNOWLEDGEMENTS | | ii |
| PREFACE | | x |
| PART I. | GREAT COMMUNICATION | 1 |
| CHAPTER 1. | COMMUNICATION THEORY AND VISUAL LITERACY | 3 |
| | Communication Theory | 3 |
| | Visual Literacy | 5 |
| CHAPTER 2. | SCRIPTWRITING | 7 |
| | Twenty-two Practical Pointers for Visual Design | 8 |
| | Writing the Script | 18 |
| | Basic Scriptwriting Checklist | 22 |
| | Advanced Scriptwriting Checklist | 22 |
| | Storyboarding | 23 |
| PART II. | GREAT COMMUNICATION WITH VIDEO EQUIPMENT | 25 |
| CHAPTER 3. | AUDIO AND VIDEO PLUGS AND JACKS | 27 |
| | Audio and Video Plugs and Jacks Checklist | 31 |
| CHAPTER 4. | THE CAMERA | 33 |
| | Camcorders | 34 |
| | Shooting an Interview | 36 |
| | White Balance, High-Speed Shutter, and Macro | 38 |
| | Depth of Field | 38 |
| | Display | 41 |
| | Back Light Function | 41 |
| | Label Tapes and Pull Tabs | 41 |
| | Shut-Down Procedures | 42 |
| | Camcorder Checklist | 42 |
| | Camera Operator's Checklist | 43 |
| | S-VHS Camcorders, Palmcorders, Digital Cameras, DVDs, and HDTVs | 44 |
| | Digital Camera for Recording Motion and Animation Checklist | 47 |
| CHAPTER 5. | LIGHTING | 49 |
| | Lighting Kits and Lamps | 50 |
| | Bounce Light | 50 |
| | Dimmers, Spots, and Barn Doors | 51 |
| | Types of Light | 51 |
| | Contrast Ratio | 53 |
| | Shooting Outdoors | 53 |
| | Lighting Checklist | 54 |
| | Sunny Day Shoot Checklist | 55 |

# Table of Contents continued

**Chapter 6. Linking Computer and Video** .................................................. 57
    Video Cards and Video-Related Peripheral Devices ................................. 58
    Putting a Still Video Image into the Computer ......................................... 58
    Putting a Visual Computer Presentation on Videotape ............................. 59
    Putting a Visual and Audio Computer Presentation on Videotape ............ 61
    Putting a Computer Presentation on Videotape while Adding Narration ...... 61
    Adding Motion Video to a *PowerPoint* Presentation on a Computer ............ 63

**Chapter 7. Switchers and Mixers** ............................................................ 65
    Video Switchers ......................................................................................... 66
    A/V Digital Mixer ........................................................................................ 66
    Video Input Switching Checklist ................................................................ 69
    Chroma Key with the A/V Digital Mixer Checklist ..................................... 69
    Strobe Effect on the A/V Digital Mixer Checklist ...................................... 70
    Split Screen on the A/V Digital Mixer Checklist ........................................ 70
    Audio Mixers .............................................................................................. 71
    Audio Mixer Checklist ................................................................................ 71

**Chapter 8. Video Editing** ......................................................................... 73
    Types of Video Editing .............................................................................. 74
    In-Camera Editing Checklist ...................................................................... 75
    Simple Two VCR Electronic Editing Checklist .......................................... 76
    Editing Using a Video Editor (No Edit Controller) Checklist ..................... 77
    Editing Using a Video (Edit Controller System) Checklist ........................ 80
    Digital Editing Using a DraCo Casablanca Digital Video Editor Checklist ...... 82
    Digital Video Editing Done on a Computer Using Digital Editing
       Software Checklist ............................................................................... 83

**Chapter 9. Presenting A Videotape** ........................................................ 85
    TV Receivers .............................................................................................. 86
    In-School Cable TV System ....................................................................... 87
    TV Receiver/Monitor .................................................................................. 88
    Data or Video Projector ............................................................................. 89
    Considerations when Presenting Video to Large Groups ........................ 89
    Presenting a Videotape Checklist ............................................................. 91

**Chapter 10. The TV Studio for the School TV News Show** .................. 93
    Things in Common for Simple and Complex TV Studios ......................... 94
    Simple TV Studio ....................................................................................... 95
    Simple TV Studio Equipment Needed Checklist ....................................... 97
    Complex TV Studio .................................................................................... 98
    The Future for School TV News Shows .................................................... 104

# Table of Contents continued

    Complex TV Studio for School News Show Checklist ............................. 105
    TV Studio Safety Checklist ................................................................... 106
    Complex TV Studio Equipment Needed Checklist ................................. 107

**CHAPTER 11. VIDEO PRODUCTION TROUBLESHOOTING** ................................ 109
    Video Production Troubleshooting Checklist ........................................ 109

**PART III.**     **GREAT COMMUNICATION AND GREAT INSTRUCTION WITH VIDEO PRODUCTION IN SCHOOL LIBRARIES** ................................................................... 113

**CHAPTER 12. LEARNING, INSTRUCTIONAL DESIGN, RESEARCH, AND VIDEO PRODUCTION** ......... 115
    Instructional Design ............................................................................ 116
    The P.I.E. Model for Instructional Design............................................. 117
    Research Findings to Justify the Use of Student Video
       and Multimedia Production ............................................................ 118
    It's Time for P.I.E........................................................................... 120
    Instructional Design for a Video Production Project Checklist ................ 120
    Video Project Evaluation Form ............................................................ 122
    Video Product Evaluation Form ........................................................... 123

**CHAPTER 13. TRAINING STUDENTS FOR VIDEO PRODUCTION** ........................... 125
    How to Select the Students Who Will Produce the Video ...................... 125
    Develop a Video Production Training System ....................................... 127
    Set Standards, Rewards, and Expectations .......................................... 127
    Let the Students Train You ................................................................. 128
    Create Training Partnerships .............................................................. 128

**CHAPTER 14. WORKING WITH STUDENT TALENT** ............................................ 129
    Selecting the Talent ............................................................................ 129
    Cueing the Talent ............................................................................... 131
    Things Talent Must Know ................................................................... 132
    Talent Checklist ................................................................................. 132
    Interviewing Techniques Checklist ...................................................... 133

**CHAPTER 15. ORGANIZING THE SCHOOL TV NEWS SHOW** ............................... 135
    Find an Audience ............................................................................... 135
    Taped, Live, or a Combination of Both ................................................. 135
    Daily, Weekly, or Monthly .................................................................. 136
    Organize a Video Production Club to Produce Your Show ..................... 136
    Find Another Teacher to Teach a Video Production Class ..................... 137
    Work with Different Classes and Teachers to Produce the Show ............ 137
    Schedule the News Show into the School Day...................................... 137
    Simple TV Studio Jobs....................................................................... 138
    Complex TV Studio Jobs .................................................................... 139

# Table of Contents continued

  Create a Spreadsheet for Job Assignments ............................................. 142
  Prepare for No Shows ............................................................................. 143
  Help Teachers Hook Up to Your Show .................................................. 143
  Have a Camcorder Lending Policy for Students ................................... 144
  Organizing the School TV News Show Checklist .................................. 145
  Daily Production Checklist ..................................................................... 146

**CHAPTER 16. THE INSTRUCTIONAL VALUE OF THE SCHOOL TV NEWS SHOW** ................... 149
  The News Show Should Promote the School Library ........................... 149
  Producing the Show Benefits Students .................................................. 151
  Keep the News Show Brief ..................................................................... 151
  Create Partnerships with Teachers ......................................................... 151
  Introduce the Notion of Service .............................................................. 152
  Strive for Excellence, but Expect Mistakes ............................................ 152
  Get Feedback .......................................................................................... 152
  Commitment to Excellence Evaluation Checklist .................................. 153
  Survey Questions for Students and Staff Regarding School TV News Show 154

**CHAPTER 17. THE LIBRARY MEDIA CENTER ORIENTATION VIDEO** ..................................... 155
  What Do Teachers Want in the Library Orientation Video? .................. 155
  Show the Orientation Video Before a Class Comes to the Library ........... 156
  Library Orientation Video Checklist ...................................................... 157

**CHAPTER 18. STUDENT-PRODUCED VIDEO BOOK TALKS** ................................................ 159
  Work with a Teacher to Identify Book Titles ......................................... 159
  Book Talk Statement .............................................................................. 160
  Student-Produced Video Book Talks Checklist ..................................... 162

**CHAPTER 19. THE COMPUTER/VIDEO RESEARCH PROJECT** ............................................. 163
  Teach Research Skills without Doing a Research Paper ....................... 163
  Start a Partnership with a Teacher ......................................................... 163
  Student-Produced Videos Are Visible Outcomes of Teaching and Learning... 164
  Provide Structure for Groups .................................................................. 164
  Creating the Final Presentation ............................................................... 165
  Computer/Video Research Project Checklist ......................................... 172

**CHAPTER 20. VIDEO ANIMATION PROJECTS** .................................................................. 175
  Computer Animation Software ............................................................... 175
  VHS or Digital Camera to Analog Video Editor .................................... 175
  VHS or Digital Camera to Computer ...................................................... 176
  Digital Camera with Animation Setting ................................................. 176
  Animation Using Drawings or Cut-Outs and Claymation ..................... 176
  VHS Camcorder to *PowerPoint* to Video Editor Animation Checklist ......... 177
  Digital Camera to Video Editor Checklist .............................................. 179

# Table of Contents continued

**PART IV: ORGANIZING FOR GREAT COMMUNICATION WITH VIDEO PRODUCTION IN SCHOOL LIBRARIES** .................................................................................................... 181

**CHAPTER 21. COPYRIGHT AND OTHER PERMISSION** ............................................................ 183
    Face-to-Face Instruction ................................................................................................ 183
    Guidelines for Using Copyrighted Materials in a Multimedia
        or Video Production ............................................................................................... 184
    Obtain Music and Sound Effects that Grant Copyright Permission for
        Use in Video Productions ...................................................................................... 184
    Copyright for Visual Materials ...................................................................................... 185
    Family Permission for a Student to Appear in a Video .............................................. 186

**CHAPTER 22. VIDEO PRODUCTION OUTSIDE SCHOOL—MEDIA FESTIVALS AND CABLE TV** ......... 187
    Media Festivals ............................................................................................................. 187
    Local Cable TV Stations ............................................................................................... 188
    Student Media Festivals Checklist................................................................................ 189

**CHAPTER 23. THE VIDEO PRODUCTION HALL OF FAME** ....................................................... 191
    Careers in Video and Multimedia Production ............................................................. 191
    Validate Former Students Who Excel in the Field of Media Production ...... 192
    Video Production Hall of Fame Checklist.................................................................... 192

**CHAPTER 24. FUNDING YOUR PROGRAM THROUGH GRANTS** ................................................. 193
    List of Grant Sources ..................................................................................................... 194
    Create a Grant Writing Partnership with a Teacher ................................................... 195
    Plan Your Grant to Solve an Educational Problem ..................................................... 195
    Grant Writing is Competitive ........................................................................................ 195
    Get Inside of the Mind of the Person Judging the Grant ........................................... 195
    If You Don't Win, Find Out Why ................................................................................. 195
    Cite Educational Research ............................................................................................ 196
    Save Receipts ................................................................................................................. 196
    Grant Writing Checklist ................................................................................................ 196

**CHAPTER 25. BUYING VIDEO PRODUCTION EQUIPMENT** ...................................................... 197
    The Video/AV/Technology Committee ....................................................................... 197
    Vendor Problems ........................................................................................................... 197
    List of Sources for Video Production Equipment....................................................... 198
    TV Production Equipment Purchase Checklist........................................................... 202

**PART V: IT'S A WRAP!** ................................................................................................... 203

**CHAPTER 26. CONCLUSION** ............................................................................................... 205
    Bibliography .................................................................................................................. 206
    Resource List ................................................................................................................. 208
    Glossary ......................................................................................................................... 209
    Index ............................................................................................................................... 222

# Table of Figures

*Figure* 1.1. The Communication Process ........................................................................... 3
*Figure* 2.1. Using the Rule of Thirds .................................................................................. 9
*Figure* 2.2. Place the Elements of a Scene Together in a Balanced Way ........................ 10
*Figure* 2.3. Style of Lettering ............................................................................................ 10
*Figure* 2.4. Use Arrows to Guide Attention ...................................................................... 11
*Figure* 2.5. Basic Angle Shots of People .......................................................................... 12
*Figure* 2.6. The Basic Shots .............................................................................................. 14
*Figure* 2.7. Never Cut Off a Subject at the Top of the Neck, Knees, or Ankles ............... 15
*Figure* 2.8. Aspect Ratio ................................................................................................... 16
*Figure* 2.9. Place Graphics in the Picture Area ................................................................ 16
*Figure* 2.10. Place the Moving Subject on the Left Side of the Screen in a Side Angle Shot ...... 17
*Figure* 2.11. TV/Computer Presentation Script ................................................................ 19
*Figure* 2.12. Simple Script Sheet ...................................................................................... 20
*Figure* 2.13. Graphic of Storyboard .................................................................................. 23
*Figure* 3.1. Plugs and Jacks .............................................................................................. 30
*Figure* 4.1. Panasonic VHS Camcorder ............................................................................ 34
*Figure* 4.2. Handheld Camera Shot .................................................................................. 35
*Figure* 4.3. The Parts of the Tripod and Dolly ................................................................. 36
*Figure* 4.4. Microphone Placement at 45° Angle ............................................................. 37
*Figure* 4.5. Interviewee Stands at 90° Angle from Interviewer ........................................ 37
*Figure* 4.6. Types of Lenses and Depth of Field .............................................................. 39
*Figure* 4.7. Size of Lens Opening and Depth of Field ..................................................... 40
*Figure* 4.8. VHS Tapes, Tab On, Tab Off ......................................................................... 41
*Figure* 4.9. JVC Digital Camera ....................................................................................... 45
*Figure* 5.1. Lowell Lights ................................................................................................. 50
*Figure* 5.2. Bounce Light .................................................................................................. 50
*Figure* 5.3. Barn Door ....................................................................................................... 51
*Figure* 5.4. Three-Point Lighting ...................................................................................... 52
*Figure* 5.5. Softening Shadows on the Subject's Face ..................................................... 54
*Figure* 6.1. "All-In-Wonder Pro" Video Input/Output Computer Device ........................ 58
*Figure* 6.2. How to Add Narration from a Microphone to a VCR While Converting a Visual Computer Presentation to Videotape ............................................................. 62
*Figure* 7.1. A Simple and Inexpensive Video Switcher from Audio Authority ............... 66
*Figure* 7.2. Panasonic A/V Digital Mixer ......................................................................... 66
*Figure* 7.3. Panasonic Character Generator ..................................................................... 67
*Figure* 7.4. Using the A/V Digital Mixer for Mixing Sound and Picture ........................ 68
*Figure* 7.5. Shure Audio Mixer ......................................................................................... 71
*Figure* 8.1. Panasonic Analog Video Editor ..................................................................... 77
*Figure* 8.2. Panasonic Analog Video Edit Controller ...................................................... 79
*Figure* 8.3. DraCo Casablanca Digital Video Editor ....................................................... 81

# Table of Figures continued

*Figure 9.1.* Radio Shack RF Splitter for Two TV Receivers .................................................. 86
*Figure 9.2.* Radio Shack RF Splitter for More Than Two TV Receivers ............................. 86
*Figure 9.3.* A Series of TV Receivers Connected with an RF Splitter ................................. 86
*Figure 9.4.* In-school Cable TV System ................................................................................ 87
*Figure 9.5.* Hooking Up a Series of TV Receiver/Monitors ................................................. 88
*Figure 9.6.* Panasonic Data Projector ................................................................................... 89
*Figure 10.1.* Simple TV Studio Connections Diagram ......................................................... 96
*Figure 10.2.* Complex TV Studio Connections Diagram ..................................................... 99
*Figure 10.3.* JVC Visual Presenter ........................................................................................ 99
*Figure 10.4.* Low Impedance Lavaliere Microphones Improve Sound Quality ................ 100
*Figure 10.5.* Hooking Up a CD/Audiocassette Player Without LINE OUT Into an Audio Mixer   101
*Figure 10.6.* Portacom Head Set and Power Supply ......................................................... 102
*Figure 10.7.* Painted Backdrop Using Two King Size Sheets............................................ 102
*Figure 10.8.* A Gobo ............................................................................................................ 103
*Figure 10.9.* Pipes Running Across Studio Ceiling............................................................ 104
*Figure 13.1.* Application for WBRN Morning News Show ............................................... 126
*Figure 14.1.* Talent Tryout Sheet ........................................................................................ 130
*Figure 14.2.* Student Using Scrolling Cue Card ................................................................. 131
*Figure 14.3.* Manipulating Cue Cards ................................................................................. 131
*Figure 15.1.* Simple News Show Jobs List ......................................................................... 138
*Figure 15.2.* TV News Show Job Description Sheet ......................................................... 140
*Figure 15.3.* Job Assignment Spreadsheet .......................................................................... 142
*Figure 15.4.* How To Get Mt. Vernon Morning News Show on Channel 6 ..................... 143
*Figure 16.1.* The Career of the Week ................................................................................. 150
*Figure 17.1.* A *PowerPoint* Slide from a High School Library Orientation Video .................. 156
*Figure 18.1.* Great Books Group Presentation Guide......................................................... 161
*Figure 19.1.* Multimedia Job Assignments ......................................................................... 166
*Figure 19.2.* Script Writer .................................................................................................... 167
*Figure 19.3.* Graph Maker ................................................................................................... 168
*Figure 19.4.* Bibliography Maker ........................................................................................ 169
*Figure 19.5.* "So What?" Statement Writer/Announcer ..................................................... 170
*Figure 19.6.* Tech Director................................................................................................... 171
*Figure 20.1.* Lights On Each Side of the Camera Improve Picture Quality....................... 176
*Figure 20.2.* Cut Out Figure With Moveable Arms and Legs for Animation ....................... 177

# Preface

Most likely, many school librarians have camcorders locked up in their equipment wardrobes. According to the American Library Association, there are over 72,000 school librarians working in elementary, middle, and secondary schools, which means there are a lot of camcorders not in use. What's to be done with all these camcorders? *Video Production for School Library Media Specialists: Communication and Production Techniques* will show you how camcorders and other video production equipment can help you communicate more effectively with students, teachers, parents, and administrators.

Information needs to be communicated to students, parents, teachers, and staff every day. All school library media specialists would probably agree. There are many ways for you to communicate the value of your library media program. For example, a newsletter in the teachers' mailboxes, a phone call, an e-mail message, or a Web page can be great ways for you, the school librarian, to communicate. Video production is another great way to communicate; it's also a great way to teach communication skills to students and to teachers. Note what the leading professional organizations, A.E.C.T. and A.A.S.L., have to say in their book, *Information Power: Building Partnerships for Learning.* "Now, as the keystone of a student-centered library media program, the library media specialist is poised to work collaboratively with teachers, administrators, and others to facilitate students' entry into the communication age" (3). Those are powerful words. It isn't enough for you to learn communication skills alone. You need additional skills that will allow you to communicate through desktop publishing and Web page creation. You, the school librarian, along with teachers and administrators, need to teach those skills to students. Your job is "to facilitate students' entry into the communication age."

One of the skills you need to teach your students is video production. Video production should be an integral part of your library media center program because learning how to produce videos is an excellent way to learn how to communicate. Video production is an instructional tool that can help you achieve traditional school library media center goals, such as encouraging reading, writing, and research. Once students have accessed information, show them how to communicate that information effectively to others using video production. Many current trends underscore the importance of teaching video production in the school library.

# Current Trends That Impact School Libraries and Video Production

Several trends impact school libraries and video production:

***Growth of cable TV in school classrooms.*** Donelle Blubaugh, director of curriculum for Cable in the Classroom, says, "More classrooms are wired for cable TV today than ever before" (Telephone interview, June 1999). In their article "The Presence of Computers in American Schools," Ronald E. Anderson and Amy Ronnkvist report on the Web page, "Teaching, Learning and Computing: 1998, a National Survey of Schools and Teachers," that 25% of all high schools, 8% of middle schools, and 3% of elementary schools nationwide have video production studios <www.crito.uci.edu/tlc/html/findings.html>. Al Race, executive editor of *Cable in the Classroom* magazine, cites a 1997 study by the Corporation for Public Broadcasting, in a December 1998 issue of the magazine, which reveals that 15% of U.S. schools have TV studios, up from 8% in 1991; 92% of U.S. schools have access to a TV camera, up from 81% in 1991. Even more surprising is the fact that 28% of U.S. schools have video editing equipment, up from less than 1% in 1991.

Race describes this growth in instructional TV production as follows: "While computers have been getting all the press, video production has become a widely available, highly motivational, and impressively adaptable instructional technology" (2). Video production in schools today is both valuable and visible.

The potential for great communication with video production in your school library media center means that library media specialists may be expected, by principals, to produce a daily TV news show for the school. This gives the school library media specialist a golden opportunity. The news show can highlight and make visible the school library media center's program.

***Growth of statewide learning standards.*** In the American Federation of Teachers' 1997 publication, *Making Standards Matter,* Gandal points out that "49 states are developing common academic standards for students...." (Adapted with permission from *A Comprehensive Guide to Designing Standards-Based Districts, Schools, and Classrooms* [Marzano and Kendall, 11-18].) Schools today are graded and get report cards and are now often evaluated by the standardized test scores of their students. Jason L. Ravitz, Yan Tien Wong, and Henry J. Becker point out in "Special Report for Participants" that 58 percent of American teachers in elementary, middle, and secondary schools feel "some" or "a lot" of pressure to prepare students for standardized tests <www.crito.uci.edu/tlc/html/findings.html>. From state to state, as the pressure to educate students increases, teachers will be looking for more effective methods of ensuring learning. Video production, when used with creative lesson plans, provides many ways of doing this.

***Integration of video technology with computer technology.*** Video production is becoming digital. Videotaped images are easily added to a visual computer presentation. Video editing can also be done on a computer. A computer presentation is easily enhanced by converting it to video and adding sound. How do you show a *PowerPoint* presentation in a classroom without a computer? You convert the *PowerPoint* presentation to videotape and show it on your VCR. The line between video production and visual computer presentation is blurry. Learning about video production today requires familiarity with computer visual presentation software, such as Microsoft *PowerPoint* and HyperStudio.

***Research studies.*** Many studies show that students can learn better with video and computer technology. The *1999 Research Report on the Effectiveness of Technology in Schools,* 6th ed., written by the Software and Information Industry Association in 1999, affirms this idea. Other studies show that teachers are overwhelmed by technology and the lack of technology training. Many teachers don't get involved with technology-based projects because they either don't have access to the technology or can't figure out how to use it. Almost one half of American teachers say they need some technical support at least once a month. According to the article "Teaching, Learning and Computing: 1998, Snapshot #4, Technical and Instructional Support for Teachers," over two thirds of these teachers say they can't get technical support when they need it for their technology <www.crito.uci.edu/tlc/findings/snapshot4/>. In his article, Don Oldenburg quotes Janet Hudgens of Arlington County Public Schools in Virginia as saying, "The technology has surpassed teachers' ability to keep up with it" (A1). To solve this problem, the school library media specialist can assist teachers with video—and computer-based—projects. School librarians can encourage teachers to assign students technology projects that require research, writing, and presentation skills. Many educators today emphasize the importance of collaboration between professionals in teaching. The isolation of the classroom teacher is considered a major problem. The school library media specialist can provide the collaboration and support classroom teachers need to implement technology into their instructional programs. This is one way that school library media specialists can stay visible in their schools.

Tangible products like videotapes serve as evidence of the learning that took place in the library media center. Student-created products of learning (videotapes) can be shown to other teachers, the principal, school board members, the PTA president, or a newspaper reporter. These videotapes will make your library media program visible.

This book provides the information you'll need to help students create a video production. Many books and magazines are available on video production. What makes this book different is that it's written from the point of view of school library media specialists, not a video production teacher or a professional video producer. You can implement a video production program in your library media program without teaching a class in video production. In fact, teaching a class in video production may be the last thing you should do. You've got a library media program to run. Because you are busy, this book is set up in a checklist format. Part I, Chapters 1 and 2, teaches you communication theory, visual literacy, and scriptwriting. Part II, Chapters 3 through 11, deals with the equipment you will need. Part III, Chapters 12 through 20, shows you how to effectively use this equipment with students and teachers in instructional endeavors. Part IV, Chapters 21 through 25, guides you on how to organize a video production program in your school. For example, if you are training camera operators, you'll turn to Chapter 4, "The Camera." You'll quickly photocopy as many copies of the "Camcorder Checklist" as you need and train your students using this checklist. You won't have to spend time creating your own camcorder checklist.

Before the checklist in each chapter, information is provided regarding the items on the checklist. For example, in Chapter 5, "Lighting," the first item on "The Lighting Checklist" deals with key lighting. If you already know about key lighting, you'll have no trouble teaching it using the lighting checklist with your students. If you don't know about key lighting, read about it in Chapter 5.

Important terms are highlighted at the beginning of most chapters. Those terms are defined in the glossary at the back of the book. You may save time by just looking up the term "key lighting" in the glossary. The glossary, like the checklists, is there to save you time.

Probably, you already are the school library media specialist or you're training to be one. If you're already in a school, you're probably one of the hardest workers there. Your time is valuable and this book helps you save it. Using our checklists in student training may prove much more time efficient than generating your own.

Reach out to your teachers as well as your students. You'll never have time to work with all of them on projects. Select teachers to work with that you suspect might be open to a new approach. Make the most of the resources you have available, and think of your video production program as one of your instructional tools to help teachers communicate information, motivate students and improve student learning, and for great communication with your students and staff!

As you do this, remember you're doing for your students what *Information Power: Building Partnerships for Learning* implores: "producing new information and creating products and presentations that communicate ideas efficiently and effectively..."(3). Your students can learn to communicate efficiently and effectively with video production.

# Great Communication

# Communication Theory and Visual Literacy

**CHAPTER 1**

## Terms

- **communication**
- **feedback**
- **visual literacy**

One way to facilitate your students' entry into the communication age is to teach them how to communicate through video production. In order to communicate effectively through video, an understanding of communication theory and visual literacy is essential.

## Communication Theory

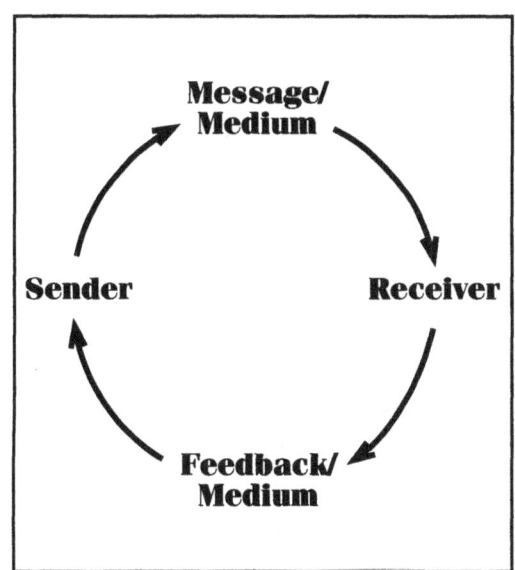

*Figure 1.1 The Communication Process*

Communication is the process of sending a message to someone through a medium and getting feedback from the receiver of the message. (See Figure 1.1.) Communication is the process of exchanging knowledge and information. One reason for your students to communicate through the video medium is that they have something important to say, a message that may enhance the lives of the people with whom they are communicating. Knowing they have an audience who may benefit from their message can inspire your students. As an educator and a school librarian, you want to set up a situation where students read, research, write, and then produce a videotape that will enhance the lives of their audience. You can help students identify an audience for their message—students in another classroom or perhaps the entire student body. Identifying a target audience will motivate your students to do the work involved in creating an effective videotape presentation. You might also want to look for opportunities where students create video productions that enhance the life of the school. For example, high school students can produce a video that helps the student body select elective classes. An example for elementary school students would be a student-produced video production shown to first graders in early September on how to safely cross the street to get to school.

Feedback is essential to the communication process. Feedback informs the video producer about how the audience responded to the message. In *Instructional Media and Technologies for Learning*, Heinich, Molenda, Russell, and Smaldino state, "A critical feature of communication, especially instructional communication, is *feedback*—the receiver's response to the message sent. After receiving and interpreting the message, the receiver may then become a source and send his or her own message back to the original source, who becomes a receiver" (13).

Even people with experience in video scriptwriting and video production can have problems communicating their message through the video medium. In a 1999 speech given at Borders Books in Virginia, the famous science fiction writer Orson Scott Card criticized George Lucas's film *Star Wars: The Phantom Menace*. He said that the weaknesses in the film were the result of a lack of feedback. According to Card, George Lucas didn't have anyone in his preliminary audience giving him appropriate feedback about how the process of producing the film was going. Who has a better track record in film production than George Lucas? Yet, Card emphasized that no one informed Lucas of critical changes that needed to be made in the production. Because of this lack of feedback, according to Card, some of the characters weren't convincing enough.

In our school, we had a similar problem when planning a TV news show. First, one teacher complained about our "Word of the Day" list. The teacher said we were using the wrong word list. Then, another teacher said the same thing. By the time the fifth teacher complained, we realized we'd better change our word list for "Word of the Day."

Why did it take so many complaints to get us to change the word list? It's very simple. Feedback isn't always easy to hear, and it may force you to admit a mistake. Most people do not like to hear criticism about their work. Who doesn't want to go through any process unblemished and untouched? The video production process, like any communication process, doesn't work that way. Scripts and productions usually need to get roughed up a bit (revised, edited, and criticized by others) before they communicate a message effectively. As your students think about, outline, write, and produce their video production, have them talk to their audience about their production ideas as much as possible. They should send up as many trial balloons as they can and get as much feedback as possible. They can ask their audience questions such as, "Would you like to see a story about a horse? What color and breed should the horse be? Did you like the way the gray horse outran the black horse in the second scene?"

Communicating to the audience is an ongoing process that starts at the beginning of a production and ends only when the videotape gathers dust on the shelf and is forgotten. Just when video producers think their productions are perfect, they get some vital feedback needed to improve their video productions. For one school's TV news show, feedback came from the audience about the poor audio quality of videotaped segments as compared to the live segments in the video. The feedback led to a new plan to boost the audio on the videotaped segments by using an audio mixer. For more information about producing a TV news show, see Chapter 10, "The TV Studio for the School TV News Show," page 93.

# Visual Literacy

To understand how to effectively communicate through the video medium, students need to understand visual literacy. The best definition of visual literacy can be found on Kent State University's Web page. "Visual literacy is the ability to understand, create and use visual images" <www.educ.kent.edu/vlo/literacy/index.html>. If you think of a visual image, such as a TV picture, a painting, an advertisement in a magazine, a photograph, or a scene from a movie, the picture you are thinking of is made up of visual elements. When you notice the visual elements of a picture, you understand the meaning of the picture. Visual images can be positive or negative. First, think of a positive visual image. For instance, Michaelangelo's painting, *The Creation of Adam*, shows Adam reaching out and almost touching God. Often, however, you see a cropped image of *The Creation of Adam*, which shows just the hands of Adam reaching for the hands of God. The message of the cropped image of the *The Creation of Adam* is different from the full painting. Is it God reaching for man? Is it man reaching for God? Is it one human trying to communicate to another? The hands in the picture are visual elements that become symbols for something more than just hands. The hands become symbols for some of the finest sentiments regarding either God and man or man and man, and a positive message using visual elements, not words, is conveyed.

Let's consider a magazine advertisement. The visual elements are a majestic mountain, a beautiful green forest, a spacious clear blue sky, and a virile young cowboy smoking a cigarette. A pack of cigarettes is seen in the lower left corner of the picture. The mountain, the sky, the forest, and the cowboy are visual elements that seem natural and healthy. These visual elements make the pack of cigarettes seem healthy. Of course, a caption in the ad would never read, "Smoking is natural and healthy." The visual elements, however, relay a positive message. When students create a visual, they should understand that each element they use can change the meaning of the visual. The visual elements of Michaelangelo's painting, the hands, seem to stand for the glory of man's relation to man or man's relation to God. The visual elements in the cigarette ad work together to create a positive image for a potentially hazardous substance. During the Civil War, photographer Matthew Brady moved bodies to gain greater visual impact in his photographs. In today's digital age, visual images are moved much more easily by copying and pasting using a computer. The power to manipulate visual images has grown exponentially since Brady's photographs were taken.

Cornelia Brunner's article, "Teaching Visual Literacy," provides a rubric for evaluating images: "Who made this image and for what purpose? What specific choices did the creator make in selecting/creating it? What specific techniques and technologies were used in its construction? What meanings, pleasures and satisfactions do I derive from the image? Why? How might other individuals interpret this image? How does this image represent its subject? What is the economic, political, and historical context surrounding the image?" (16)

Both Brunner and another expert in the field of visual literacy, Paul Messaris, believe visual literacy should be taught in schools. In his article, Messaris states, "There is considerable evidence that such educational efforts can be effective…especially when they actively engage students in the production of videos or other visual formats" (79).

When students themselves create and select the elements of their visuals, they begin to understand how others do it and how visual images can influence an audience.

# Scriptwriting

**CHAPTER 2**

## Terms

- aspect ratio
- background (BG)
- close-up (CU)
- closure
- composition
- cutaway
- depth of field
- dissolve
- Eisenstein's Law
- establishing shot
- exterior (EXT)
- extreme close-up (ECU)
- extreme long shot (ELS)
- foreground (FG)
- hook
- interior (INT)
- long shot (LS)
- medium close-up (MCU)
- medium shot (MS)
- objective angle
- oblique angle
- parallel action
- picture area
- rule of thirds
- segue
- sequencing
- sound effects (SFX)
- subjective angle
- transition
- voice-over (VO)

To be able to produce a video, your students need to know how to write a video script. The video script is the way your students plan to communicate their message to their audience. Scriptwriting for video production is an important skill and puts visual literacy and communication theory into practice. Writing a script, and creating a video production from that script, is a powerful experience for your students. They not only absorb knowledge, but they also are able to communicate that knowledge to others. Writing a script and producing a video orients a student to the communication age. When writing a script, the scriptwriter is trying to make an impact on the audience. An effective script may start out with a hook, something that surprises or piques the interest of the audience. Sometimes the script may start out with an intriguing question; the audience keeps watching to find an answer.

## Twenty-two Practical Pointers for Visual Design

In order to write a script, students need to know some important ideas about visual design. The following 22 ideas for visual design will help students create effective visual images for their videos. These 22 practical pointers are guidlines, not laws carved in stone.

### 1. Use the Rule of Thirds

When students are creating visual images for their videos, they should select the important visual elements of each scene and place these elements on the screen according to the rule of thirds. (See Figure 2.1.) According to the rule, the most important element of a picture should be one third of the distance from the top of the screen. The next time you go to the movies or watch TV, note that the eyes of the actors or announcers in any given scene are one third of the distance from the top of the screen. Using the rule of thirds, the centers of interest in a picture are placed at the intersection of horizontal and vertical lines one third of the distance from the top, bottom, and sides of the TV screen.

### 2. Make Images on Screen Clearly Visible

Images and text on the screen should be clearly visible to the audience. Words on the screen should be big enough to be read from the back of the classroom, and the camera work should be focused so that the images can be clearly seen. Not only should the images be in focus and the text legible, they should also be placed on the screen in a manner that is easy to see. For example, if you put red images on a green background, the colorblind segment of your audience will have a difficult time seeing your visuals. If the skin tone of the narrator blends in with the wall behind him, it will be difficult for the audience to see him.

*Incorrect*

*Correct*

*Figure 2.1 Using the Rule of Thirds*
*From "Looking Great with Video Production" by Augie Beasley*

### 3. Balance the Visual Elements

The elements of a scene should be placed together in a balanced way. (See Figure 2.2.) Do the shapes in the visual complement each other? Are the shapes arranged to attract the viewer's attention? Do the images on the right side of the picture enhance or detract from the images on the left side of the screen? Since we read from left to right, a visual element on the left side of the screen should be of more importance than the visual elements on the right side of the screen.

### 4. Make the Visuals as Complex as Necessary

Visuals should be as complex as needed. If the audience is learning something for the first time, a simple drawing may be best. For a person more familiar with the information in the video, a detailed photograph may be a much better visual.

### 5. Select Appropriate Lettering Style

Have students be aware of the style of lettering they use in their videos. One font may convey their message better than another one. For example, if they were inviting people to a birthday party, they would select a font that would give the guest a happy feeling. If displaying a school rule in their video, they would select a font that would convey a much more serious feeling. (See Figure 2.3.)

*Figure 2.2 Place the Elements of a Scene Together In a Balanced Way*

For a happy experience like a birthday party use a font like Paisley ICG 02 or Schwarzwald.

Example:

# Come to the Party!

For something more serious, like a statement of school rules, use a font like AGarmond Bold.

Example:

## No running in the hall!

*Figure 2.3 Style of Lettering*

*Figure 2.4 Use Arrows to Guide Attention*

### 6. Use Arrows

Encourage students to use arrows to guide attention to important information in their videos. (See Figure 2.4.) For example, in a computer training video, arrows can be used to illustrate a sequence of actions that need to be taken. An arrow can point out where to type in an Internet address or what key to press to perform a certain action.

### 7. Keep Visuals Consistent with Other Visuals

Are the visuals consistent with each other? If your students are introducing a series of concepts in text, they should place the text pertaining to each concept in the same part of the screen. This will direct the audience to the message, and they will spend less mental energy figuring out where to look for the important information in the visual.

### 8. Shoot at Eye Level

When shooting scenes for a video, the camera should be set up at the eye level of the talent. Shooting at the eye level of the talent gives the audience the feeling of actually being there and makes the experience of watching the video more real. If students are filming a TV news show, have them set the tripod so the camera is at eye level with the announcer sitting at the news desk. The camera should not be looking up or down at the talent. The next time you watch a TV news show, check to see if the anchorperson is at your eye level.

### 9. Minimize Camera Movement

For the camera shot to be effective, the attention of the audience should be on the subject, not camera movements. Zooms, pans, and tilts should be used sparingly. Whether the camera is handheld or mounted on a tripod, the picture should not shake.

### 10. Use Camera Angles

Camera angles should be used for effect. For a TV news show, a subjective camera angle is much more useful than an objective angle. In a subjective angle, the person on camera looks directly at the audience. In a dramatic work, the objective angle is usually used, and the actor does not look at the camera but at the other actors. Whether the angle of the camera is subjective or objective, however, the audience expects to see both eyes of the subject, not a silhouette. Using a low angle makes the subject look more powerful; a high angle makes the subject look weak. An oblique angle is also a nice change; the actor, announcer, or person being interviewed is seen at a slanted angle. MTV viewers are used to seeing oblique angle shots. When using any camera angle, students should avoid cutting off the subject at the neck, knees, or ankles to improve picture composition. (See Figure 2.5.)

*Subjective Angle*

*Objective Angle*

*Low Angle*

*High Angle*

*Oblique Angle*

*Figure 2.5 Basic Angle Shots of People*
*From "Looking Great with Video Production" by Augie Beasley*

**11. Use Depth of Field**

Depth of field is very important when students envision a scene that they will use in their script. They shouldn't stand their subjects up against a blank wall, giving very little depth of field. Instead, subjects should be given a three-dimensional background. Have you ever wondered why there are people working on computers in the background of CNN's Headline News? The background makes the TV screen look three-dimensional and is very interesting to the human eye. This is the essence of depth of field. The more depth of field in the picture, the more three-dimensional the picture looks. Using more light in the picture also gives more depth of field. For more information on depth of field, see Chapter 4, "The Camera, page 33."

**12. Understand Basic Camera Shots**

To write a script and produce a video, students need to know basic camera shots and when to use them. (See Figure 2.6.) Basic camera shots are as follows: (1) The extreme long shot (ELS) shows the entire subject on the screen with room to spare above the head and below the feet. (2) The long shot (LS) shows all of the body, with little room on the screen above the head and below the feet. (3) The medium shot (MS) cuts off the subject at the waist. (4) The medium close-up (MCU) of a person shows the entire head and cuts off the body at the chest. (5) The close-up (CU) of a subject shows the head and cuts off the body at the lower part of shoulders. (6) The extreme close-up (ECU) cuts off the top of the subject's head and shows the rest of the head and neck. When framing shots, remember this basic rule—never cut off a subject at the top of the neck, the knees, or the ankles. (See Figure 2.7.) Each type of shot serves a specific purpose and helps scriptwriters communicate their message. A beginning shot for a script is called an establishing shot. An establishing shot is one form of an extreme long shot (ELS.) An extreme long shot might not contain any people or the people might look like ants as seen from the top of a skyscraper. One rule of thumb to remember about an ELS is that the entire subject is shown in the shot. In *Total Request Live* on MTV, the establishing shot shown in the beginning of the show is the New York City skyline followed by crowds of young people on Times Square. In the TV show *Family Matters*, the establishing shot shows an outdoor view of Urkle's attractive home. *The Mary Tyler Moore Show* begins with a long shot of Mary walking down a street in downtown Minneapolis, Minnesota, throwing her hat into the air. The establishing shot is a long shot that "establishes" the setting for the show. Long shots are usually followed by medium shots. Medium shots are followed by close-up shots. A close-up or extreme close-up communicates emotion and sincerity.

Video scenes change every few seconds. Establishing shots usually last about five or six seconds. If students are using many close-up scenes with dialogue, each scene should last four or five seconds. An action shot would last longer, possibly 10-15 seconds. Each long shot should last five seconds. To give students a sense of how quickly video scenes change, videotape some advertisements and play them back to the students with the sound off.

Extreme Long Shot ELS

Medium Shot MS

Long Shot LS

Medium Close-Up

Two Shot

Extreme Close-Up

Close-Up CU

Establishing Shot

*Figure 2.6 The Basic Shots*
*From "Looking Great with Video Production" by Augie Beasley*

*Correct*  *Incorrect*

*Figure 2.7 Never Cut Off a Subject at the Top of the Neck, Knees or Ankles*
*From "Looking Great with Video Production" by Augie Beasley*

### 13. Use Transitions

Use transitions to prepare the audience to go from one scene to another. To signal the end of a scene, the screen may fade out as another scene fades in. This transition is called a dissolve, and a dissolve connects two scenes.

Transitions are the glue that gives the entire script a sense of purpose and direction. As in any writing, each statement needs to be connected to the next. Either each statement fits into the whole or the audience is lost. Here's an example of a school TV news show transition between a football game and a student government election. "Not only did our football Tigers, enjoy victory last week, so did Elaine Jones, our newly elected student government president." Another term for a transition is "segue," which means to "proceed without pause." A good segue relates what you just said to what you're going to say, like relating a football story to a student government story.

After a few transitions, a video script needs closure. Sometimes the ending can be as simple as saying "good-bye for now" or "thanks for watching."

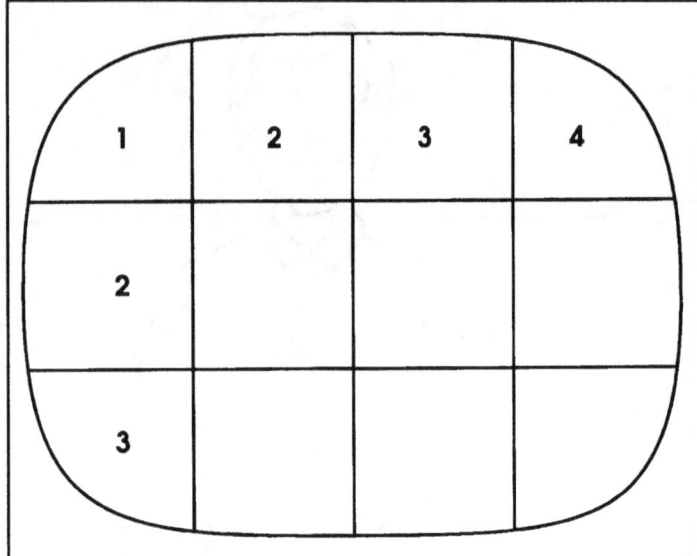

*Figure 2.8 Aspect Ratio*
*From "Looking Great with Video Production" by Augie Beasley*

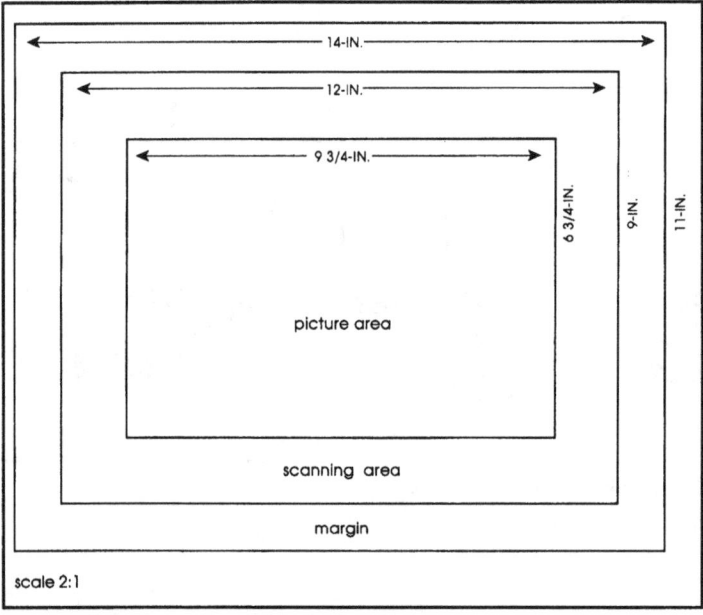

*Figure 2.9 Place Graphics in the Picture Area*
*From "Looking Great with Video Production" by Augie Beasley*

### 14. Understand Aspect Ratio

When planning a visual image for a script, it is important to understand aspect ratio.(See Figure 2.8.) The visuals that students create will have a ratio of four vertical units to three horizontal units. The image will be wider than it is tall, like a TV screen. For instance, you can get a better close-up of the entire White House than the entire Washington Monument on the TV screen. Also, visuals and text should be in the "picture area," not the "margin." Because TV monitors vary, what's visible in the margin of one TV screen might not be visible on another TV screen. (See Figure 2.9.)

### 15. Use Cutaways

Sometimes a series of scenes can get boring. Let's say you are videotaping a concert. Going from a long to a medium to a close-up of a musician can get a bit monotonous after a while. Cut aways can be used to make the video more interesting. A cutaway shot would be of someone in the audience watching the concert. Later, that audience shot will be added to the video. The music can still be heard as the shot of a member of the audience listening to the music is shown. This is called a "video insert" and is explained in further detail in Chapter 8, "Video Editing, page 73."

### 16. Use Voice-over

Another important technique to understand in scriptwriting and video production is voice-over. When a voice-over is used, the audience is watching something on the screen while listening to a voice that is not in the picture. One simple way to do voice-over is to tape an activity in one area of the room while the narrator stands in another part of the room off camera and describes the activity into a handheld microphone. An audio dub achieves the same effect. Audio dubbing is an editing technique that will be described in detail in Chapter 8, Video Editing, page 73. For now, students should understand that an audio dub can be added to a videotaped segment. The scriptwriter's abbreviation for voice-over is (VO).

### 17. Use Parallel Action

In "parallel action," video producers switch back and forth between two events happening simultaneously, thus creating suspense. The following scenes are classic examples of "parallel action." The first scene is a close-up of a bomb with 10 seconds showing on the timer. The second scene is a long shot of the hero running toward the bomb. In the third scene, a close-up of the bomb with five seconds on the timer is shown. The fourth scene is a medium shot of the hero gripping the bomb. The fifth scene is a close-up of the bomb with one second on the timer, the sixth scene is a close-up of the hero's hand stopping the timer and preventing an explosion.

### 18. Use Sequencing

Sequencing would be critical in an instructional videotape on hitting a baseball. The first scene would be of the batter's stance before the ball is pitched. The next scene would show the batter's front leg moving toward the pitcher as the bat is cocked. The next scene would be the swing itself, and the last scene would be of the follow through.

### 19. Use Eisenstein's Law

Eisenstein's law is also called the "one plus one equals three" law. For example, if there is a scene in a script of a close-up shot of a man looking longingly in a particular direction, then the next scene would show what the man is looking at, a medium shot of a beautiful woman. The scene of the close-up of the man looking longingly at something comes directly before the scene of the medium shot of the beautiful woman. These scenes would have a profound effect on the viewer. Viewers will get the image of a man with romantic intentions when they watch the video. Now, if the scene of the man looking longingly at something is followed by a scene of a close-up of a big, thick, juicy steak and a baked potato with butter on a plate, the viewer will now get the image of a man who is hungry for dinner. This is Eisenstein's law. After the viewer sees the first scene followed directly by the second scene, a third image takes shape in the viewer's mind. A very powerful scriptwriting technique, Eisenstein's law allows a scriptwriter to convey an idea without words. The scriptwriter can show how hungry a man is without incorporating the sentence, "I'm hungry," in the audio section of the script.

### 20. Include Motion

Camera directions for a script should deal with motion. If the narrator in a scene is walking toward the camera, that should be noted in the script. If the subject is running or walking in the scene and the camera angle is from the side, place the subject more to the left side of the screen. This gives the subject room to run. If you place the subject on the right side of the screen, it will seem that the subject is about to crash into the right side of the TV screen. Place a moving subject on the left side of the screen in a side angle shot. (See Figure 2.10.)

*Figure 2.10 Place the Moving Subject on the Left Side of the Screen in a Side Angle Shot*

**21. Use Lighting**

Lighting effects can be noted in the script. Lighting a subject from below will give the subject an eerie or gothic effect. If the scene is to take place at night, dusk, sunrise or midafternoon, that must be noted in the script.

**22. Don't Break the Illusion**

Remind students not to design a scene in their scripts where a person walks out of the scene; an exception would be walking out a door. Remember, television is an illusion of reality. In real life people don't "walk off the screen." The TV screen provides a very narrow perspective. When the main character in a video production walks off the left or right side of the screen, you draw the audience's attention away from your story, the illusion you are creating. If a character walks off the left or right side of the screen, the audience is made aware of the limitations of the perspective of television.

# Writing the Script

As a library media specialist, you may not have time to cover all of the 22 Practical Pointers for Visual Design mentioned in this chapter, which is why we have provided two checklists for your use when teaching scriptwriting to your students: "Basic Scriptwriting Checklist" and "Advanced Scriptwriting Checklist." However, the more practical pointers you can teach your students, the better. The students should understand these visual design ideas before they begin writing their scripts. If you only have time to teach one practical pointer, teach the rule of thirds. Then have the students use the rule of thirds as they plan out the visual scenes of their scripts.

**Tools for Scriptwriting**

Having a single-page script sheet for each scene helps sequence the presentation. There isn't any cutting and pasting. Students can just change the scene number in the upper right corner of the script sheet. (See Figures 2.11 and 2.12.)

When writing a script using the "Simple Script Sheet," students plan the camera shot in the box under "visual" and put the narration or dialog under the "audio" section. Abbreviations can help them save time when scriptwriting. They can use EXT for an exterior shot and INT for an interior shot in the box under "visual." Also, in the box under "visual," they can use BG for the background of a scene and FG for the foreground of a scene. In the "audio" section, they can use SFX for sound effects. When writing the narration or dialogue in the "audio" section, have the students use simple sentences with a subject, verb, and object. Long sentences with dependent clauses do not work well in video productions. Also, have students keep the audio narration or dialogue simple and to the point.

# TV/Computer Presentation Script

Script Scene # _____

## Visual

A. **Pictures from Other Sources**

    Magazine or Newspaper _____ Page# _____ Date _____
    Book _____ Page # _____
    Clip Art Software _____ Category _____ Filename _____
    Video Disk _____ Code# _____
    Video Tape _____ Hr. _____ Min. _____ Sec. _____
    Internet Site _____ CD-ROM _____

B. **Visual Text** _____

    Font Style _____ Font Size _____ Animation Type _____

C. **Camera Shot- (Circle One)**    long      medium      close-up
    Duration in Seconds _____ Draw shot in box below.

```
┌─────────────────────────────────────────────────────┐
│                                                     │
│                                                     │
│                                                     │
│                                                     │
└─────────────────────────────────────────────────────┘
```

## Audio

Title of Cassette _____ Title of Selection _____
Title of CD _____ Title of Selection _____
Narration/Interview Questions/Dialogue

_____
_____
_____
_____
_____
_____

*Figure 2.11 TV/Computer Presentation Script*

# Simple Script Sheet

Scene___

```
                          Visual




















Type of Camera Shot _____     OR      Source of Picture -_____
```

Dialogue or Narration
_____
_____
_____
_____
_____
_____
_____
_____
_____
_____
_____

Music/Sound Effects_____
_____


*Figure 2.12 Simple Script Sheet*

## The SWEET Method

Scriptwriting is the most difficult aspect of video production to teach. You could teach each visual principle discussed in this chapter and have the students go through both of the checklists and still find that many of your students are not writing effective scripts. A system of writing scripts, the "SWEET" method, can help your students write better scripts. After you try it with your students, we hope you'll say, "How sweet it is." Use the SWEET method with the "Simple Script Sheet," Figure 2.12, page 20.

1. **SKETCH.** Have students sketch the visual with a pencil in the box in the "Simple Script Sheet." If possible, have them go to the place where the video will be shot and select the key visual elements to include in their picture. Have them follow the principles of the rule of thirds as they sketch. If they are interviewing the choral music teacher, for example, have them go to this teacher's classroom and note what is there. Do they see a piano? If yes, that piano should probably be one of the visual elements included in their first scene. Then have them draw the music teacher, interviewer, and piano. Including the piano in the scene helps establish and introduce the video. This first scene will probably be a long shot.

2. **WRITE.** Have students write down what needs to be said in the audio section of the script. There would not necessarily be dialogue in the first scene. It may be enough just to write down that the sound of the piano being played will be heard.

3. **EXCHANGE IDEAS**. Have student share the first draft of their script with you and other students. Make suggestions, and offer encouragement.

4. **EDIT.** Have students think about the suggestions others have made and then rewrite and redraw their scripts.

5. **TELEVISE.** Have students begin producing their scripts so they can be shown to an audience on video at the school.

When you use the SWEET method for scriptwriting, implement it in 10 minute blocks. Allow your students 10 minutes to sketch a scene or two and 10 minutes to write down what words, sound effects, or music will go with that scene. Then allow 10 minutes for the students to discuss each other's work and 10 minutes for students to revise their scripts. You might repeat this process two or three times on different days before you allow the students to begin producing their scripts.

The "Simple Script Sheet" could be made into a template for your computer. Then the resulting script could be typed and will be easy for the narrator or actors to read.

Teach your students at least some of the 22 Practical Pointers for Visual Design and then get your students to write scripts using the SWEET method. Scriptwriting is a powerful tool for teaching students how to write and plan.

They might then design a storyboard for the entire presentation. (See graphic of storyboard on page 23.)

# Basic Scriptwriting Checklist

_____ 1. Write a paragraph regarding the purpose of the video production.

_____ 2. List the people, visual images, and type of information needed.

_____ 3. Take notes if information is needed. (See the "Research Helper" sample note taking form at the end of the chapter.)

_____ 4. Begin writing the script. Each scene for the script is a separate page. The most important thing about scriptwriting is to visualize what the audience will see in the "visual" section and describe what the audience will hear in the "audio" section. (See "TV/Computer Presentation Script," page 19, and "Simple Script Sheet," page 20.)

_____ 5. Under "Visual" in scene one, draw an establishing shot.

_____ 6. Under "Audio" in scene one, write what will be said and what sound effects or music will be used.

_____ 7. Under "Visual" in scene two, draw a medium shot.

_____ 8. Under "Audio" in scene two, write what will be said.

_____ 9. Under "Visual" in scene three, draw a close-up shot.

_____ 10. Under "Audio" in scene three, write what dialogue or narration will be said.

# Advanced Scriptwriting Checklist

_____ 1. Create a hook in the first scene.

_____ 2. Create an effective transition between the first and second scene.

_____ 3. Create closure in scene three.

_____ 4. Write a series of parallel action scenes.

_____ 5. Write a series of scenes demonstrating Eisenstein's Law.

_____ 6. Write a series of scenes that show sequencing.

_____ 7. Select a picture from a book to use in the visual section of a script. Be sure the name of the book and page number are noted on the script sheet.

_____ 8. Select a CD or audiocassette to use in the audio section of a script. Be sure the name of the CD or cassette, and the name of the selection from the CD or cassette to be used, are noted in the script sheet. Write the counter number for a cassette or selection number for a CD.

# Storyboarding

Storyboarding is similar to scriptwriting. Both use a separate page for each scene. In storyboarding, the visual or picture is going to be more elaborate than the one in scriptwriting. Storyboarding is an excellent way to plan a video production, and it is especially important when you design a *series* of pictures. In an action sequence of a sword fight, storyboard card #1 might be a long shot showing both swordsmen drawing their swords; storyboard card #2 could be a medium shot of the swordsmen with their swords clashing; and storyboard card #3 could be a close-up of the wrist of one swordsman, showing him losing the grip on his sword.

The storyboard technique is used extensively in both the film and video production industries. It gives you time to be creative, to arrange, rearrange, and organize an entire sequence of pictures, small drawings, or "thumbnail sketches."

In storyboarding, you sketch the picture you plan to use with your narration. After making a series of these storyboard sketches on cards, arrange and organize them in a rough sequence on some sort of firm paper. Many people use plain old index cards for storyboarding because they are small, cheap, and durable, and you can buy them in a variety of sizes and colors. Many professionals even use "Post It" notes, the self-sticking removable notes that are so popular because they will stick to almost anything.

You will want to organize each individual storyboard card into sections that represent the picture, the narration, the music, and your other production notes. Remember, the exact format of the storyboard cards should always fit your own personal needs and instructional objectives. (See Figure 2.13.)

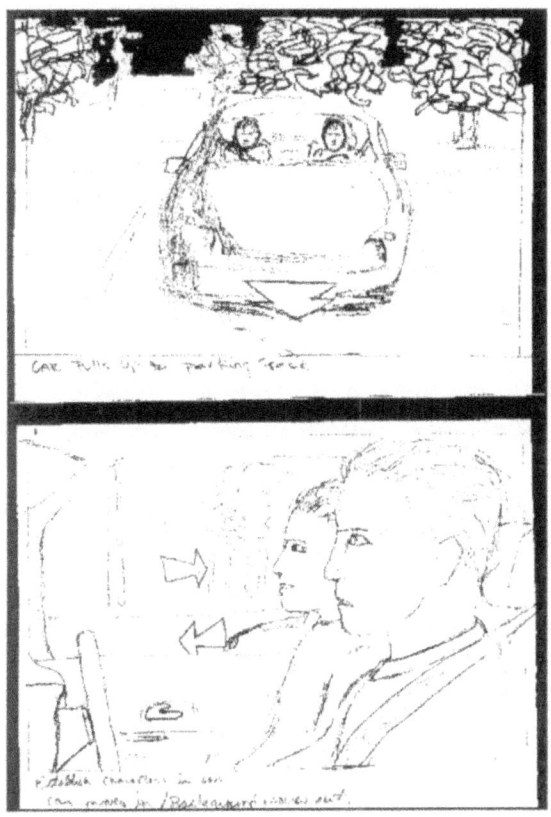

*Figure 2.13 Graphic of Storyboard*
*Artwork by Brandon Roberts*

To make a good storyboard you don't have to be a great artist. Just draw as much detail as possible and apply the "22 Practical Pointers for Visual Design" as you sketch your storyboard. If you don't want to sketch the shots you want, shoot the shots you want using some type of camera. You can take instant still camera shots from a Polaroid type camera and paste them (real paste, the white, sticky stuff in a tube) to your storyboard cards. Or use your camcorder and a computer with video capture software to create still pictures for your storyboard. (See Chapter 6.) Just print these pictures out on your computer printer and paste them (again, real paste) to your storyboard cards.

Once you have created a series of cards, lay them all out on a table. Next, you will want to place each card in a tentative order and this activity will give you a rough idea of what the finished presentation might look like. This storyboarding technique will save you time by allowing you to add, delete, replace, revise, and make refinements in the sequence of the cards. By displaying your cards in this manner, you allow others, including teachers, students, and production staff, to review the presentation in its early planning stage. You will want to number your cards so they can be rearranged to suit your instructional objective(s). Mark the cards on the front or back, but use a pencil in case a card needs to be renumbered.

Thanks to computers and software companies, the work of storyboarding is now easier. Now, with only the "click" of a computer mouse and the right software, you can create your own storyboard. Storyboard software provides you with pre-drawn images, graphics, backgrounds, and other types of pictures that you will want to utilize for detailed descriptions. With storyboarding software, you are the "designer" and you will want to add narration, script notes, and camera shots and movements. As the designer, you may also want to import "digital" images that will make your storyboard seem even more realistic and natural. There's storyboard software available that will actually "play" sounds for you, make transitions from scene to scene, and even perform like a real slide show. Anyway, you will want to take your images, **link** them to your text, "save" them to computer files, and later arrange and organize them in different sequences with the help of your computer software, according to your instructional objectives.

The Board Master company makes storyboarding software. For order information go to their Web site <http:www.boardmastersoftware.com>. The PowerProduction Software company also offers storyboarding software. Their Web site is <http://www.powerproductionsoftware.com>.

Remember, storyboarding techniques are important and are widely used by teachers and others, not only for their own planning, but also as a learning and teaching tool for their students. Also, you will want to see how just by using these same storyboard techniques with your students you can help them do instructional activities like "inferencing" and sequencing of events.

**Tell a Story Using Storyboarding and Scriptwriting**

In conclusion, storyboarding and scriptwriting may seem boring to some of your students. Yet, you can't create an effective video production without planning. Storyboarding and scriptwriting are two excellent ways to plan; they are planning tools that help you tell your story.

Harry Sprouse says, "The story is the thing. Everyone has a great story to tell someone. Stories have been told and recorded since the beginning of time. Curiosity makes us want to acquire knowledge and learn about people, places, and things. Mankind has always used **stories as a way to teach.** That's the way we still teach today. Remember, the medium is determined by the message. You deliver the message through the story, and that folks, is what great communication is all about."

We still use *stories as a way to teach.* **We use storyboarding and scriptwriting as a way to teach and to create great communication.**

# Great Communication with Video Equipment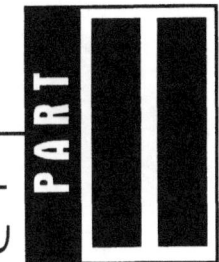

# Audio and Video Plugs and Jacks

**CHAPTER 3**

## Terms

- audio line cable
- BNC jack
- connector
- female
- high level signal
- jack
- low level signal
- male
- microphone cable
- mini plug
- phone plug
- plug
- RCA (phono) cable
- RF cable
- RF signal
- S-Video cable
- Video Line cable
- XLR cable

To begin training students in video production, you need to teach them terms related to video and audio inputs and outputs. What are the different types of video and audio signals? What is the function of the different cables and plugs used for video production? Throughout this book we refer to various types of cables, plugs, jacks, and microphones used in video production, which we will define in this chapter.

First, there is the basic cable that sends the TV picture and sound from the VCR, the TV antenna, or the cable TV hook-up to the TV receiver that will display the image. This cable is called an RF (*radio frequency*) cable. RF stands for radio frequency and RF signals contain the sound and picture for what you see and hear on each TV channel. An RF cable transmits a specific signal for each TV channel. These signals run on the RF cable from the antenna, cable box, or VCR to your TV receiver. The end of the RF cable is called an RF plug and that plug fits into a hole on the back of the TV called an RF jack. When you record a TV program on your VCR, you use an RF cable with an RF plug that fits into the RF jack of your VCR. The sound and picture you record runs on one type of cable, an RF cable.

When you create your own video production, one type of cable is not enough. In video production work, the sound and the picture run on separate cables. The sound runs on a microphone cable or an *audio line* cable. On the end of the microphone cable is the microphone plug, which enters into the VCR, audio mixer, or camcorder at the MIC hole or jack. The plug for a microphone is either an XLR plug with three holes, an XLR plug with three prongs, a mini (1/8") plug with a small prong, or a phone (1/4") plug with a larger prong. Another name for the plug at the end of a cable is a connector. A plug at the end of any cable may be male or female. If it has one or more prongs, it is male. If it has one or more holes, it is female.

The sound in video production work that does not come from a microphone is called an *audio line* input or an *audio line* output. The plugs for *audio line* inputs and *audio line* outputs are called RCA (phono) plugs. These plugs fit into RCA (phono) jacks on camcorders, microphone mixers, or VCRs. Microphone plugs will not fit snugly into RCA (phono) jacks. The microphone plugs will be mini-plugs, phone plugs, or XLR plugs. None of the *audio line* plugs will fit into the microphone jacks. The microphone cable is sending a low-level signal. The VCR *audio line* cable is sending a high-level signal.

Two types of cables carry video signals from one VCR to another VCR or from a VCR to a camcorder. The first type is a *video line* cable. This is the same type of cable as the *audio line* cable. It has RCA (phono) plugs and fits into an RCA (phono) *video in* jack on the VCR. *Video line* cables sometimes use BNC connectors. The second type of cable is an S-Video cable. Some VCRs, especially VCRs used in video editing, will accept S-Video cables, which carry a better quality video signal than *video line* cables. An S-Video cable has an S-video plug and fits into an S-video jack on a VCR or camcorder.

These cables are available at stores that sell electronic equipment. Adapters are available as well. For example, if your VCR accepts only an RCA or phono cable and your camera has only an S-Video connector, an adapter plug is available so you can use the camera and VCR together. A library media specialist should have a supply of extra plugs and adapters for the purpose of using various pieces of video, audio, and computer equipment together. Radio Shack is an excellent source for all these cables and adapters.

## What Cable Goes with What Equipment?

**A BNC cable** is used with a VCR, TV monitor and editor VCR. A BNC cable carries TV picture only. This cable hooks up a VCR to an editor VCR, a VCR to a TV monitor and one editor VCR to another.

**A mini (1/8") cable** is used with a microphone, microphone or audio mixer, head set, camcorder, editor VCR, digital video editor and computer used in digital editing. A mini (1/8") cable carries sound from a microphone to a camcorder

**A phone (1/4") cable** is used with a microphone, microphone or audio mixer, head set and a/v digital mixer. A phone (1/4") cable is used when duplicating an audiotape with two cassette recorders. A phone (1/4") cable also carries sound from the microphone to the a/v digital mixer.

**A RCA (phono) cable** is used with a VCR, microphone or audio mixer, TV monitor, camcorder, a/v digital mixer, digital video editor and computer used in digital editing. This cable can carry either sound or TV picture. When duplicating a videotape with two VCRs, one phono (RCA) cable is used to carry the video signal and another phono (RCA) cable is used to carry the audio signal. A phono (RCA) cable is used to hook up an a/v digital mixer to an editor VCR, a camcorder to a VCR and a microphone or audio mixer to an editor VCR.

**An RF cable** is used with a TV receiver, VCR, cable drop and head end of cable system. An RF cable carries sound and picture. An RF cable is used to carry the sound and TV picture from the head end of the in school cable TV system to the cable drop in a classroom and then to a TV receiver. An RF cable carries the sound and TV picture from a VCR to a TV receiver.

**An S-Video cable** is used with an S-VHS VCR, TV monitor, editor VCR, a/v digital mixer and S-VHS camcorder. An S-Video cable carries the TV picture only. This cable hooks up a VCR to a TV monitor, an a/v digital mixer to an editor VCR, a VCR to a digital editor, an S-VHS camcorder to a TV monitor and a computer to a TV monitor.

**An XLR or Cannon cable** is used with a microphone and a microphone or audio mixer. An XLR cable carries sound only. This cable hooks up a microphone to a microphone or audio mixer.

(See Figure 3.1 for examples.)

# Plugs and Jacks

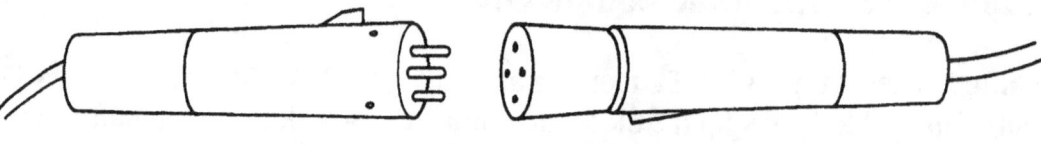

XLR or Cannon Plug

XLR or Cannon Jack

Mini Plug

Mini Jack

Phone Plug

Phone Jack

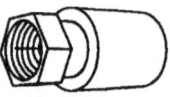
RCA or Phono Plug

RCA or Phono Jack

RF

RF Jack

BNC

BNC Jack

S-Video

S-Video Jack

*Figure 3.1 Plugs and Jacks*
*From "Looking Great with Video Production" by Augie Beasley*

# Audio and Video Plugs and Jacks Checklist

When discussing audio and video plugs and jacks, have a TV and VCR on a cart with all the cables talked about in this chapter available.

_____  1. Identify a BNC cable.

_____  2. Identify a cable that carries a low-level signal.

_____  3. Identify a cable that carries a high-level signal.

_____  4. Identify a microphone cable with a mini plug.

_____  5. Identify a microphone cable with an XLR male plug.

_____  6. Identify a microphone cable with an XLR female plug.

_____  7. Identify a microphone cable with a phone plug.

_____  8. Identify a phono (RCA) cable with a male plug.

_____  9. Identify a phono (RCA) cable with a female plug.

_____ 10. Identify an RF cable.

_____ 11. Identify an RF jack.

_____ 12. Identify an RCA (phono) jack.

_____ 13. Identify an S-Video cable.

_____ 14. Identify an S-Video jack.

_____ 15. Identify an audio line cable.

_____ 16. Identify a video line cable.

# The Camera

## Terms

- camcorder
- charge-coupled device (CCD)
- digital
- digital versatile disk (DVD)
- dolly
- electronic news gathering (ENG)
- extended play (EP)
- eye level
- fluid head
- handheld shot
- high-definition television (HDTV)
- Hi 8 Videos
- palmcorder
- pan
- pedestal
- slow play (SLP) speed
- standard play (SP) speed
- super video home system (S-VHS)
- tilt
- tripod
- truck
- video home system (VHS)
- video home system, compact (VHS-C)
- zoom in
- zoom out

## Camcorders

The camcorder isn't the only camera used in video production, but it's by far the most important. We will discuss the VHS camcorder first. Later in the chapter, we will discuss S-VHS camcorders, palmcorders, digital cameras, DVDs, and HDTV. VHS, video home system, is a type of videotape used for recording. It was introduced in the late 1970s by JVC (Japanese Victor Corporation). The VHS camcorder is the workhorse of video production and can be used as your ENG (electronic news gathering) camera for portable use outside the building, or it can be used as a TV studio camera. The VHS camcorder can also be used to digitize a visual image for a computer presentation. If you have a small budget for your program, we suggest buying one VHS camcorder. Some common features on VHS camcorders are auto and manual focus, zoom and macro (close-up) lenses, and *video out* and *audio out* jacks.(See Figure 4.1.)

The development of the camcorder was a major turning point in the history of video production. Early TV cameras used video tubes that were very sensitive to light. In the early 1980s, manufacturers began making TV cameras and camcorders with digital chips called CCDs (charge-coupled device). The CCD was less subject to light damage than the old video tube, but it was still very sensitive. Also, cameras with CCD were much smaller; large tubes for red, blue, and green colors were no longer required. Thus, the camera could be combined with the recorder in one unit.

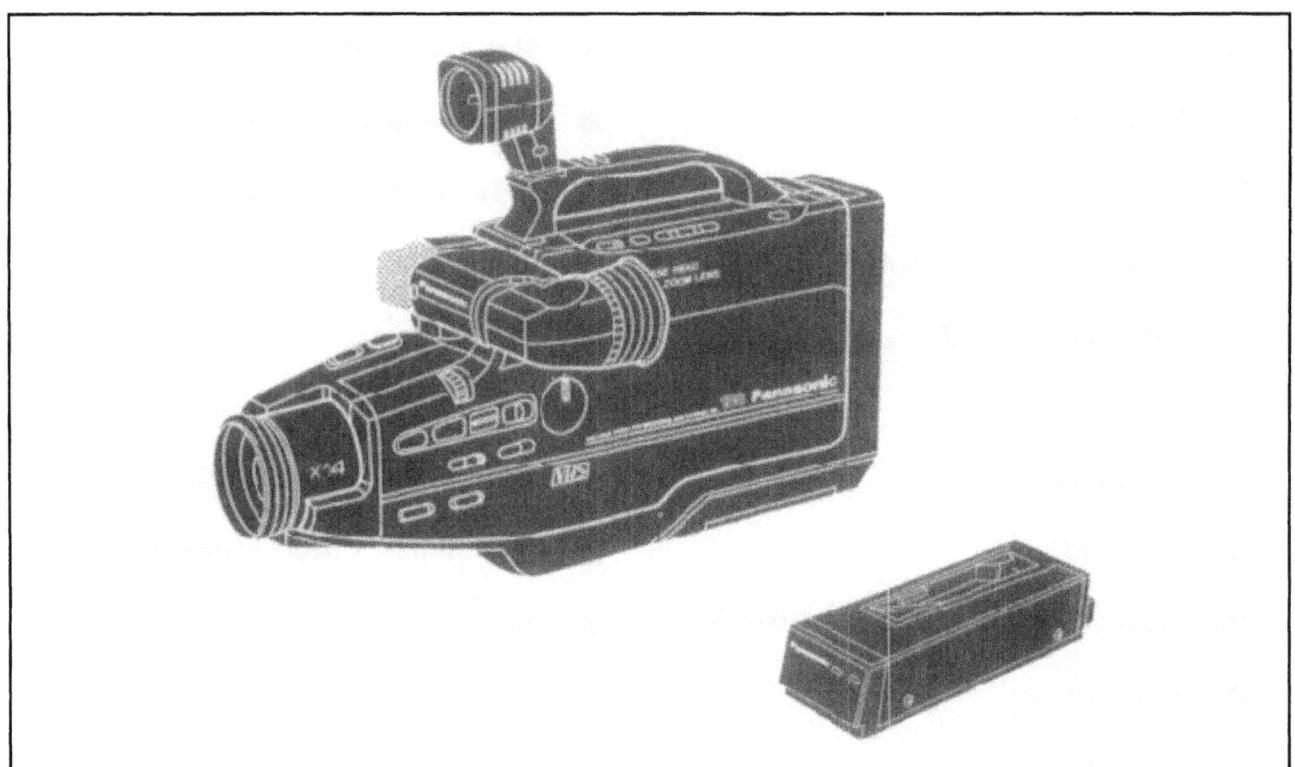

*Figure 4.1 Panasonic VHS Camcorder*

## VHS Videotapes

Of course, with regular VHS camcorders, you need to use VHS tapes. There are many opinions about which VHS tape is best. We've found that as long as you buy a tape with the official VHS symbol, you probably won't go wrong. A more expensive, higher quality videotape would be best if the tape were going to be played back constantly. However, in 20 years of working with VHS tapes, we've never encountered this problem.

Since you are running a library media center, you are using videotapes for different purposes: recording shows off the air, legally copying tapes, and producing short or long videos. Since the cost of tapes has gone down, a 30-minute or 60-minute videotape is not that much cheaper than a 120-minute tape. There's nothing worse than putting a 60-minute tape in your VCR to record a two-hour show using the SP (standard play) speed and discovering that only half of the show was taped. Also, EP (extended play) and SLP (slow play) speeds have lower picture quality than SP speed, so you must tape only at the SP speed. Make it easy on yourself and buy only 120-minute VHS tapes for video production work. We can't recommend T-160 tapes because we've never used them.

## Camcorder Batteries

There is a great deal of misunderstanding about camcorder batteries. Generally, recharging a camcorder battery before it is totally run down isn't recommended. When the battery is recharged too soon, the battery will not function properly. When you charge the battery before the charge is totally run down, the battery thinks it has less operating power and therefore does not provide full power. When on location outside your TV production area, always have at least one spare fully charged battery. Check with the vendor regarding your specific battery and camcorder.

*Figure 4.2 Handheld Camera Shot*

## Holding the Camcorder

Teach students how to use the camcorder so they can learn basic camera shots. (See Figure 2.6. "The Basic Shots," page 14.) First, have the camera mounted to a tripod. Then teach the proper technique for shooting without a tripod, the camcorder mounted on the camera operator's shoulder. A steadier shot is obtained with a tripod because it's tiring to the arms and shoulders to hold a camcorder in your hand. If the camera shot is not steady, it becomes very distracting to the audience. Anyone who has watched a few birthday party videos knows this is true. At times, however, it's awkward to use a tripod so students should know how to shoot from the shoulder. This is called the "handheld shot." In the handheld shot, the camera should rest between the shoulder and the cheekbone of the camera operator. (See Figure 4.2.)

# Shooting an Interview

One of the most important lessons a student should learn is how to shoot an interview. The camera operator needs to understand how to move the zoom lens of the camera to get close to the subject, T for tight shot on the zoom lens, and how to move the lens farther away from the subject, W for wide on the zoom lens. Have the students learn how to focus the camera by zooming in on a close-up of the face and shoulders of the person being interviewed, making sure to get the person's face in focus. The camera should be set on the manual focus setting so if the subject moves during the interview, the focus won't go out of adjustment. Once the students have achieved sharp focus on the close-up, have them zoom out to a medium shot. In the medium shot, only the top half of the interviewee and interviewer, their waists to the tops of their heads, can be seen. Have the students begin the interview with a two shot (medium shot of two people). Once the interviewer asks the interviewee a question, have them zoom in on a close-up of only the interviewee. The eyes of the subject on the screen should always be one third of the way from the top of the TV screen. (See Figure 2.1 "Using the Rule of Thirds," page 9.)

**Using the Tripod when Shooting an Interview**

To use a tripod, students need to learn how to loosen the tilt knob on the tripod so the camera can rotate up or down. This is a good time to also teach the students how to pan, moving the camera horizontally from a stationary position, with the camera. The ability to tilt or pan with a tripod is made possible at the top or head of the tripod. Tripods of good quality have a fluid head. The fluid head has a thick, oily substance that makes smooth pans and tilts easy to do. It's harder to do a smooth tilt or pan with a tripod that does not have a fluid head.

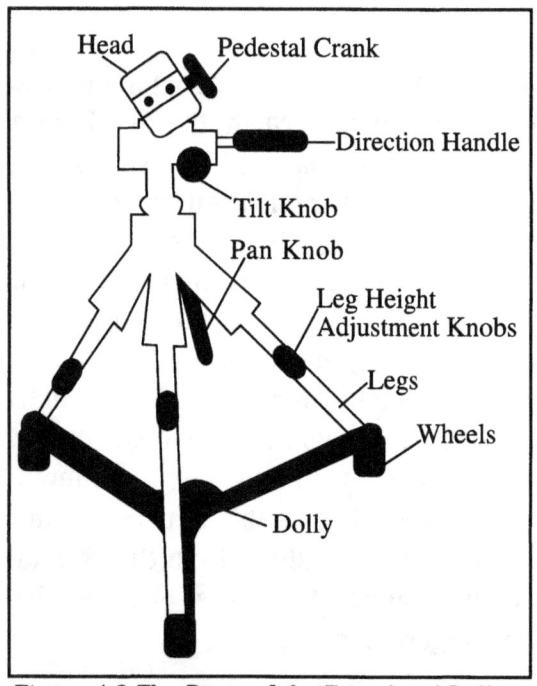

*Figure 4.3 The Parts of the Tripod and Dolly*

In general, camera movements such as zoom in, zoom out, pan, tilt, should be done before the scene is shot. The primary purpose of these functions is to set up the scene before shooting takes place. The audience should be aware of the action in the scene, not the action of the camera. However, when shooting an interview, camera movements are often necessary.

It's very important for the student camera operator to know how to adjust the height of the camcorder. Generally, the height of the camcorder should be at the eye level of a person with average height. Shooting at eye level makes the scene seem more real to the audience. The height of the camera can be adjusted two ways. First, the tripod legs can be extended. Second, the head of the tripod can be raised or lowered. This up or down placement of the tripod head holding the camera on the tripod is called *pedestal*. Teach the students where the

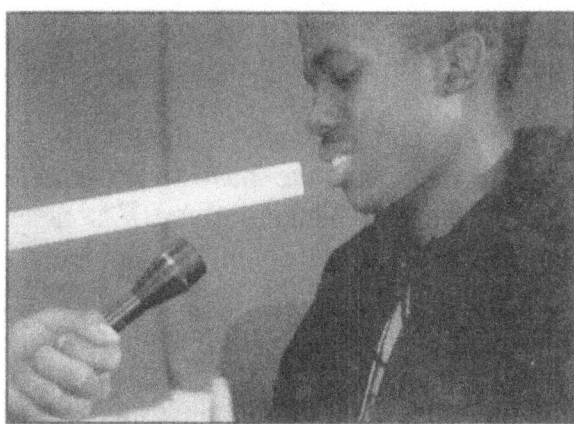

*Figure 4.4 Microphone Placement at 45° Angle*

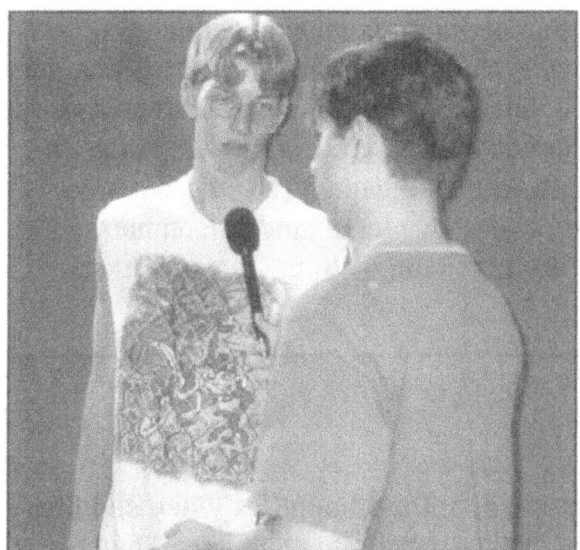

*Figure 4.5 Interviewee Stands at 90° Angle from Interviewer*

pedestal knob is on the tripod. Don't confuse the pedestal with the tilt knob. The tilt knob only changes the up or down angle of the camera. The pedestal knob changes the up or down placement of the entire camera on the tripod head.

## Positioning the Interviewer and Interviewee

Have the students plug a microphone into the external microphone jack, and train the interviewer to hold the microphone at all times during the interview. The students should position the microphone about 6" and at a 45° angle from the mouth of the person talking. (See Figure 4.4.)

If the interviewer and interviewee stand at a 90° angle from each other, it's easier for the camera operator to zoom in on the interviewee during the interview. The interviewee would face the camera, and the interviewer tilts his head sideways to look at the camera. The interviewee should look at the interviewer, not the camera, when speaking. Because the camera faces the interviewee, the audience is able to see both eyes of the interviewee. A silhouette of the interviewee should not be seen when talking on camera. (See Figure 4.5.)

After the camera operator has practiced zooming in and out to get medium and close-up shots on the interviewee, videotaping can begin. Instruct the camera operator to place the videotape in the camcorder, and hit the RECORD button. After pressing the RECORD button, the camera operator should wait 10 seconds before pointing to the interviewer to begin the interview. The practice of shooting an interview is an effective way to teach camera movements, camera shots, and camera operation simultaneously.

## Dolly and Truck with the Tripod

It is rare that an interview would be done while the interviewer and interviewee are walking or running. However, to capture subjects walking or running, the camera operator needs to know how to truck and dolly with the tripod. The word "dolly" has two meanings in video production. First, a dolly is a set of wheels that the tripod rests on allowing the camera to move. Second, a dolly is a camera movement where the camera moves forward or backward into the scene. Trucking involves moving the camera on a dolly in a direction that runs parallel to the scene.

# White Balance, High-Speed Shutter, and Macro

One important operation available on some camcorders is white balance, adjusting the camera's color response to the existing light. To adjust the white balance, have students hold a white piece of paper in front of the camera and press the white balance button. On some cameras there are different white balance settings for different lighting conditions. Be sure the appropriate setting has been chosen.

Also, another important adjustment on the camcorder is high-speed shutter, a feature on the camera that allows fast-moving objects to be captured with more detail. High-speed shutter is used most effectively in outdoor action shots on sunny days. If students press the high-speed shutter button, the picture won't be overexposed. An iris inside the camcorder will let in the appropriate amount of light.

A much overlooked and very useful camera function is macro, a lens adjustment on the camera that allows close-up objects to be captured with more detail. Anything, including fine print from a page, can be brought into sharp focus. Using the macro function to get a close-up of a section of a computer screen can be very helpful when making a training videotape on computer operations. To activate the macro setting, have the students press the W (wide) button until they have zoomed out as far as possible. Then have them move the camera as close as possible to their subject and set the focus to the manual setting. They can then adjust the focus knob until the subject is focused.

# Depth of Field

Remind students of this visual principle they learned about in Chapter 2. When shooting an interview, students shouldn't shoot their subjects against a wall. Instead, have them use a room or hallway as a background for their interview. This gives the picture more depth of field. The type of lens they use also effects the depth of field. A telephoto (zoom) lens decreases depth of field; a wide-angle lens increases depth of field. (See figure 4.6.)

The amount of lighting used in a scene also affects depth of field. A well-lit scene results in the lens aperture (hole letting light in camera) becoming smaller; a smaller lens aperture results in greater depth of field. A poorly lit scene results in the lens aperture becoming larger; the larger lens aperture results in less depth of field (See Figure 4.7.)

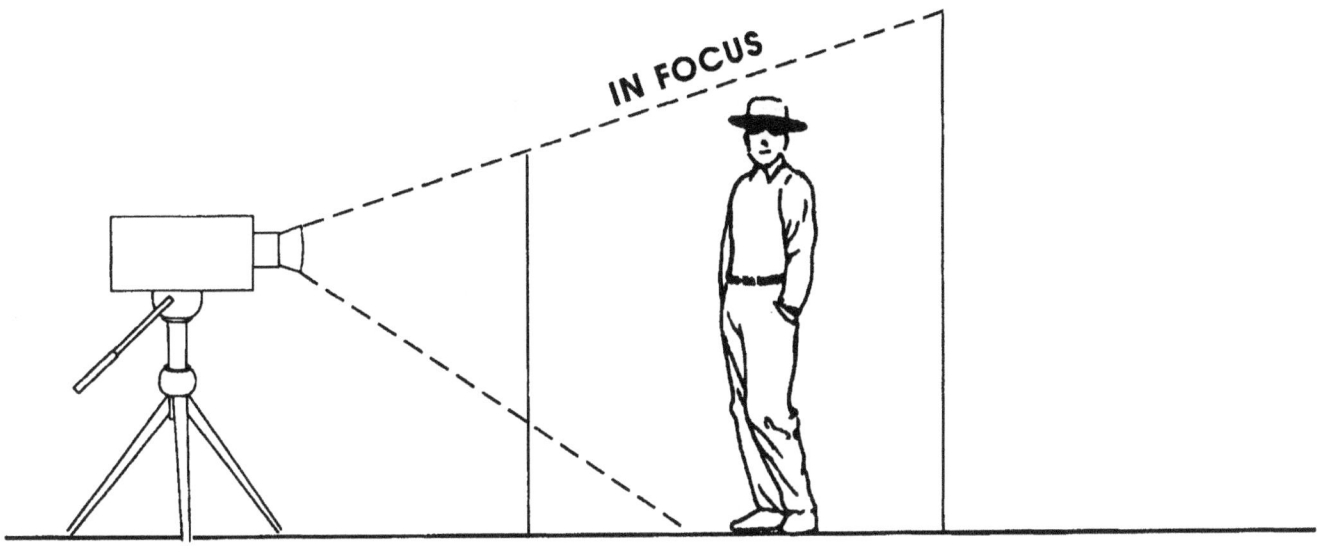

*When you use a wide-angle or short focal lens, you increase the depth of field.*

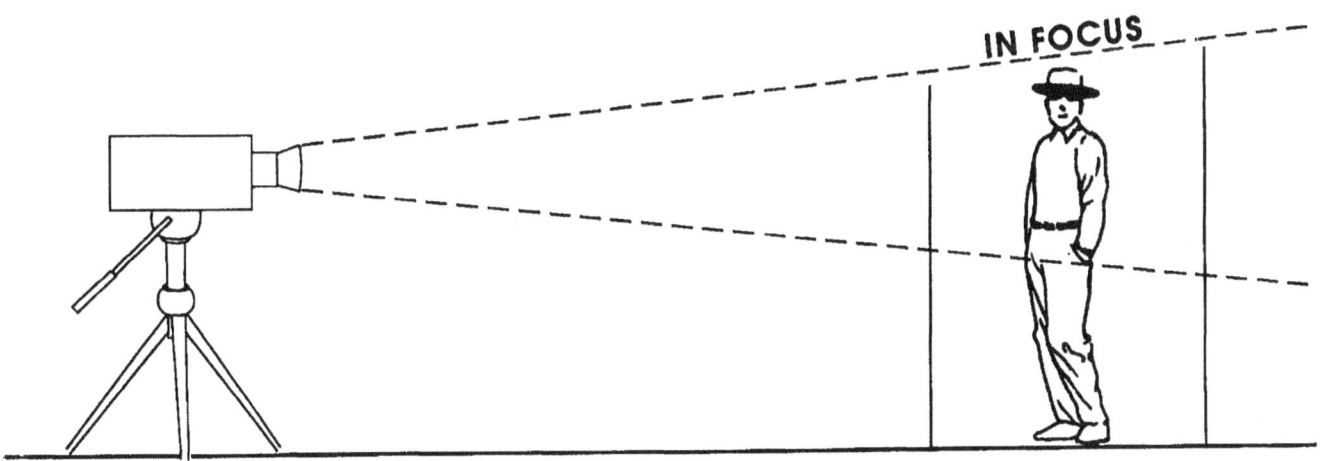

*When you use a telephoto lens you decrease the depth of field.*

*Figure 4.6 Type of Lenses and Depth of Field*
*From "Looking Great with Video Production" by Augie Beasley*

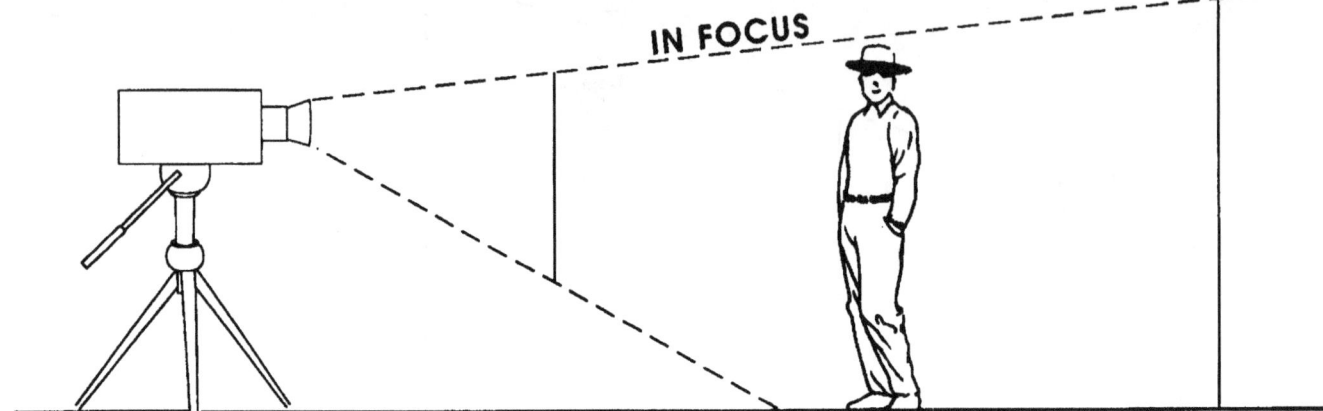

*Small Aperature*

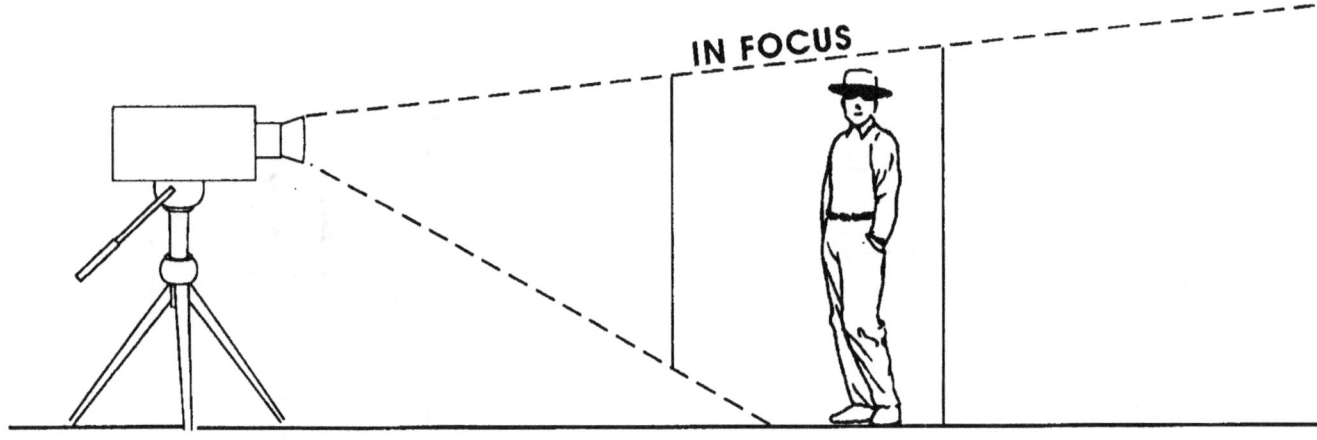

*Large Aperature*

The smaller the lens opening, the greater the depth of field. The larger the lens opening, the less the depth of field.

*Figure 4.7 Size of Lens Opening and Depth of Field*
*From "Looking Great with Video Production" by Augie Beasley*

# Display

Knowing how to eliminate time, date, and other graphics from the viewfinder is a vital skill for students to learn. On many camcorders, pressing the DISPLAY button will turn the time and date on or off. Showing the date and time on a home birthday party videotape may be nice. Showing it on a school production, however, makes the production look unprofessional. When adding a picture from a camcorder to a computer visual presentation, all graphics must be removed from the camcorder viewfinder or they will be seen on the computer visual presentation, which can be very distracting. Consult your camcorder manual to figure out how to eliminate viewfinder graphics. On some camcorders, pressing PAUSE and DISPLAY for six seconds removes viewfinder graphics.

# Back Light Function

The back light function allows the camera operator to shoot into a bright light and still be able to see the subject. Generally, shooting into a bright light isn't recommended. The most common mistake made by beginning camera operators is shooting into a window. On a sunny day, a window constitutes a very bright light source. In daylight hours, it's best to never shoot into a window. The result of shooting into any bright light is that the subject of the shot loses light and can't be seen very well.

# Label Tapes and Pull Tabs

Instruct the students to always label videotapes as soon as the shooting is finished. Have a designated person return the tapes to the place where they are kept. Tell students never to leave a videotape that's just been recorded in the camcorder. The next person using the camcorder may think the tape is not important and might tape over the valuable material that your students have just shot. It's a good idea to pull the tab on a VHS tape right after important footage has been shot so that the footage won't be inadvertently erased. Later, when the footage is no longer needed, place a video label over the square hole where you pulled the tab. That way the tape can be reused. (See Figure 4.8.)

*Figure 4.8 VHS Tapes, Tab On, Tab Off*

## Shut-Down Procedures

One of the most important steps in camcorder shut down is to take the videotape you just recorded out of the camcorder. If you don't do this, the next person who uses the camcorder may record over what you've just recorded. The more important your videotape, the worse you will feel. Teach your students to get into the habit of removing the videotape from the camcorder as soon as they finish videotaping. Also, teach the students to give their finished videotape to you. Have a specific place to store videotapes that have just been shot.

Next, if you used AC power, shut down procedure entails turning the power switch on the camcorder off, disconnecting the camcorder from the AC adapter, putting the lens cap on the lens, detaching the camcorder from the tripod and putting the camcorder and AC adapter in the carrying case. Last, lock up the camcorder in your equipment wardrobe or other secure area. Camcorders are often stolen so be sure you've left your camcorder out of sight and locked up.

If you used battery power, shut down procedure is more complicated. VHS camcorders use lead acid batteries. These batteries should be fully discharged before they are recharged. If the battery is not dead when you are finished shooting, it needs to be drained of power. To do this, put an old VHS videotape in the camcorder. Put the camcorder in the record mode. When the record light stops flashing, take the battery out of the camcorder and recharge it. Then follow the same shut down procedures you'd follow when using the camcorder with the AC adapter.

## Camcorder Checklist

_____ 1. Be aware of camcorder safety. The lens cap should always be on when the camera is not in use so the lens does not get scratched. The camera should never be dropped or operated in the rain or in temperatures below 40° F or above 100° F.

_____ 2. Pick up the camcorder and hold it firmly on your shoulder so you can see into the viewfinder. Attach camcorder to the tripod.

_____ 3. Locate the POWER button. Check to see if the battery is charged. Place the battery in camcorder. Eject the battery from camcorder. Connect camcorder to the power adapter. Connect power adapter to the extension cord and surge protector.

_____ 4. Place the VHS tape in the camcorder. Put the camcorder in the RECORD mode. Press the RECORD button. Note the signal light and the REC graphic in the viewfinder to confirm that recording is taking place. Press the RECORD button again to put the camcorder back in PAUSE mode.

_____ 5. Demonstrate camera moves to be done prior to recording using a tripod and dolly:pan, tilt, zoom in, zoom out, pedestal, dolly, truck.

_____ 6. Demonstrate camera shots—extreme long shot, long shot, medium shot, close-up, extreme close-up, and two shot. Videotape each shot for 20 seconds.

_____ 7. Set the tripod so the camera is at the eye level of a person of average height.

_____ 8. Shoot the following camera angles of a subject–low, high, and oblique.

_____ 9. Shoot a scene that has good depth of field.

_____ 10. Shoot this same scene following the rule of thirds.

_____ 11. Demonstrate white balance, high-speed shutter, auto focus, manual focus, and macro focus.

_____ 12. Demonstrate a shot where you hold the camera steady for one minute.

_____ 13. Demonstrate how to eliminate time and date from the viewfinder.

_____ 14. Demonstrate eliminating all graphics from the viewfinder.

_____ 15. Demonstrate using the back light function when shooting into a bright light.

_____ 16. Demonstrate camera shut down procedures–lens cap on, camera back in case and returned to the media center, tape labeled and returned to media center, and dead batteries labeled and placed in recharger.

## Camera Operator's Checklist

_____ 1. Is microphone plugged in and turned on?

_____ 2. Is tape rewound to the place you want it to be?

_____ 3. Is the camcorder in the camera-recording mode?

_____ 4. Does the tape have its tab in place?

_____ 5. Does your battery work? Is an extra, charged battery available?

_____ 6. Is your subject in focus?

_____ 7. Is your medium shot framed correctly?

_____ 8. Is the room light sufficient?

_____ 9. Do you need extra lighting?

_____ 10. Is your contrast ratio between background light and the subject correct?

_____ 11. Does the subject blend into the background too much?

_____ 12. Do you need a tripod to hold the camera steady?

_____ 13. Does your camera shot have sufficient depth of field?

_____ 14. Is your shot at eye level?

_____ 15. Are the eyes of the talent one third of the distance from the top of the screen?

_____ 16. Are you following the rule of thirds in your picture composition?

_____ 17. Did you record for 10 seconds before signaling the talent to speak?

_____ 18. Did you play back the tape after recording to be sure it is usable?

_____ 19. Did you label your tape?

_____ 20. When finished, did you take tape out of camcorder and give the tape to the person in charge?

# S-VHS Camcorders, Palmcorders, Digital Cameras, DVDs, and HDTVs

The VHS camcorder is a reliable piece of equipment that serves many needs. However, other related emerging technologies can be very useful when producing a video.

## S-VHS Camcorders

S-VHS and S VIDEO are commonly confused terms. S VIDEO refers to a type of video input that has a better picture quality than the RCA (phono) input. S-VHS is a type of videotape and camcorder setting that has a somewhat better picture quality than VHS. The advantage to an S-VHS camera is better focus, and picture quality. Our new S-VHS camera renders a sharper focus and better picture quality than our new VHS camera. Our S-VHS cameras have white balance buttons, but our VHS cameras do not. For TV studio work, it's a tremendous advantage to have white balance capability. When you have a multi-camera set-up, it's important that each camera's picture have the same tint. If one camera looks bluer and the other looks redder, switching from one camera to the other looks terrible. It becomes painfully obvious to the audience that one camera has a bluish tint while the other camera has a reddish tint. If both cameras in a TV studio have white balance capability, the color on both cameras can be easily adjusted to look the same. An S-VHS camera usually costs a few hundred dollars more than a VHS camera, but it is an excellent camera to have. For best results, use an S-VHS camcorder, setting it to the VHS setting and using VHS tapes with it. S-VHS camcorders can use either S-VHS or VHS videotapes.

S-VHS videotapes cannot be used with regular VHS camcorders. This lack of compatibility between VHS and S-VHS tapes may cause problems when you produce a video on an S-VHS tape. When you play this tape on a VHS VCR, you won't be able to watch it. A well-produced video production recorded with an S-VHS camcorder on an S-VHS videotape looks a *little* better than it would using a VHS videotape and the same S-VHS camera—but only a *little*, not significantly better. An important S-VHS tape can cause you a lot of embarrassment if you don't have an S-VHS VCR handy to show it. To make your life easier, you may want to use only VHS tapes with your S-VHS and VHS camcorders.

## Palmcorders

Palmcorders use VHS-C (Video Home System-Compact) videotapes, which are smaller than VHS tapes and require special adapters for playback on VHS VCRs. Most of your students have VHS VCRs at home and can take a VHS videotape they produce at school and show it to their parents on their home VCR. Why complicate a convenient situation by introducing a new format into your video production program? An elementary school library media specialist whose students do a great deal of camera work reports that her students enjoy using a VHS camcorder much more than a palmcorder.

The 8mm palmcorder produces a sharper image and better sound quality than a VHS camcorder because the 8mm videotape does not use iron oxide particles like a VHS tape. Instead, it uses metallic particles. An advanced form of 8mm is Hi 8. Picture quality on

Hi 8 is better than VHS. Hi 8 videotapes do not lose their picture quality when they are edited, which is one advantage of the camcorder. However, with the advent of digital video editing, this feature is of less importance. If you have a digital video editor, you do not have to worry about loss of picture quality. (For more information on how to digitize the picture from a VHS camcorder, see Chapter 6, "Linking Computer and Video," page 57.)

## Digital Cameras

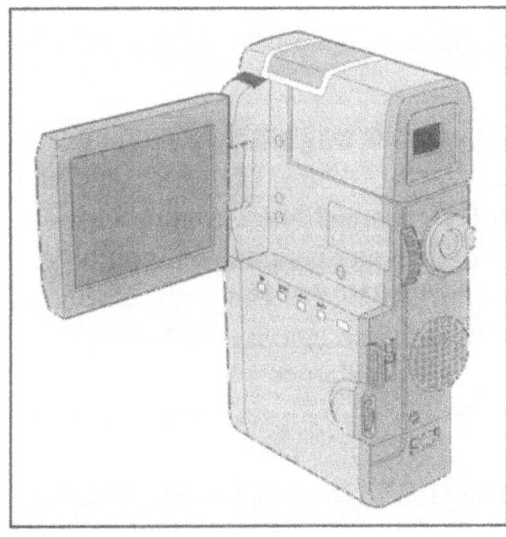

*Figure 4.9 JVC Digital Camera*

The digital camera is like a regular VHS camera in that the picture is captured by a digital chip, the CCD (charge-coupled device) in the camera. In the type of digital camera that we use regularly, the small tape that records the image is digital, whereas in a regular VHS camcorder, the tape that records the image is not digital. Instead, the tape consists of iron oxide particles. The video outputs from both our digital and VHS cameras are not digital. Instead they both send out a regular analog video signal. Hence, the biggest difference between our digital camera and VHS camcorder is that the digital camera is smaller. Our digital camera has an animation setting that does a much better job with animation than our VHS camcorder. (See Figure 4.9.) For the purpose of taking still pictures, a digital camera with a zoom lens would be best. Also, the camera should have large control buttons that are easy to manipulate and a floppy disk drive. The floppy disk for this camera can be used in either an IBM-compatible or a Macintosh computer. The picture can be saved on the floppy disk in the camera; then it can be taken out of the camera and inserted in the computer's floppy disk drive. The picture is opened like any other file and can then be printed. If you have a color printer, you can print a color picture. If there are five teachers who want to add a picture of a student to a computer presentation on the same day, the teachers can take their shots, save them on a separate floppy disk, take out the floppy disk, use it with their own computer, and allow the next teacher to use this digital camera. A digital camera with a floppy disk feature is an excellent choice for a school library media center. One school librarian had taken pictures of her TV news team with a digital camera, printed them out and placed them on a bulletin board. The pictures of the students looked great!

Another type of digital camera that is good for taking still pictures does not have a floppy drive. Instead, it has a device called a flash card that attaches to the camera. A second device, a flash card reader, attaches to the computer at the parallel port. After a picture is taken, it is downloaded from the flashcard to the flashcard reader on the computer. Then the file for the picture is opened in the computer and can be printed in color from the color printer.

The disadvantage of some digital cameras is their size. Because they are so small, they are a little harder to manipulate than a camcorder. The digital camera's small size can also be an advantage. When people are aware of a camera, they sometimes become very shy or overly active. To capture a spontaneous scene of a crowd, you'd have more success with a digital camera. No one would notice that you were recording.

Another digital camera to consider is one without recording features or a zoom lens. It looks like a small desk lamp and is called a flexcam. These have a gooseneck feature so they are easy to manipulate. The focus is not as good as a regular VHS camcorder, and the cost is almost as much as a VHS camcorder. This type of digital camera has an S VIDEO and RCA (phono) output cable. If you have a camcorder with good focus and an RCA (phono) *VIDEO OUT* jack, don't bother with this type of digital camera because it won't offer you any new features not on the camcorder.

### DVD

At this time, DVD (digital versatile disc) has become a popular way to use a computer to watch full motion video along with audio on a computer. A DVD disc is the same size and shape as a CD or CD-ROM disc. Unlike CD or CD-ROM, a DVD disc can hold a number of feature films with high-quality sound, a great deal of music, or many gigabytes of computer software information. However, there isn't a DVD camcorder available at this time. For student video producers, the only use for DVD is to play back what someone else has produced.

### HDTV

Another video technology breakthrough on the horizon is HDTV (high-definition television). HDTV offers a TV picture with twice the picture resolution quality. A TV picture seen in North America today has 525 lines of resolution. With HDTV, the number of lines of resolution is doubled. A camcorder today records an image on videocassette with 240 lines of resolution. It seems clear that at some point, the video productions students produce will have much better picture resolution because the TVs and videocassettes will probably have more lines of resolution.

# Digital Camera for Recording Motion and Animation Checklist

_____ 1. Set up the digital camera for recording with a battery. Turn on the power.

_____ 2. Place a tape in the digital camera.

_____ 3. Operate the zoom lens. Demonstrate auto and manual focus and brightness control.

_____ 4. Record a scene. Rewind and play it back inside the digital camera.

_____ 5. Turn off the camera and remove the battery.

_____ 6. Set up the digital camera for recording from AC power.

_____ 7. Set up the digital camera on a tripod. Record a snapshot of a student. Record another student walking around the room. Have students repeat their names and grades in school.

_____ 8. Put the digital camera in the animation mode. Don't move the tripod or the camera. Shoot the object you want to animate and record one animation scene. Move the object you want to animate just a bit. Shoot the next animation scene. Continue doing this until you've shot five animation scenes.

_____ 9. Set up the digital camera for playback into a TV monitor. Go from Video Out and Audio Out on the digital camera to Video In and Audio In on the TV monitor.

_____10. Remove the date and time from the digital camera's view screen.

_____11. Rewind the snapshot of the student, the recording of the student in motion, and the animation sequence you shot. Play them back on the TV monitor. Note both sound and picture.

_____12. Demonstrate how to charge the battery.

# Lighting

CHAPTER 5

## Terms

- back lighting
- barn doors
- bounce lighting
- contrast ratio
- depth of field
- dimmer
- fill lighting
- floodlight
- florescent light
- incandescent light
- iris
- Kelvin Scale
- key lighting
- neutral density filter
- reflector
- scrim
- spotlight

The camera operator must be trained to produce a visual image that effectively communicates a message to an audience. To do this, knowledge of lighting is required. Poor lighting distracts the audience from the message the video producer is trying to communicate. Good lighting is taken for granted. The viewers are so focused on your message that they fail to notice your technique.

There are two types of light: hard and soft. Hard lighting produces harsh shadows that do not flatter your subject. How can light be adjusted so that it flatters the subject?

## Lighting Kits and Lamps

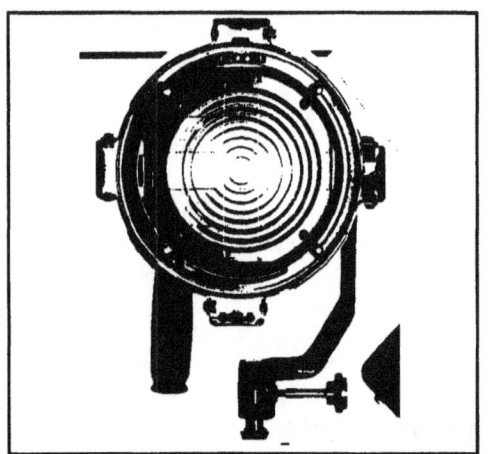

Lighting kits help adjust light to flatter the subject. The lights that attach on top of the camcorders give video shots a flat look. Use a lighting kit instead to achieve well-lit scenes. (See figure 5.1.) The lamps used for some lighting kits may be the same lamps that many of your overhead projectors use. You may already have some lamps like this on hand. Keep this in mind when you are ordering supplies and equipment for your library media center.

*Figure 5.1 Lowell Lights*

## Bounce Light

One easy way to create a well-lit scene is to use bounce light! You can bounce light off of a ceiling, a wall, or a reflector on to your subject. (See Figure 5.2.) When bouncing light off a ceiling you need a relatively low ceiling. A reflector is a large piece of white poster board.

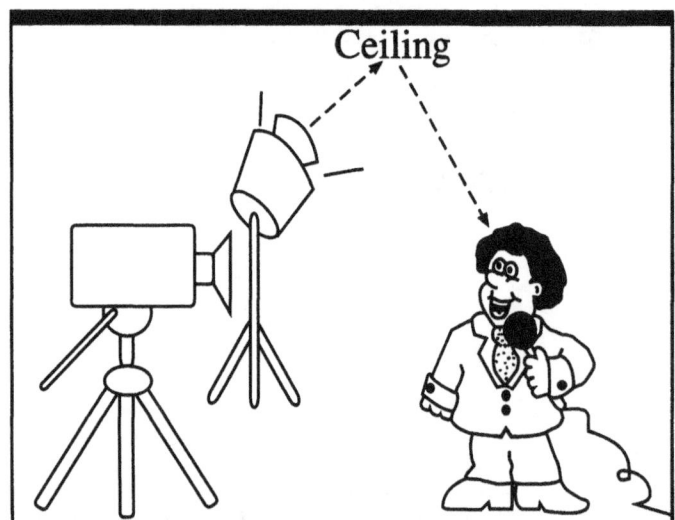

A suggested size to use is 24" x 36." The reflector is used to bounce or reflect light back on to the subject's face. Some people like to wrap aluminum foil, dull side out, on the poster board for even more reflection. By changing the angle at which the reflector adjusts light from the light source, you can soften the shadows on the subject's face. Another way to adjust lighting is to put an umbrella lighting attachment over the light. The umbrella uniformly bounces the light to minimize the shadows on the subject's face.

*Figure 5.2 Bounce Light*

# Dimmers, Spots, and Barn Doors

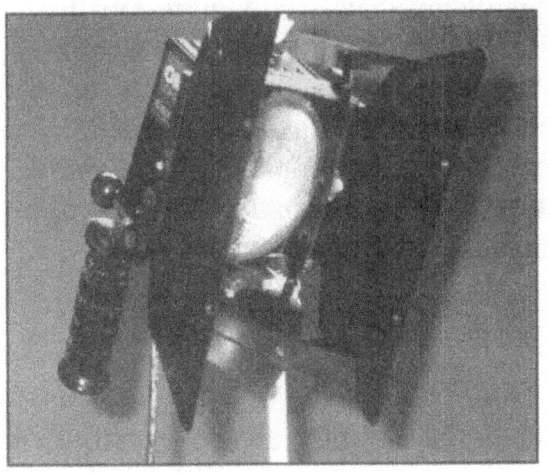
*Figure 5.3 Barn Door*

There are other ways to adjust lighting. Some lights come with a dimmer switch that controls the intensity of the light, and some lights have flood and spot light adjustments. A floodlight will create shadows on the subject less harsh than the spot setting. Barn doors are attachments on the sides of a TV studio light that can be opened or closed, either blocking the light or allowing the light to show on the subject. Barn doors on the sides of the light can be adjusted to bounce the light to soften shadows on the subject.(See Figure 5.3.) If your students are going to adjust the barn doors of a light, be sure to provide them with leather gloves so they won't burn their hands when they touch the hot metal of the barn doors. Moving the light farther back from the subject is another way to adjust shadows.

# Types of Light

Natural lighting for video means lighting that is flattering to skin tones. Light is measured in the Kelvin (K) Scale. Typical indoor incandescent light is rated at 2,500K and has a red tint. Typical florescent light is rated at 4,800K and has a green tint. Typical sunlight has a blue tint and is rated at 5,600K. Natural lighting for video should be 3,200K with a red tint. When shooting outdoors, the best time to shoot on a sunny day is late afternoon. Film producers call this "the magic hour" because the light temperature is much closer to the ideal 3,200K at 5 PM on a summer day then it is at noon. When shooting in a TV studio, camera operators can use the lighting kit's key, back, and fill lights to create a natural light around 3,000K without too many distracting shadows. When in a room with fluorescent light, camera operators can use a bounce light from the lighting kit to counteract the green tint of fluorescent light.

**One-point Key Light**

In one-point lighting, the key light is placed in front of the subject at a 45° angle and above the subject, aimed down at a 45° angle. If the lighting equipment has a focus knob, a spotlight or floodlight effect can be created. Spotlight is focused and creates harsh shadows. Floodlight is unfocused and creates soft shadows. Generally, a harsh shadow distracts the audience more than a soft one.

## Two-point Key and Fill Light

In two-point lighting the fill light and the key light work together. The fill light is placed closer to the subject than the key light. Since the fill light is less powerful than the key light, it should not be pointed directly at the subject. Place the fill light on the opposite side of the camera from the key light at a 45° angle. The angle of elevation for the fill light is 10° to 20°. The fill light should be a floodlight, not a spotlight. The light from the floodlight is more diffuse. The purpose of the fill light is to soften the harsh shadows from the key light. Some shadow is needed to give a feeling of depth in the picture. You want to control shadows in lighting, not get rid of shadows all together. Also, keeping the subject away from a wall helps minimize shadows.

## Three-point Key, Fill, and Back Light

In three-point lighting place the back light above and in back of the subject at a 60° to 70° angle of elevation. This separates the subject from the background, adds highlights to the subject's hair, and creates a three-dimensional effect. The back light should be a spotlight, not a floodlight. This is the basic lighting technique for a TV studio. (See Figure 5.4.)

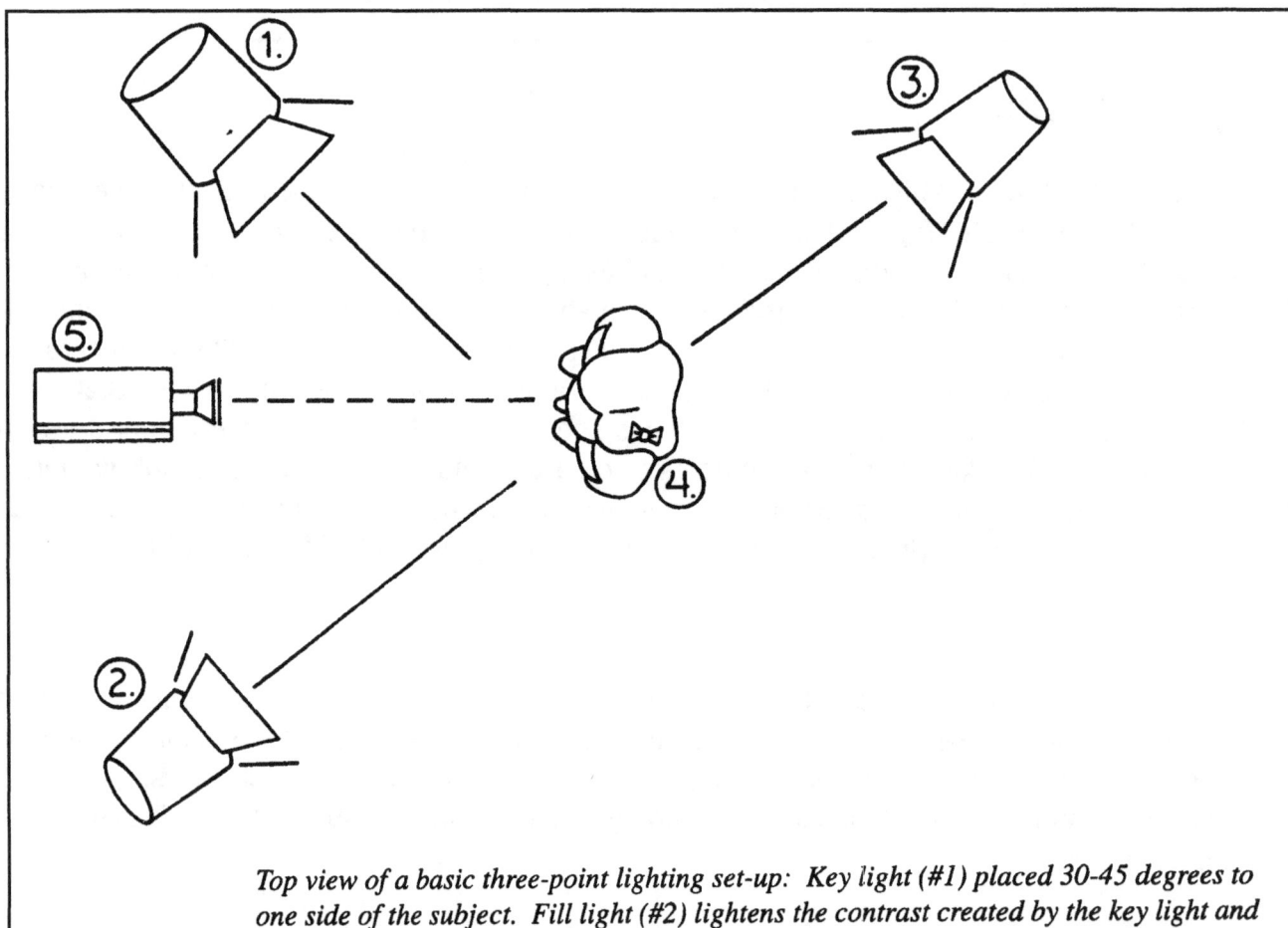

*Top view of a basic three-point lighting set-up: Key light (#1) placed 30-45 degrees to one side of the subject. Fill light (#2) lightens the contrast created by the key light and is usually on the opposite side of the key light. Back light (#3) is located above and behind the subject. (#4) Subject. (#5) Video camera.*

*Figure 5.4 Three-Point Lighting*
*From "Looking Great with Video Production" by Augie Beasley*

# Contrast Ratio

Having different elements of the picture contrast too much can be a real problem. The human eye can view great detail in bright and dark areas in the same picture. A video camera can't do this. The contrast between lights and darks needs to be less, which is why a window on a sunny day should not be used as a background. It makes for a bad contrast ratio. Keep the contrast ratio or difference between lightest and darkest elements of your picture to no more than 15 to 1. Here's an example of a contrast ratio problem. Let's say the walls of your school library are painted a bright white. If you are recording some students with dark skin against this bright white background, the students' faces will seem too dark and hard to see when you play back the tape. The solution to this problem is to pick a less bright background for the shot of the dark-skinned students. There will be better contrast ratio between the light and dark elements of the picture. The dark-skinned students' faces will be brighter and easier to see.

# Shooting Outdoors

Shooting talent on a bright sunny day is a real problem. A cloudy day will, in most cases, allow you to shoot a videotape with more realistic looking colors. Sunlight works best for video shoots two hours after sunrise and two hours before sunset. However, these are often inconvenient times to shoot video outdoors. You may have to shoot your outdoor scene when the sun is brightest in the early afternoon. Your first strategy to get the best lighting is to position the talent at a 45° angle from the sun. You may need to use a reflector to shoot the talent on a bright sunny day. You can adjust the angle at which the reflector reflects light from the sun to soften the shadows on the subject's face.

Obtaining a neutral density filter can also help. The neutral density filter is placed over the lens of the camcorder. It reduces the amount of light entering the lens. When a camera operator uses a neutral density filter on a bright sunny day, the colors in the video production will not look washed out. Instead, the colors will look more natural. The reds will look redder; the blues will look bluer.

Another solution to shooting in bright sunlight is to find a shady area. Shoot your shot under a tree or in the shadow of a building. When shooting in a shady area, be sure you don't include bright blue sky in the picture. That will make your subject's face harder to see. (See Figure 5.5.)

The worst problem when shooting outdoors occurs when the subject can't be moved and the light is directly in back of the subject. To help with this problem, you can use the back light switch on the camcorder, if you have one. Also, a reflector can be used to soften the shadows. The manual iris control will help too. The iris is the part of the camera that lets in sufficient light to videotape a scene. The manual iris control will let in enough light to illuminate the subject. The automatic iris control on most cameras is bad for this situation. The automatic iris control responds to the bright back light, not the subject, so the automatic iris control does not let in enough light to see the subject. A bright blue sky, a lake, or the ocean will not be a good background for a subject on a sunny day. When the sun is bright, bodies of water and sky reflect too much light and cause back lighting problems. Instead, trees or buildings can be used for the background.

*Figure 5.5 Softening Shadows on the Subject's Face*
*From "Looking Great with Video Production" by Augie Beasley*

## Lighting Checklist

_____ 1. Shoot a shot using only a key light: one-point lighting.

_____ 2. Shoot a shot using key and fill light: Two-point lighting.

_____ 3. Shoot a shot using key, fill, and back light: Three-point lighting.

_____ 4. Adjust the spot/floodlight control to a spot setting and then to a flood setting.

_____ 5. Shoot a shot using bounce light off a ceiling.

_____ 6. Shoot a shot using bounce light off a reflector.

_____ 7. Demonstrate how to reduce a shadow in key lighting.

_____ 8. Demonstrate videotape shots with good and bad contrast ratio.

# Sunny Day Shoot Checklist

_____ 1. Bring two working batteries, a camcorder, a reflector, and a videotape.

_____ 2. Screw a neutral density filter onto the camera lens.

_____ 3. Use a windscreen for the handheld microphone if doing an interview.

_____ 4. Position the talent at a 45° angle from the sun.

_____ 5. Have an assistant adjust the reflector to soften shadows on the talent.

_____ 6. If you have to shoot into the sun, use your back light setting.

_____ 7. Don't use a bright blue sky for a background. Use trees or buildings instead.

# Linking Computer and Video

CHAPTER 6

## Terms

- floppy disk
- font
- hard drive
- HyperStudio
- NTSC
- PAL
- parallel port
- peripheral device
- pixel
- point
- port
- PowerPoint
- RAM
- resolution
- ROM
- SECAM
- video card
- zip disk

Today, many people use computers and video images to enhance computer presentations. However, a computer signal and a video signal are quite different. The video signal is an older signal, called an analog signal. It was invented before World War II. The computer signal, a digital signal, was developed more recently and renders a picture image with greater resolution. The digital video signal is in a binary form of computer bits. It can be added to a computer software presentation like *PowerPoint*. In North America and Japan, the analog video signal that flows through VCRs and videotapes is called NTSC (National Television System Committee). In other parts of the world, different video signals are used, such as PAL (Phase Alteration Line) or SECAM (Sequential Color and Memory).

When working with computers and videos, there are two problems: (1) How do you convert a video image from a videotape using an analog NTSC video signal into a computer that accepts digital signals? (2) How do you transfer the digital computer signal into the analog NTSC format so it can be recorded onto videotape?

## Video Cards and Video-Related Peripheral Devices

Video cards and video-related computer peripheral devices enable the user to go back and forth between the computer and video. Sometimes VIDEO IN and VIDEO OUT devices are separate devices. Sometimes, one device does both jobs in a video card that is built into the computer.

## 1. Putting a Still Video Image into the Computer

Adding a picture, especially the picture of a person, greatly enhances a visual computer presentation. Most people enjoy seeing pictures of themselves and their associates in visual presentations. In the world of education, as in the world of business, people expect to see computer presentations created on *PowerPoint*. A new digital camera is not needed to add pictures to a *PowerPoint* presentation. A camcorder will work as long as it has a VIDEO OUT or S VIDEO OUT device. Either Macintosh computer VIDEO IN cards or IBM-compatible VIDEO IN cards can be used. (See Figure 6.1.)

*Figure 6.1 "All-In-Wonder Pro"*
*Video Input/Output Computer Device*

## Putting a Still Video Image into the Computer Checklist

_____ 1. Obtain the appropriate VIDEO IN device and attach it to your computer.

_____ 2. Load any software necessary to operate this device.

_____ 3. To add a still video image to a computer presentation, run an RCA (phono) cable or S VIDEO cable from the camcorder or VCR to the VIDEO IN jack on the computer's video card or the VIDEO IN jack on the peripheral VIDEO IN device.

_____ 4. Use the VIDEO IN computer software to capture the image you want. Click on the SNAP or CAPTURE icon.

_____ 5. Use the VIDEO IN device's computer software to save the image to the computer's hard drive. Be sure to use a "filename" when you save.

_____ 6. Save the image you want in a visual presentation program on your computer, such as *PowerPoint* or HyperStudio.

## 2. Putting a Visual Computer Presentation on Videotape

Putting a computer presentation on a videotape is a very useful skill to master. If the computer presentation has many visuals, it probably won't fit on a floppy disk. Therefore, you may not be able to take that computer presentation from the library computer to a classroom computer. If the libary computer has a zip disk drive, the presentation can be saved on a zip disk, then shown in a classroom equipped with a computer with a zip disk drive. Sure, you can move the computer from the library to the classroom. However, that wastes time. Also, moving computers from room to room can easily cause breakdowns.

The expensive solution to this problem is to buy plenty of laptops with abundant memory of 128 MB of RAM or higher. Visual presentations with many pictures can be created on a laptop and saved to the hard drive. When the presentation needs to be made in a specific classroom, the laptop can be taken to that classroom. Most schools, however, don't have enough laptops to make this feasible.

Another solution is to create your presentation on your computer and save it on a CD-recorable disk. This requires a computer with a CD-recordable disk drive. What about the computer in the room where your presentation will be? Does that computer have a CD-ROM drive? If so, this solution may work. Be sure to test your newly created CD ahead of time on the computer in which you will be presenting.

What if you don't have laptops or computers with zip disks or CD-write recorders in your school? The next best thing to do is create the visual presentation on the hard drive of a computer in the library and convert the presentation to a videotape. Most classrooms have access to a TV and VCR. When creating a presentation to be placed on videotape, you must keep two things in mind.

First, when creating a computer presentation, use large size fonts. When showing your presentation on a TV receiver or TV monitor with a 25" screen size, you shouldn't use font sizes smaller than 60 point. Students in the back of the classroom won't be able to see font sizes smaller than 60 point. Also, font sizes of 60 point and above convert from computer to videotape with excellent quality. Small font sizes (below 30 point) convert from computer to video with very poor quality.

Second, do not put text or pictures on the edges of the computer screen. TV monitors vary in the section of the picture they pick up. Visual information on the edge of the picture is easily cut off. (See Figure 2.9, "Place Graphics in the Picture Area," page 16.)

## Putting a Visual Computer Presentation on Videotape Checklist

_____ 1. Obtain the appropriate VIDEO OUT device and attach it to your computer.

_____ 2. Connect the RCA (phono) cable or S VIDEO cable to the VIDEO OUT or S VIDEO OUT jack on the computer video card or computer peripheral device.

_____ 3. Connect the other end of the RCA (phono) or S VIDEO cable to the VIDEO IN or S VIDEO IN jack on the VCR.

_____ 4. Be sure the appropriate input select option has been selected on your VCR. For example, be sure you're using LINE, not TUNER. Be sure you've selected S VIDEO, not LINE if you're using S VIDEO cables.

_____ 5. Be sure your VCR is connected to your TV correctly.

_____ 6. You may have to adjust your computer screen monitor. For example in Windows adjust the monitor by going to choices like PROGRAMS, SETTINGS, CONTROL PANEL, and DISPLAY. Adjust the monitor to a lower number of pixels.

_____ 7. Put the videotape in your VCR and press RECORD button.

_____ 8. Open your computer presentation and move through it to completion.

## 3. Putting a Visual and Audio Computer Presentation on Videotape

Sometimes, it is necessary to put an entire multimedia presentation including sound, text, graphics, stills, and motion video onto videotape. Perhaps the appropriate computer is not available at the site where the presentation will be taking place. If you are not sure about how the computer equipment works at the location of a presentation, consider converting the entire presentation, both sound and picture, to videotape. The video picture will not be as sharp as the computer picture. However, the picture will be acceptable as long as font sizes don't go much below 60 point. The audience members will enjoy seeing your presentation on videotape much more than they will enjoy twiddling their thumbs for an hour while you tear your hair trying to get your computer presentation to work on someone else's computer.

### Putting a Visual and Audio Computer Presentation on Videotape Checklist

_____ 1. Connect the RCA (phono) cable to the AUDIO OUT jack on the computer video card or computer peripheral device.

_____ 2. Connect the other end of the RCA (phono) cable to the AUDIO IN jack on the VCR.

_____ 3. Repeat Steps 1-8 from "Putting a Visual Computer Presentation on Videotape."

## 4. Putting a Computer Presentation on Videotape while Adding Narration

Audio takes up a great deal of memory on a computer. Putting sound for a computer presentation on a videotape is a convenient way to store the sound. Many computers will not have enough memory to easily store and play the audio portion of a presentation. Every VHS VCR in your school will be able to play the sound portion of your presentation on VHS videotape.

If you have a VCR with a microphone input, you convert the computer material to video using a video output device. The cable is run from the VIDEO OUT on the computer to the VIDEO IN on the VCR. Insert the microphone in the MIC jack on the VCR and press RECORD. As you are recording the visual material, you can add an audio narration by speaking into the microphone.

However, most VCRs on the market today do not have a microphone input. Camcorders have microphone inputs but often the newer models don't allow the user to add sound while also adding the picture in the line input, VIDEO IN.

The technique of using the cassette recorder to add sound from a microphone is very valuable. (See Figure 6.2.) It would cost five times the regular cost of a VCR to find a new VCR with a microphone input. Another solution to this problem would be to hook up a microphone to a microphone mixer and go from the microphone mixer to the, AUDIO IN jack of the VCR as you add the visual computer presentation in the VIDEO IN jack.

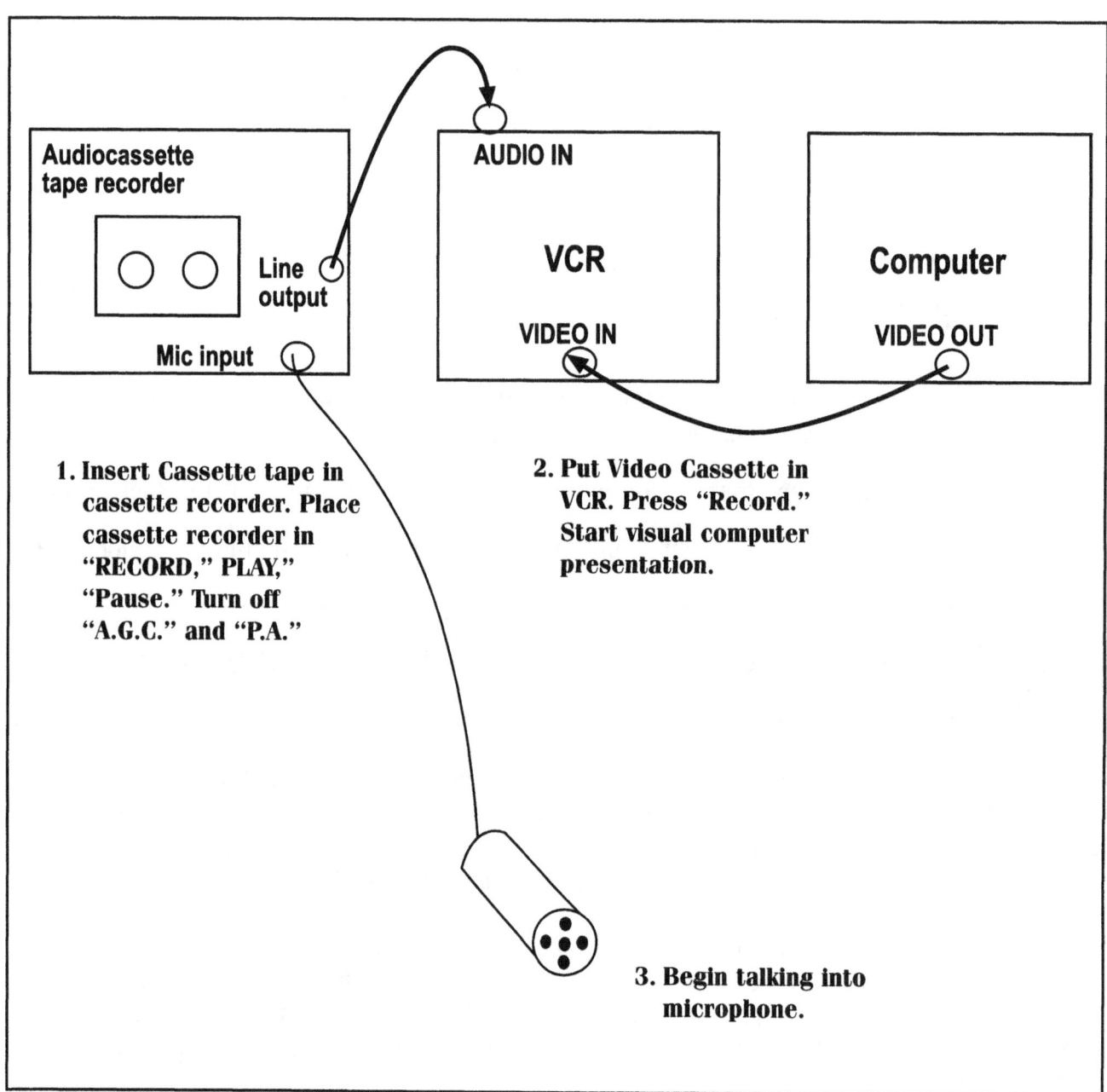

*Figure 6.2 How to Add Narration from a Microphone to a VCR While Converting a Visual Computer Presentation to Videotape.*

## Putting a Computer Presentation on Videotape while Adding Narration Checklist

_____ 1. If the VCR has a MIC jack, insert the microphone.

_____ 2. Follow Steps 1-8 from "Putting a Computer Presentation on Videotape."

_____ 3. If the VCR does not have a MIC jack, insert the microphone in a cassette recorder's MIC jack.

_____ 4. Place a cassette tape in the tape recorder and place the cassette recorder in the PAUSE/RECORD mode.

_____ 5. Be sure the A.G.C. (Automatic Gain Control) and P.A. (Public Address) switches are turned off.

_____ 6. Connect an RCA (phono) cable in the LINE OUT jack of the cassette recorder.

_____ 7. Connect the other end of the RCA (phono) cable to the AUDIO IN jack of the VCR.

_____ 8. Follow Steps 1-8 from "Putting a Computer Presentation on Videotape." As you record each section of the computer presentation, speak into the microphone to add narration.

## 5. Adding Motion Video to a *PowerPoint* Presentation on a Computer

A computer presentation can be greatly enhanced by adding motion video shots with a camcorder or digital camera. Perhaps a *PowerPoint* presentation is on a subject involving motion, such as a presentation on modern dance or how to hit a baseball. A video sequence of a hitter's swing or a dancer's routine would greatly enhance the presentation.

In order to import the video from a camcorder, you would need to install a video card in your computer.

# Adding Motion Video to a *PowerPoint* Presentation on a Computer Checklist

_____ 1. Connect the VIDEO OUT or S VIDEO OUT of your camcorder or digital camera to the S VIDEO IN or VIDEO IN of the video card.

_____ 2. In Windows, go to START.

_____ 3. In Windows, go to PROGRAMS.

_____ 4. Go to multimedia player program.

_____ 5. Click on TUNER MODE button on upper part of screen.

_____ 6. Select S VIDEO IN connector icon or VIDEO IN RCA (phono) connector icon on the lower left section of screen.

_____ 7. Begin playing a tape in camcorder or digital camera.

_____ 8. Click camcorder icon button in upper right of screen.

_____ 9. Click red button with camcorder icon on the lower left of screen.

_____ 10. Click OK in dialog box.

_____ 11. Click same button as in # 9 to stop recording.

_____ 12. Note SAVE AS box comes up. Type in filename. Select drive and save to it.

_____ 13. Click yellow arrow to play back the video you've recorded on the computer's video player.

# Switchers and Mixers

## CHAPTER 7

## Terms

- audio mixer
- a/v digital mixer
- character generator
- chroma key
- decibels
- graphic
- internal synchronization
- line input
- MIC input
- mosaic
- over modulation
- split screen
- strobe
- superimpose
- switcher
- VU meter

# Video Switchers

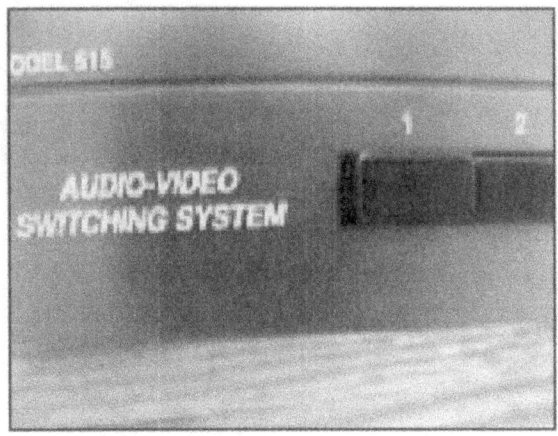

Figure 7.1 A Simple and Inexpensive Video Switcher from Audio Authority

Training students to operate switchers and mixers will help them produce professional looking videos. A video switcher allows students to switch between at least two video cameras or other video inputs. For a switcher to do this it needs "internal synchronization." Some video switchers are relatively inexpensive (about $100). If you buy one like this, be sure it has internal synchronization.(See Figure 7.1.) There are video switchers on the market that will not let users switch between different TV cameras because they don't have internal synchronization.

# A/V Digital Mixer

A high quality switcher for a TV studio will have four inputs and will accept both the regular video signal, VIDEO IN, and the higher quality S VIDEO signal. Usually, this type of a switcher is called an a/v digital mixer, which costs between $1,000-$2,000. The "a/v" means that the switcher has both audio and video inputs and outputs. Not all video switchers accept audio inputs and outputs. If there is an S VIDEO input and a Y/C next to it, the switcher can accept and process a high quality S VIDEO signal. Y stands for the brightness of the picture, and C stands for the color. In an S VIDEO signal, these elements are processed separately by the switcher. In the regular video signal, VIDEO IN, the brightness and color parts of the signal are not split. Hence, the regular VIDEO IN signal is called a composite signal.

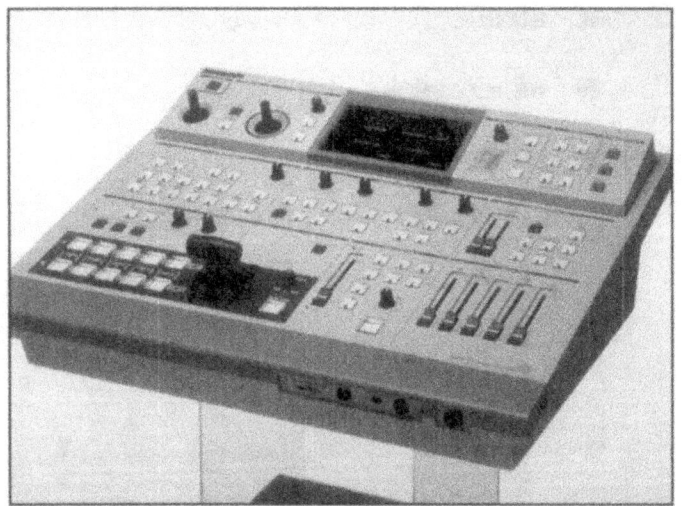

Figure 7.2 Panasonic A/V Digital Mixer

### Chroma Key and Split Screen

The chroma key and split screen effects work on the principle of the A BUS and the B BUS. The A BUS and B BUS are simply different ways for the TV picture to come into the a/v digital mixer. TV pictures from the A BUS and B BUS can be combined in many ways. One example of combining the A BUS and B BUS is chroma key. Chroma key adds an entirely new dimension to video productions by allowing the insertion of an image from one video source into the picture of another video source. In one video source all the visual material of one color is removed. For example, if a person is shot in front of a blue background, the entire blue background can be removed from the picture. The part of the image that remains, the person, is inserted into the other video source; the blue background is deleted and the person in front of the blue background is now seen in the picture of the other video source. If that other video source were a picture of a forest, the person would appear in front of the forest.

The split screen effect is great when doing educational quiz shows. The quiz master is seen in a close-up shot from one camera asking questions on one side of the screen on the A BUS while the contestant is seen in a close-up shot from another camera on the B BUS giving answers on the other side of the screen. (See Figure 7.2.)

## Fade, Dissolve, Wipe, and Still

In a "fade," the picture gradually goes to black. To create a "fade," press the FADE button on the a/v digital mixer. For a "still," press the STILL button. There is usually one button for MIX and WIPE. "Mix" is another term for "dissolve" and means one picture gradually blends into another. For a mix or dissolve from camera one to camera two, the light for camera one would be lit on the A BUS, and the light for camera two would be lit on the B BUS. Then the A BUS/B BUS lever would be moved from the A BUS to the B BUS. For a "wipe," a specific wipe pattern must be chosen. It could be horizontal or vertical. Then, the MIX/WIPE button must be pressed to enter the wipe mode. Then, switch from one camera to the other the same as for a dissolve. However, the scenes don't blend now. In a wipe, the scene from camera one gradually or quickly pushes the scene from camera two away. How fast the "wipe" happens depends on how quickly the A BUS/B BUS lever is moved.

## Strobe and Mosaic Effects

The strobe effect is another special effect made possible by the a/v digital mixer. To strobe a person standing in front of the camera, have him look left, look right, wave, and take a bow. With the strobe effect, these actions will appear as still shots, each lasting about one second.

The mosaic effect is great for disguising the identity of a person. The mosaic, which looks like a pattern of mosaic tiles, is simply positioned over the face of the person whose identify needs to be hidden.

## Character Generator

Switchers or a/v digital mixers should be compatible with character generators. The character generator is a device that makes it easy to type title graphics into a TV show and superimpose them over any video scene. A character generator that has a keyboard at least a foot long is best. Some character generators are only about two inches square. They are very cumbersome to work with.

Figure 7.3 Panasonic Character Generator

## Using the A/V Digital Mixer for Mixing Sound and Picture

The audio from a microphone would enter a camcorder's MIC input when using the a/v digital mixer to mix both picture and sound. The sound from the microphone would leave the camcorder as a line output at the camcorder's AUDIO OUT. The sound would then travel into one of the a/v digital mixer's AUDIO IN jacks and finally from the a/v digital mixer's AUDIO OUT to the AUDIO IN on the VCR. A word of caution is called for here. Mixing sound from different sources is done more effectively on a separate audio mixer because it's easier to control the volume level for sound with a separate audio mixer. (See Figure 7.4.)

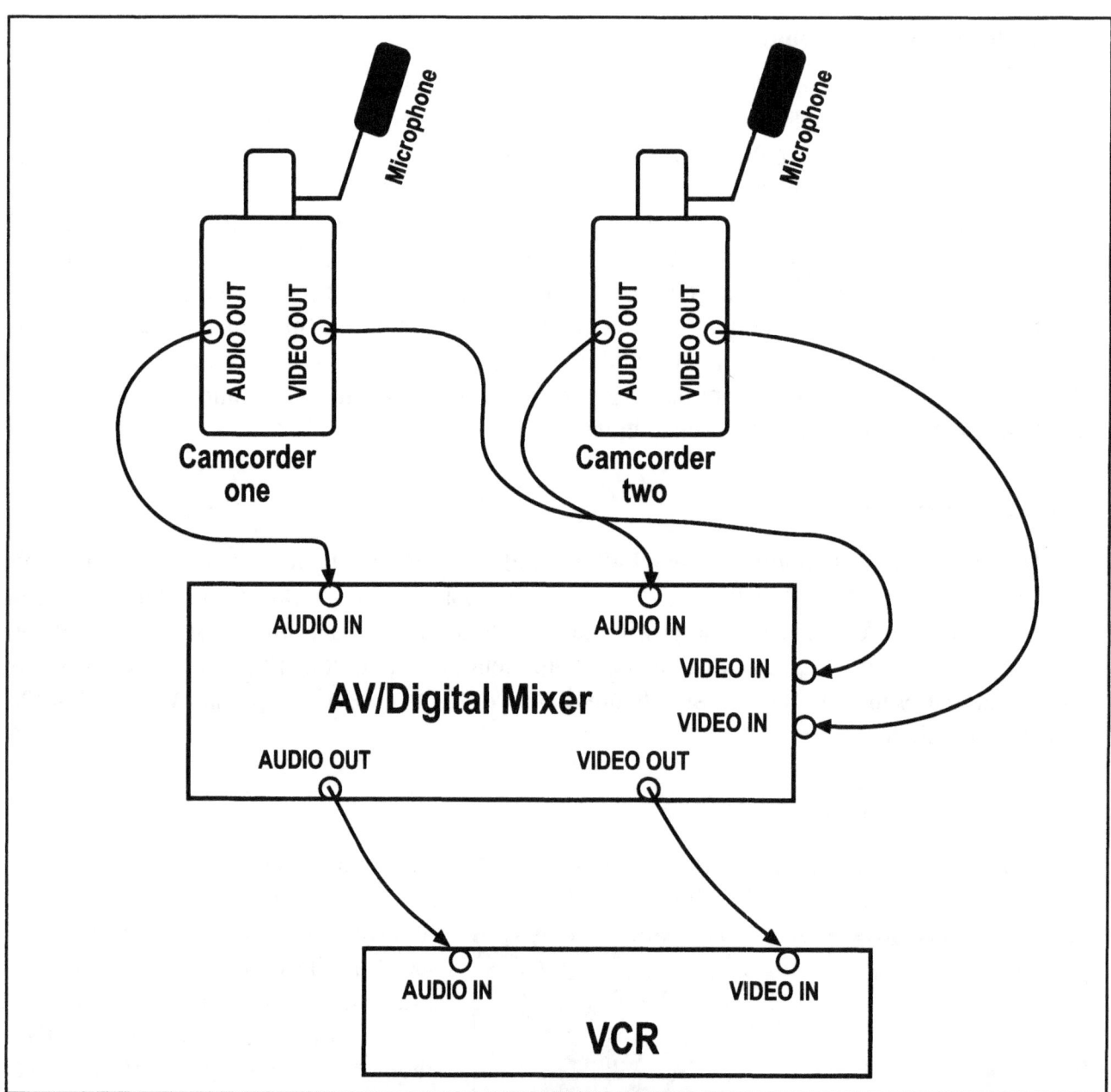

*Figure 7.4 Using the A/V Digital Mixer for Mixing Sound and Picture*

## Video Input Switching Checklist

Use a video switcher or a/v digital mixer to create the following effects so they can be seen on the recorder VCR monitor.

_____ 1. Select the picture on video input 1.

_____ 2. Do a camera switch to video input 2.

_____ 3. Do a camera switch to video input 3.

_____ 4. Do a camera switch to video input 4.

_____ 5. Do a "wipe" between video inputs 1 and 2.

_____ 6. Do a "fade" from video input 3 to black (no picture).

_____ 7. Do a "dissolve" between video inputs 3 and 4.

_____ 8. Do a "still" effect for a camera or camcorder input.

_____ 9. Create a title using the digital mixer's character generator. Superimpose the title over the talent on camera 1 at the bottom of the screen.

## Chroma Key with the A/V Digital Mixer Checklist

_____ 1. Select camera 2 on the A BUS for the background.

_____ 2. Press STILL.

_____ 3. Select camera 1 on the B BUS for the talent.

_____ 4. Press SET. Note the white plus sign on the preview monitor.

_____ 5. With the joystick on the left side of the a/v digital mixer, move the white plus sign to the biggest area of the background scene.

_____ 6. Press ENTER. The talent can now be seen in front of background on the preview monitor.

_____ 7. Move the white plus sign with the joystick to an area of the background that looks distorted.

_____ 8. Press ENTER. Note that the distortion disappears.

_____ 9. Repeat Steps 7 and 8 until all distortion has been removed.

_____ 10. Press CHROMA KEY. Note that the chroma key effect can now be seen on both the preview monitor and the TV monitor for the recorder VCR. If it is not seen on the TV monitor or the recorder VCR, move the A BUS/B BUS lever until it can be seen.

## Strobe Effect on the A/V Digital Mixer Checklist

_____ 1. Press EFFECT in the upper right corner of the a/v digital mixer. Note the graphic display on the preview monitor.

_____ 2. Use the right number pad arrow on the a/v digital mixer to move "A" next to EFFECT on the preview monitor.

_____ 3. Use the down arrow on the a/v digital mixer's number pad to STROBE on the preview monitor.

_____ 4. Use the a/v digital mixer's right arrow to select a strobe speed of 1-5 on the preview monitor. The "5" speed renders the fastest strobe effect.

_____ 5. On the A BUS, push the button for the camera to be used. That button will flash.

_____ 6. Push the EFFECT button on the upper right section of the a/v digital mixer so the graphic on the preview monitor can no longer be seen.

_____ 7. Push the EFFECT button on the A BUS. Have the talent move around on the camera you selected for strobe. Note the strobe effect.

## Split Screen on the A/V Digital Mixer Checklist

_____ 1. Set up shot for camera one on A BUS.

_____ 2. Set up shot for camera two on B BUS.

_____ 3. Press WIPE/MIX button. Note the graphic comes up on the preview monitor.

_____ 4. Press WIPE.

_____ 5. Look at the preview monitor to note wipe patterns. Use the up/down or right/left buttons on the a/v digital mixer to move the desired pattern onto the preview monitor.

_____ 6. Press the SELECT/UNDO button repeatedly to get the direction you want.

_____ 7. Move the A BUS/B BUS lever to the middle.

_____ 8. Look on the recorder TV Monitor. Note the split screen effect.

# Audio Mixers

Quality audio can greatly enhance a video production. An audio mixer should have at least four inputs. These inputs should be able to accept either a MIC or LINE source. A MIC source is from a microphone; a LINE source is from a CD or cassette player. A typical audio mixer allows the user to flip a switch to either the LINE or MIC setting for each input.

The audio mixer should accept low impedance microphones. Low impedance microphones render better sound quality than high impedance microphones. In addition, an audio mixer should have one *audio output*. When doing a TV production, the sound goes from the *audio output* of the audio mixer to the LINE IN audio input of the recorder VCR.

An audio mixer should have a VU (volume unit) meter that tells the strength of the audio signal in decibels. Generally, a quality audio signal should fluctuate between +4 and +10 decibels. It should bounce into the upper levels of the "red" zone but not stay in the upper levels of the "red" zone. If it stays in those upper levels over modulation takes place. The sound source is so strong that it is distorted. To check to be sure that each audio input is set at the appropriate level, each audio input should have a dial next to it that can be adjusted. The *audio output* should also have a dial. To adjust these dials, look at the VU meter and move the dial until the meter shows the correct setting. It helps if the recorder VCR also has a VU meter. All audio coming from various audio inputs needs to be adjusted so each sound source has the same volume level. That way, people watching the video do not have to continually turn their TV volume level up or down. (See Figure 7.5.)

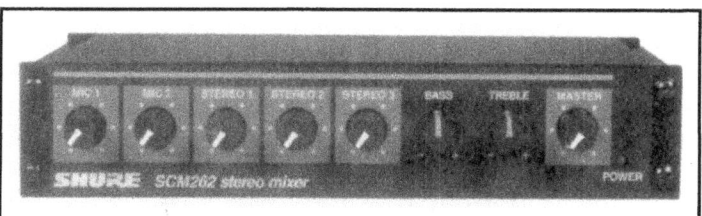

*Figure 7.5 Shure Audio Mixer*

# Audio Mixer Checklist

_____ 1. Adjust the VU (volume unit) meter on the audio mixer for first microphone, INPUT 1, to the optimum level (approaches 100% mark on the meter periodically but does not stay a 100%).

_____ 2. Repeat for second microphone, INPUT 2.

_____ 3. Repeat for third microphone, INPUT 3.

_____ 4. Adjust the VU meter on the audio mixer for the CD/cassette sound source to the optimum level for INPUT 4.

_____ 5. Adjust the VU meter for OUTPUT from the audio mixer to the recorder VCR so that the optimum audio level is achieved on the VU meter of the recorder VCR.

_____ 6. Make a recording on the recorder VCR that mixes narration with music so that the announcer's voice is clearly heard with a musical background.

# Video Editing

**CHAPTER 8**

## Terms

- A/B roll editing
- analog
- assemble
- audio dub
- control track
- digital video
- dissolve
- edit controller
- footage
- generation (editing)
- hi-fi
- jump cut
- non-linear
- snow
- transition
- video insert

Just about every staff member, teacher, and student needs to do some video editing at some point. The football coach may want to edit some football plays from a recent game. A student may want to edit an video project for English class. An art teacher could possibly want to create a short video on brush stroke technique using as little editing as possible.

You, the library media specialist, don't have time to edit everything for everybody. However, if you can show the staff, teachers, and students how to edit their videos, you'll be doing them all a great service. You don't want to teach everyone the same type of video editing. There are six types of editing for different needs and levels of experience.

Some or all may have a place in your library media center. The type of editing used depends on the simplicity or complexity of the project, how much time the person has to spend editing the video, and how comfortable the person is with technology.

Any video editing should be seamless. This means there should be good transition from one scene to the next. You never want to see snow in the picture between scenes or the jerky kind of transition between two scenes that's called a jump cut.

## Types of Video Editing

The six types of video editing that are going to discussed in this chapter are:
1) In-Camera Editing, 2) Simple Two VCR Electronic Editing, 3) Editing Using a Video Editor (No Edit Controller), 4) Editing Using a Video Editor (Edit Controller System), 5) Digital Editing Using a DraCo Casablanca Digital Video Editor, and 6) Digital Editing Done on an IBM-Compatible or Macintosh Computer using Digital Editing Software.

In all six types of video editing, VHS videotapes are used at some point for playback and recording. Be sure all VHS recording is done at the SP speed. Video footage shot at the SLP or EP speed will not edit well. In-Camera Editing and Simple Two VCR Electronic Editing have a major weakness. With these editing systems, audio dub or video insert cannot, sometimes, be done. Some older model camcorders, widely used in the early 1990s, allowed audio dubbing. In the more recent camcorders, audio dubbing cannot be done. The audio dub feature, adding additional sound, can really improve a video. The video insert feature can also improve a production a great deal. Using video insert, new video can be added to a scene while keeping the old sound. The new video footage you add is called B roll. Audio dubs and video inserts can be added to a video by using the other types of video editing. The first four types of editing are analog. This means the editing process is an electronic process whereby iron oxide particles on a videotape are changed. Digital editing using a DraCo Casablanca Digital Video Editor is done on a digital editing machine, and digital editing done on an IBM-compatible or Macintosh computer using digital editing software is done with special editing software. In both types of editing, binary computer bits of information are edited, not iron oxide particles. The advantage of this method is that digital editing provides a more attractive edit.

The use of any of the first four types of video editing, such as analog editing, diminishes picture quality each time the tape is edited. In other words, each time the video image is copied in the editing process, the quality of the image goes down. A scene that has never been edited (copied) is called first-generation. The edited copy of the first scene is called second-generation. When the second-generation copy is edited again it is called third-generation. By the time you get to the third-generation copy of an edited videotape, the picture quality is considerably poor.

By the time a tape has been edited four times in the analog process, the picture quality looks terrible. This effect is only true of the video element of a TV production. The quality of audio does not change very much with each additional edit. Six different checklists for video editing are listed below. Before using these checklists with students and staff, you'll probably want to change them to account for your video equipment. Every model has some unique qualities.

### 1. In-Camera Editing

This type of editing will only work if the video is scripted when shooting begins. Every scene must be shot in sequence. If a mistake is made, it has to be corrected immediately; nothing can be added or edited out later. In-camera editing saves a great deal of time editing later. This is the high planning, low-tech option.

## In-Camera Editing Checklist

_____ 1. Be sure the videotape is rewound to the beginning. Be sure the tab on the front of the tape to be recorded is not missing. You cannot record if the videotape is missing its tab. Put the lens cap on the camera. Pick a quiet location. Record 10 seconds of a blank screen.

_____ 2. Shoot the first scene. Dialogue should not be spoken or important events should not take place until the recording has been going for six seconds. Pause camcorder at end of scene.

_____ 3. Follow Step 2 for each scene.

_____ 4. Play back tape to be sure nothing important was left out of the production. Check for other serious mistakes as well. In this type of editing, if a serious mistake is made in scene one, the entire video will have to be shot again. If a serious mistake is made in the last scene, go back to the end of the second to last scene PAUSE, PLAY and RECORD. Shoot the last scene again, correctly, and the video production will be successfully edited.

### 2. Simple Two VCR Electronic Editing

With this type of editing, a tape is copied from one VCR to the other. The PAUSE mode on the recorder VCR is pressed at the right moment to eliminate unwanted images. The advantage of this type of editing is that a great deal of video footage can be edited out. This is also a very low-tech option. It is a good idea to play the videotape before editing to note which sections of the original videotape needs to be eliminated. If the VCR has a counter, it should be set at zero at the beginning of the tape. As the tape plays, note the counter numbers for the sections that need to be eliminated when editing. In this type of editing, the STOP button on the recorder VCR should not be pressed in the middle of the editing. If the STOP button on the recorder VCR is pressed to check edits in the middle of the editing, some distracting colored lines in the picture might appear when the edited videotape is played back.

# Simple Two VCR Electronic Editing Checklist

_____ 1. Set up two VHS VCRs with TVs side by side in a room that can be locked.

_____ 2. Post a sign nearby that states, "It is illegal to duplicate copyrighted material without permission from the producer."

_____ 3. On the left-side VCR, place a sign that says, "PLAYBACK." This is the playback VCR.

_____ 4. On the right-side VCR, place a sign that says "RECORDER." This is your recorder VCR.

_____ 5. Switch the recorder VCR from the TUNER mode to the LINE or AV mode. Consult the instruction manual for the recorder VCR to do this. THIS IS A VITAL STEP. This type of editing can't be done unless you do this.

_____ 6. Connect an RCA (phono) cable from the VIDEO OUT jack on the playback VCR to the VIDEO IN jack on the recorder VCR.

_____ 7. Connect an RCA (phono) cable from the AUDIO OUT jack on the playback VCR to the AUDIO IN jack on the recorder VCR.

_____ 8. Place a blank tape in the recorder VCR. Place the tape with the video footage you want to edit in the playback VCR.

_____ 9. Set the recorder VCR to the SP speed.

_____ 10. Be sure the tape in the recorder VCR is rewound to the beginning. Be sure the tab on the front of the tape to be recorded is not missing. You cannot record if this videotape is missing its tab.

_____ 11. Record 10 seconds of blank tape on the recorder VCR and leave the recorder VCR in the PAUSE/RECORD mode.

_____ 12. Place the video footage tape in the playback VCR. Use the counter numbers on the playback VCR to find the first footage that needs to be edited into the video.

_____ 13. Rewind the video footage tape on the playback VCR at least 10 counts past the footage that needs to be edited in.

_____ 14. Start the footage tape on the playback VCR. When the counter on the playback VCR is three counter numbers away from the footage that need to be recorded, release PAUSE on the recorder VCR so it's recording. At the place where the footage ends, press PAUSE on the recorder VCR.

_____ 15. Continue this process until all the video footage has been edited.

_____ 16. Play back the edited tape to be sure the inappropriate material was edited out and the necessary material was left in.

### 3. Editing Using a Video Editor (No Edit Controller)

This process allows the editor to pinpoint exactly where edits will be made. Each scene can be checked after each edit by pressing STOP on the recorder VCR. Colored lines will not appear in the picture as they would in the second type of editing. This type of editing also allows the person editing to audio dub and video insert. This option will help create a high quality finished product. Also, the person editing does not need to learn how to operate an edit controller, which can take hours to learn. The same principles are followed as in the second type of editing, but better equipment is used. Students can be trained to do this type of editing quickly. One disadvantage of this type of video editing is that it produces no control track; a videotape edited this way may cause a few technical problems if taken to a TV station to be edited into a program for cable TV. Another disadvantage of this type of editing is that when the tape is played back on the recorder VCR where video inserts or audio dubs were made, the hi fi audio needs to be turned off. Otherwise, the appropriate audio will not be heard when the videotape is played.

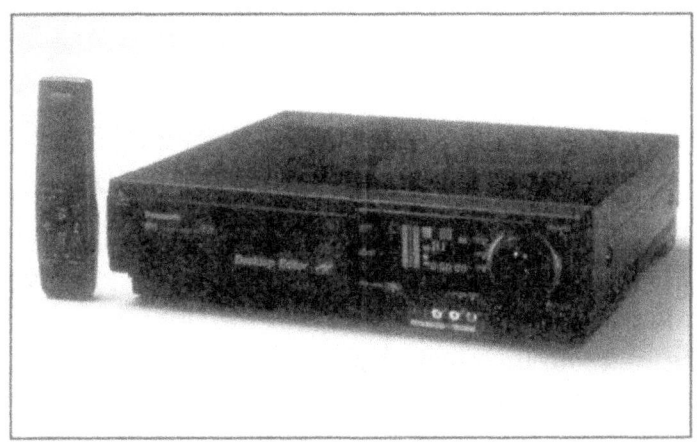

*Figure 8.1 Panasonic Analog Video Editor*

If the procedure of locating the exact end point of the scene and then putting the recorder VCR in the PAUSE/RECORD mode is not followed, unrecorded sections of videotape, snow, will appear throughout the video. Snow makes the video look very unprofessional. If recording does not begin within five minutes of setting up the edit, the record function goes off. If RECORD is pressed again without locating the exact endpoint of the last edit, something important will be cut off or snow will appear in the tape. (See Figure 8.1.)

## Editing Using a Video Editor (No Edit Controller) Checklist

_____ 1. Be sure the tape in the recorder VCR is rewound to the beginning. Record 10 seconds of blank tape on the recorder VCR. Be sure the tab on the front of the tape to be recorded on is not missing.

_____ 2. On playback VCR find the counter number for the beginning of the first scene. Rewind the playback VCR tape 10 counts from where the first scene begins.

_____ 3. Be sure recorder VCR is in the RECORD mode. If it isn't, go back to the last part of the first scene recorded and press PAUSE. Then press RECORD.

_____ 4. Start the playback VCR. When the counter number on the playback VCR is three counts on the counter from the beginning of the first scene, release PAUSE on the recorder VCR. When the first scene on the playback VCR is finished, press PAUSE on the recorder VCR.

_____ 5. Edit the next scene by repeating Steps 2-4.

_____ 6. Check the edit. Hit STOP on the recorder VCR. Rewind the tape and play back what was recorded. Was anything important cut off? Is there too much of a pause between the first and second scene? If the edit is not correct, do it over.

_____ 7. Attempt the edit again. If you cut off something important, release PAUSE on the recorder VCR a second earlier than you did last time. If there is too much of a gap between the first and second scene, release PAUSE on the recorder VCR a second later.

_____ 8. Continue in this fashion until the videotape is edited.

_____ 9. A new picture can be added to replace the picture previously recorded while keeping the previously recorded audio. To do this, press PAUSE on the recorder VCR at the place on the videotape where you want the new picture to begin. Now press Video Insert.

_____ 10. On the playback VCR, play the videotape with the new picture to be added to the video production. When the new picture is found, release PAUSE on the recorder VCR. When done adding new video to the scene, press STOP on the recorder VCR.

_____ 11. A similar process works for audio dubbing. Hit PAUSE on the recorder VCR at the place on the videotape where the new audio is to be added. Press AUDIO DUB.

_____ 12. The sound being added is probably coming from a sound source like a CD player, cassette recorder, or VCR. Determine the counter number for the beginning point of your sound source. Rewind the tape or CD three counts before the spot where the new material begins. Press PLAY on the sound source. Release PAUSE on the recorder VCR. When finished, press STOP on the recorder VCR.

_____ 13. Check the edits. For both video inserts and audio dubs, a remote unit may have to be used to remove the hi-fi L and R audio symbols on the recorder VCR's front panel. The hi-fi L and R symbol needs to be removed in order to hear the new sound added with audio dub or the correct sound that should go with the video insert. IT IS EXTREMELY IMPORTANT TO REMOVE THE HI-FI L AND R SYMBOLS DURING AND AFTER AUDIO DUBBING AND VIDEO INSERTING. IF THIS ISN'T DONE, THE CORRECT AUDIO WILL NOT BE HEARD.

## 4. Editing Using a Video Editor (Edit Controller System)

This system requires two analog VCR editors of the same model and an edit controller unit. Put the tape of the video footage already shot in the playback VCR. Put a brand new tape in the recorder VCR. It's important to use a new tape so that the finished product does not have any bits of information left over from a previous recording. If a used tape must be used, be sure that the tape is rewound to the beginning and the tab on the front of the tape to be recorded is not missing. You cannot record if the videotape is missing its tab.

It's a good idea to record over the tape that will be the edited master before editing. This is called "blackening" the tape. Put the tape in a camcorder with the lens cap on in a quiet room and press RECORD. There will be no snow on this tape so there will be no chance that snow will appear on the finished production.

Once the tapes have been placed in the VCRs, all editing is done by manipulating the edit controller. The VCRs are not touched again until the finished master tape and the video footage tape are taken out of the VCR. It takes a while to learn this type of editing. This system of editing is useful if the needed equipment is on hand and a great deal of editing needs to be done. One great advantage of this type of editing is that the edit controller has an audio dub and video insert edit feature. Another advantage is that the edit controller puts down a control track. This means that if the edited video is shown on a local cable TV channel the quality will be better. The biggest disadvantage of this system is that it takes time to become comfortable using the edit controller. It might not be beneficial to teach students the edit controller system because this technology has been replaced by digital computer video editing. However, if a Video Editor/Edit Controller System is the best editing system you have, use it. Note Figure 8.2 shows the Panasonic Analog Vdeo Edit Controller that controls two analog video editors referred to in Figure 8.1. (See Figure 8.2.)

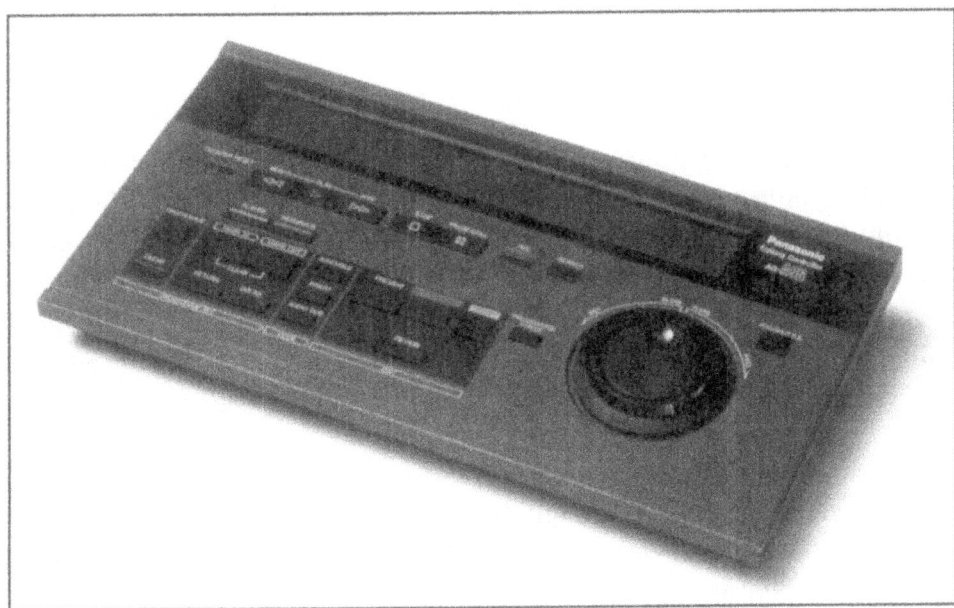

*Figure 8.2 Panasonic Analog Video Edit Controller*

# Editing Using a Video Editor (Edit Controller System) Checklist

_____ 1. Press the button that clears out information from previous taping. It's called "AC" for all clear.

_____ 2. Press the PLAYER button to control the playback VCR.

_____ 3. Press the PROGRAM button.

_____ 4. Press PLAY, REW or FF to find the video footage needed. Press PAUSE at the exact spot where the first scene begins. As in all six types of editing, the first scene should be 10 seconds of blank.

_____ 5. Press the INSET button.

_____ 6. Press PLAY, REW, or FF to find when the first scene ends. Press PAUSE at the exact spot on the tape where the first scene ends.

_____ 7. Press the OUTSET button.

_____ 8. Press RECORDER to control the recorder VCR.

_____ 9. Press PLAY, REW, or FF to find the exact spot on the tape where the program should begin. Press PAUSE at the exact spot on the tape where the program should begin.

_____ 10. Press INSET.

_____ 11. Press ASSEMBLE.

_____ 12. Press EDIT. There may be a pause of about a minute before the VCRs go into action The recording will take place automatically. The VCRs or edit controller should not be touched while the editing is taking place.

## 5. Digital Editing Using a DraCo Casablanca Digital Video Editor

Digital editing using a computer video editor is an excellent choice for students. Because of digital editors, analog editing will be used less and less in the coming years. Students should become familiar with digital editing. Digital editing is non-linear. In the first four types of editing, each segment needed to be edited in the sequence that it is to be shown. This is called linear editing. Digital editing allows editors to do edits in any sequence. Think of linear analog editing like laying bricks. Once a brick had been laid, it cannot be taken out unless the wall is torn down. Once an analog video edit has been made, it's very difficult to undo it later.

On the other hand, with digital editing, re-edits can be done in any way. What is put in the introduction can be re-edited into the middle of the show. The process is similar to writing a research paper on a word processor. A sentence can easily be taken out of the first paragraph and inserted into the last paragraph.

A digital editing system like the DraCo Casablanca isn't an IBM-compatible or a Macintosh-compatible computer. It's a computer-like piece of equipment with memory and a hard drive that does only one thing: edits video. We purchased one of these systems (DraCo Casablanca) for about $7,000, and we're happy with it. The Casablanca School Edition (SE) is now available for under $4,000.

In the "Digital Editing Using a DraCo Casablanca Digital Video Editor Checklist," there isn't any mention made to the playback VCR and the recorder VCR. In digital editing, the same VCR is used. The editor inputs the video and audio signal onto the digital editor. Everything is edited on the Casablanca. The editor uses a mouse just as he would with a Macintosh or IBM-compatible computer. The mouse has a trackball on top. The pointer on the screen is moved by the trackball. The editor outputs the finished video production to the same VCR used for input. Only one TV monitor is used for the entire process. Whether playing the tape on the VCR or looking at an edited scene from the Casablanca, you'll be watching it on the same TV monitor sitting on top of the Casablanca. We've had better results in our video productions edited on the Casablanca when we used a VCR with S VIDEO jacks and cables. When we used RCA (phono) cables and jacks we lost color on our video. Be sure you have one VCR with S VIDEO IN and OUT jacks to use with your digital Casablanca system.

The DraCo Casablanca system has removable hard drives. It's a good idea to have a few extra hard drives available. On the Casablanca hard drive we've been able to store and edit only one video production at a time. Having a removable hard drive would allow us to do two productions concurrently on the same Casablanca unit. For example, the removable hard drive would allow us to work on one production during first period and another production during second period for a few days until editing was completed on both productions.

Editing is not an easy skill for either a library media specialist, a teacher, or a student to learn. A few people pick up editing skills quickly and easily. For the rest of us, a list of steps may make editing on the Casablanca much easier. For a unit like the Casablanca, such a list may be of great help. The Casablanca has system settings, language settings, and a time setting that must be set up before editing can begin. There are project settings to set up, such as audio level and brightness. Sharp looking graphics can be generated on the Casablanca to enhance productions. Pictures, motion media, graphics, and text from a computer can be imported into the Casablanca, or pictures, motion media, graphics, and text can be exported from the Casablanca to a computer. An item from DraCo called PC Link is needed to do this. The training video supplied by DraCo, Inc., is very helpful in this regard. We set up our Casablanca so the audio and video would be inputted in the front of the machine and outputted in the back of the machine. There are other ways to set up the Casablanca. If using the following checklist, understand that it describes the way we use the Casablanca, input in front and output in back.

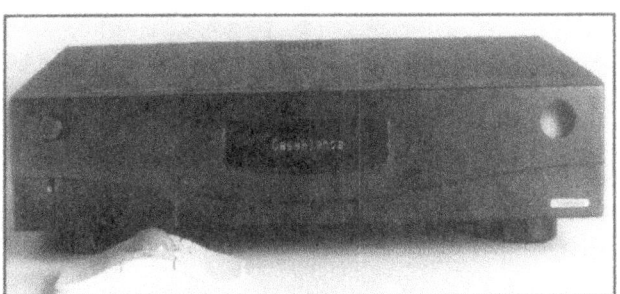

*Figure 8.3 DraCo Casablanca Digital Video Editor*

It took us a while to understand the Casablanca well enough to teach its use effectively to all the students in our program. The checklist below shows you how to do a simple edit with a transition. Remember how you felt the first time you could ride a bicycle? That's how you may feel the first time you successfully complete an editing job on the Casablanca with transitions. (See Figure 8.3.)

# Digital Editing Using a DraCo Casablanca Digital Video Editor Checklist

_____ 1. Set up the Casablanca inputting from S VIDEO OUT and AUDIO OUT from the VCR into the S-VHS IN and AUDIO IN of the Casablanca.

_____ 2. At the main menu of the Casablanca, click on RECORD.

_____ 3. Place the videotape into the VCR connected to the Casablanca. Press PLAY on the VCR. Search for the first scene on the VCR.

_____ 4. When the beginning of the first scene to be used is seen, click on the red circle RECORD function on your Casablanca. When the first scene ends, press the black square to stop recording. Note the "Name of Scene" is "S1."

_____ 5. Repeat Step 4 for the second scene. Note the "Name of Scene" is "S2."

_____ 6. Click on the tan square with black lines on lower right of screen.

_____ 7. At the main menu, click on EDIT.

_____ 8. Click on "S1." Note it is highlighted in blue. Click on ADD. Note "S1" is now on the storyboard at the top of the screen.

_____ 9. Repeat Step 8 for "S2."

_____ 10. At INSERT WHERE? box, click on FRONT or BEHIND.

_____ 11. If a scene needs to be removed from the storyboard, move the pointer with the trackball to the scene on the storyboard, click on that scene and then click on REMOVE.

_____ 12. If the correct scenes appear in the storyboard in the right order, click the tan box with black lines on the lower right of the screen. Note SAVING PROJECT as appears on screen.

_____ 13. At the main menu, click on TRANSITIONS. At the next screen, click on INSERT.

_____ 14. On the lower left of the screen, use the trackball in the center of the mouse to scroll to the desired transition. Click on the desired transition effect. Note the transition on the storyboard between scenes.

_____ 15. Click on RENDER to save the transition. This takes a few minutes.

_____ 16. Click on "X."

_____ 17. Highlight the yellow box above OK. Note it turns blue.

_____ 18. Scroll with the trackball on the mouse until you get to the amount of time you want your transition to take.

_____ 19. Click on the mouse.

_____ 20. Click OK.

_____ 21. Click on RENDER. It takes a few minutes.

_____ 22. Click on the tan box with the black lines in the lower right of the screen.

_____ 23. Click on FINISH at main menu.

_____ 24. Change the hookups so the cables are coming from the S-VHS Out and AUDIO OUT jacks of the Casablanca to the S VIDEO In and AUDIO IN jacks of the VCR.

_____ 25. Place a blank videotape in the VCR. Don't record over the original video footage tape. It may be needed later. Record for 10 seconds on the VCR.

_____ 26. Select the function on the Casablanca that says, RECORD TO VCR.

## 6. Digital Editing Done on a Computer Using Digital Editing Software

As with the Casablanca, editing on a computer requires the use of only one VCR. First the editor inputs the videotape footage into the computer. Then the editor edits footage in the computer and outputs the edited video presentation into the same VCR. To output the edited video presentation into the computer, the editor places a videotape in the VCR and presses PLAY and the RECORD on the VCR. Computer-editing software can be purchased to be used with a computer as a digital video editor. A Video/Audio Input/Output card needs to be installed to the computer. (See Chapter 6, "Linking Computer and Video," page 57.) Digital video editing requires a computer with a very large hard drive, 128 MB or more of RAM (random access memory), and a high-speed processor. Video and audio take up an enormous amount of RAM. Because digital video editing on a computer takes up a great deal of memory, save to the hard drive and/or a zip disk, not a floppy disk. If you already have a computer with the necessary components for video editing and you do not have the funds to buy a Casablanca system, this type of editing may be your best editing choice.

# Digital Video Editing Done on a Computer Using Digital Editing Software Checklist

_____ 1. Install a video card that allows the input and output of audio and video into computer.

_____ 2. Install an editing program by placing a video editing CD-ROM in the CD-ROM drive, go to PROGRAMS and then to RUN in Windows. Program automatically is installed.

_____ 3. In Windows go to PROGRAM, CONTROL PANEL, DISPLAY, and SETTING. Under COLORS, select "32 bit color" and under SCREEN AREA select "800 x 640 pixels."

_____ 4. Connect RCA (phono) plugs from VIDEO OUT and AUDIO OUT on VCR to VIDEO IN and AUDIO IN on computer's video card.

_____ 5. On computer, click on VIDEO EDITING program.

_____ 6. Select the output device for "videotape."

_____  7. For American users, select NTSC.

_____  8. For video quality, select PREMIUM.

_____  9. Click on CABLE icon.

_____ 10. Select video card driver.

_____ 11. Select VIDEO.

_____ 12. Begin playing the first section of video footage to be used from the VCR.

_____ 13. When the first section of video footage has been played, press the SPACE BAR on the keyboard.

_____ 14. Select LIBRARY.

_____ 15. Note the frame of the "story board" at the top of the screen. The first section of footage has been edited into the computer.

_____ 16. Continue adding video footage segments into the computer repeating steps 11-13 until all the video segments have been edited into the computer.

_____ 17. Go back to LIBRARY. All the segments of the program can be seen at the storyboard at the top of the screen.

_____ 18. To move through any of the segments, select the icons for PLAY, FAST FORWARD, or REWIND on the right of the screen.

_____ 19. Select TRANS for transitions. Select the transitions desired between scenes.

_____ 20. Select ABC for titles. Type the title on the keyboard.

_____ 21. Press START.

_____ 22. Press HOLD. Select the amount of time for the title.

_____ 23. Select APPLY.

_____ 24. Save the edited video production to the hard drive of the computer and the zip drive if available.

_____ 25. Reconnect the RCA (phono) cables, so they are going from VIDEO OUT and AUDIO OUT on the computer's video card to VIDEO IN and AUDIO IN on the VCR.

_____ 26. Be sure VCR is in LINE or AUX, not the TUNER mode.

_____ 27. Insert a new tape in the VCR, and press PLAY and RECORD.

_____ 28. Wait 10 seconds and select the forward arrow on the computer screen.

# Presenting a Videotape

## Terms

- cable drop
- closed circuit TV
- data projector
- head end
- in-school cable TV system (closed circuit)
- lower tier channels
- remote unit
- RF splitter
- TV monitor
- TV receiver
- upper tier channels
- video projector

How are the students going to present the videotape they worked so hard to produce? It's an important question. Think of presentation as an approach to a spectrum of audiences. At one end of the spectrum, there is one person sitting a few feet in front of a TV screen in a quiet room. That person can see every detail on the screen and distinctly hear all sounds coming from the TV. At the other end of the spectrum, there are over a thousand people, many over 100 feet away from the TV picture in a very noisy auditorium.

There are four different types of TV presentation equipment needed to accommodate the spectrum of audiences: (1) TV receivers, (2) in-school cable TV systems (closed circuit), (3) TV monitor/receivers, and (4) data or video projectors.

# TV Receivers

Figure 9.1 Radio Shack RF Splitter for Two TV Receivers

TV receivers are similar to the TVs in most homes. In many schools, the screen size generally ranges from 17" to 25." The size of a TV is determined by the measurement of a diagonal straight line from the lower left corner of the screen to the upper right corner of the screen. TV receivers accept only an RF (Radio Frequency) cable. The signal of the RF cable carries both audio and video and is delivered on a channel, usually channel 3 or 4, on a typical TV/VCR videotape playback. A series of TV receivers can be hooked up together using an RF splitter. An RF splitter can be found at any Radio Shack. (See Figures 9.1, 9.2 and 9.3.)

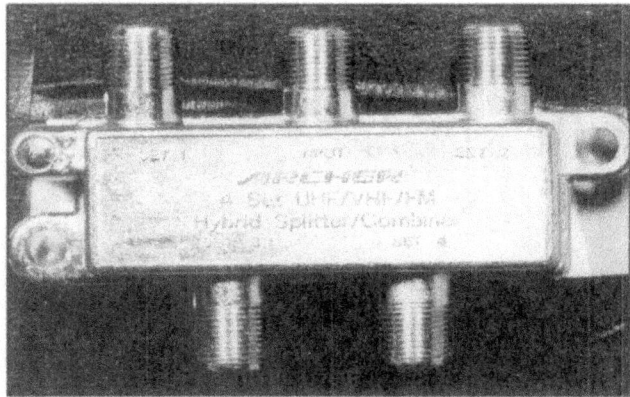

Figure 9.2 Radio Shack RF Splitter for More Than Two Receivers

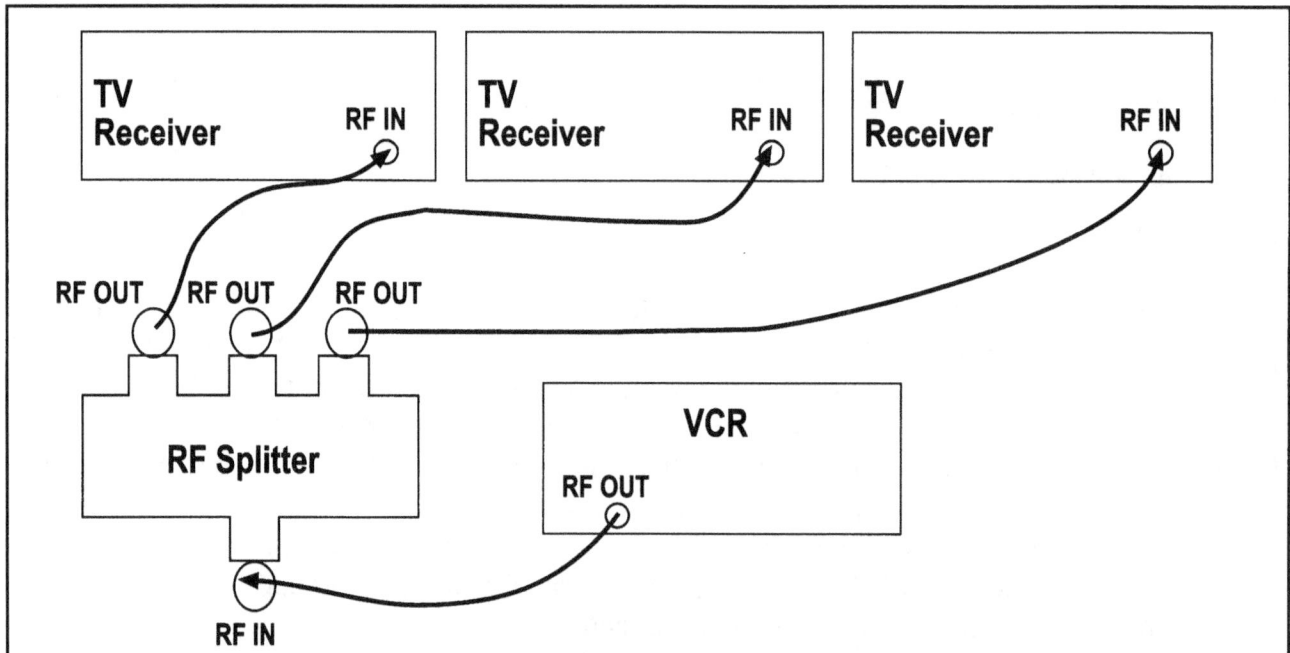

Figure 9.3 A Series of TV Receivers Connected with an RF Splitter

## In-School Cable TV System

An in-school cable TV system (also called closed circuit video distribution system) delivers a number of channels to a classroom. These channels travel to the classroom through an RF cable. Each TV channel has a different frequency or signal called an RF signal. RF signals for different TV channels are received by the TV receiver in each classroom and office via an RF cable. Each location where a TV receiver can be hooked up to the in-school cable TV system is called a cable drop. In a typical in-school cable TV system, the classroom TV receiver would receive about nine channels. The channels that are received are determined by the head end of the system. The head end is the device that receives television channels from a cable that comes from the cable TV provider. After the head end receives the television channels, it relays these channels to classrooms via an RF cable. If the school is hooked up for cable, generally, only the lower tier channels on the cable system would be sent from the head end to the classroom. Lower tier channels are the channels that the cable provider does not charge extra for. The cable company charges the viewers extra for upper tier channels. In other words, NBC would probably be sent to the classroom because it's considered lower tier. The Disney Channel would probably not be sent to the classroom because many cable providers consider it upper tier. If 100 channels are coming into the school from the cable provider, about eight of those channels can be selected at the head end for use in classrooms. It's easy to switch the channels at the head end. In the head end one channel is reserved as the local origination channel from the school's TV studio.

In some schools, Channel 6 is the channel on which shows can be originated from the school's TV studio via the in-school cable TV system. RCA (phono) cables for audio, AUDIO OUT and video, VIDEO OUT go from the TV studio to the head end of the cable system. From the head end, the TV news show goes out to the classrooms on a certain channel. An RF cable in each classroom connects the TV receiver's RF jack to the RF jack in the wall. The RF jack on the wall is called a cable drop.

The in-school cable TV system can be used for purposes other than the school TV news show. This system can be used for any large group purpose. An advantage of this system is you don't have to move all the students to one large room. All the students can watch the presentation on the TV receiver in each of their classrooms. (See Figure 9.4.)

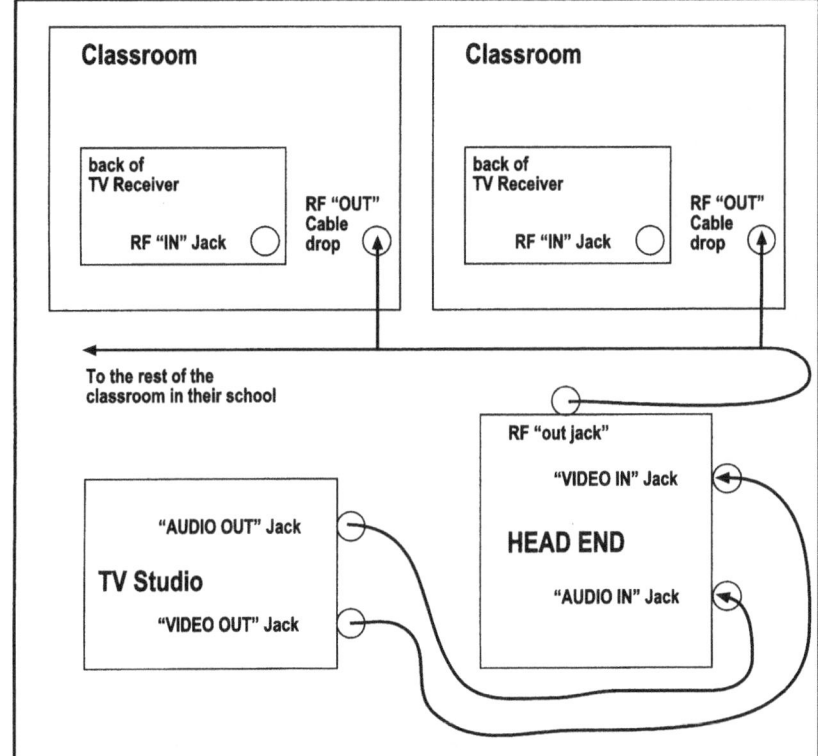

*Figure 9.4 In-School Cable TV System*

# TV Receiver/Monitor

Generally, TV receivers are being replaced in classrooms by TV receiver/monitors. The TV receiver/monitor can function as a receiver, if it has an RF jack. The TV receiver/monitor also has a VIDEO IN jack and AUDIO IN jack. This is a great advantage to the classroom teacher. With a TV receiver, the teacher can play a videotape from a VCR hooked up to the TV receiver's RF in jack. The teacher can also receive at least 9 cable channels from the school's head end, including the school TV news show. Also, with the TV receiver/monitor, the teacher can hook up the computer screen to the TV, using the appropriate device. (See Chapter 6, "Linking Computer and Video," page 57.) With the TV receiver/monitor the VIDEO OUT and AUDIO OUT jacks can be hooked up to another TV receiver/monitor's VIDEO IN and AUDIO IN jacks so a string of TV receiver/monitor's can be hooked up for a large group presentation. RCA (phono) cables are used to connect the TV receiver/monitors. The biggest problem in dealing with TV receiver/monitors is figuring out how to switch from the receiver mode to the monitor mode. On some TV receiver/monitors you need a remote unit. The remote unit has a TV/VIDEO button, which is pressed each time you want to switch from receiver to monitor. Other TV receiver/monitors have an INPUT SELECT switch on the front of the TV. By pressing that switch, you'll get to the monitor mode. When a new TV receiver/monitor arrives in your school building, you may have to consult the instruction manual to figure out how to switch from receiver to monitor. (See Figure 9.5.)

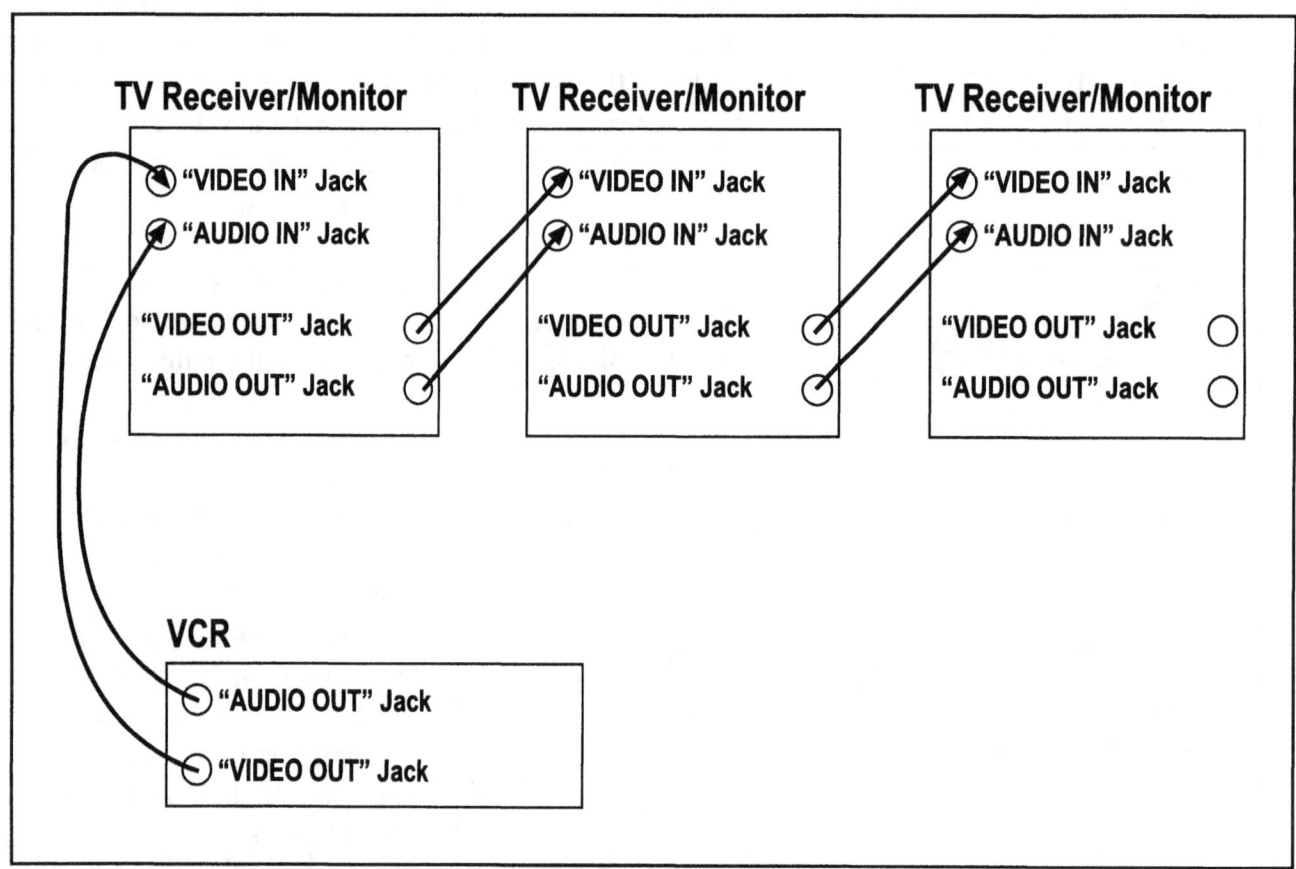

*Figure 9.5 Hooking Up a Series of TV Receiver/Monitors*

# Data or Video Projector

*Figure 9.6 Panasonic Data Project*

Another device used to present a video to a large group is the data projector or video projector. A data projector can be hooked up to a VCR or a computer and can play either a computer or video presentation to a large group. A video projector can only present what's on a VCR. A video projector can't present what's on a computer unless you use a scan converter. Since these devices are projectors, the size of the image is only limited by the size of the screen or wall. Like a film projector, the data projector is moved farther back from the wall to get a bigger image on the screen. These projectors have their own speakers that are adequate for a classroom-size group. For a presentation in an auditorium for a larger group, the data or video projector's audio can be hooked up to a separate speaker. (See Figure 9.6.)

# Considerations when Presenting Video to Large Groups

With a large group, use a 25" or 28" TV receiver or monitor. Keep the following things in mind. The font size for graphics should not be smaller than 60 points. In the back of a typical classroom, the student will be about 10 yards from the TV screen. From 10 yards distance, titles in a 60-point font will be readable to a student with 20/20 vision. If you are using *PowerPoint* slides and transferring them to video, the font size should not be smaller than 60-point. You can always create more *PowerPoint* slides to fit the information into a 60-point size.

Here are some general guidelines for large group presentations using video. These guidelines have been taken from Heinich, Molenda, Russell and Smaldino's *Instructional Media and Technologies for Learning, 6th Edition.* "Seat no one closer than twice the inches of screen size. For example for a 23-inch monitor, the closest viewer would be 46 inches (or about four feet) from the screen. Seat no one farther *in feet* than the size of the screen in inches. For example, for a 23-inch monitor, the farthest viewers would be 23 feet away." (380) (*Instructional Media and Technology for Learning 6/E* by Heinreich et al., © 1999. Reprinted by permission of Prentice-Hall, Inc., Upper Saddle River, NJ) The total number of viewers per TV screen should be no more than the number of inches of screen size for the TV. Make sure that the audience members do not have to tilt their heads to see the screen more than 30°. The audience should watch the TV production in normal room light or dim light, not in total darkness. When using a video projector or data projector that displays the image on a wall screen, the room should be dimly lit or totally dark. Set the volume level loud enough so the audience in the back of the room can hear. At the same time, don't have the volume so loud that it makes the audience in the front uncomfortable.

Any fine details are going to be hard to see in any large group video presentations. Video images are still not as sharp as 16mm or 35mm film.

Large group presentations require very clear audio. Things you can hear easily when standing close to a TV monitor are impossible to hear when you are 50' away in a crowded room. For a large group presentation, the video should have one narrator with a very clear and distinct voice. Very deep voices are often difficult to hear on a videotape. A video with interviews with many people will be much harder for your audience to hear than the narration of one narrator with a clear and strong voice.

If the videotape has been created from a *PowerPoint* presentation and is made up of graphics and still video images, it will work better using a data projector and a computer. Data projectors can project the computer image directly without changing it to the NTSC video format. The computer screen image is sharper on the screen than the video image. When you display the computer screen using a data projector, you can display graphics with a smaller font size effectively. You might be able to get by with a 28-point font size using this method. However, the 28-point font size wouldn't be sharp enough to see on the NTSC video format.

# Presenting a Videotape Checklist

## A. Your Audience and Your Videotape

_____ 1. How many people will be watching at one time?

_____ 2. How far away from the screen is the viewer sitting in the last row?

_____ 3. Will the audience be noisy or quiet?

_____ 4. Is the audio a narrator's voice, music, interviews with many people, or a combination of all three?

_____ 5. Will the video use graphics, a talking head, pictures with fine details, or a combination of all three?

## B. Your Presentation Equipment Options

_____ 1. Do you have an in-school cable TV system for the classrooms in your school?

_____ 2. Do you have large screen TV receivers (23" to 28")?

_____ 3. Do you have a splitter to link two TV receivers and at least two 25' RF cables and one 2' RF cable? (RF cables and splitters are available at Radio Shack for a few dollars.)

_____ 4. Do you have at least four 25' RCA (phono) cables and two 2' RCA (phono) cables to link two TV monitors?

_____ 5. Do you have a video projector or a data projector with video and audio outputs and computer screen output? Two 2' RCA (phono) cables will be required. You will also need a large front projection movie screen at least 60" x 60."

## C. Presentation Decisions

_____ 1. If you are showing a presentation to a group larger than 40 people, you may need either multiple TV receivers linked with a splitter or multiple TV receiver/monitors linked with RCA (phono) cables. Figure a ratio of one TV for every 40 people. Some video splitters can accommodate up to four TV receivers. If there is a lot of important detail in the TV picture, and the audience will be close to the TVs, this may be the best solution.

_____ 2. If you can split your group up into classrooms and the classrooms are all equipped with an in-school cable TV system, that may be your best solution.

_____ 3. If you will have hundreds of people in a large auditorium with many people over 100 feet from the screen, the video or data projector is the best choice.

# The TV Studio for the School TV News Show

**CHAPTER 10**

## Terms

- acoustics
- anchor desk
- backdrop
- complex TV studio
- control room
- cue
- flat
- floor
- gobo
- high impedance microphone
- Intranet
- lavaliere microphone
- low impedance microphone
- macro
- simple TV studio
- streaming technology
- surge protector
- visual presenter

The TV studio is the place where video production programs are created. It can also be the place where the school TV news show originates. It would be convenient to have the video production equipment set up and ready to record at a moment's notice. The TV studio can be as simple as hooking up a camcorder to the cable system in the library. Library media specialists have done that with great success.

A special place for TV production, a TV studio facility, may be created. The TV studio can be simple or complex. A simple TV studio uses only one camera and one microphone. A complex TV studio uses more than one camera and more than one microphone. At the end of this chapter, checklists are provided for both types of studios. A TV studio can be a regular classroom-sized room where live and videotaped segments are produced using a lighting kit, audio and video mixers, and a cable TV outlet. It can also be a small room with a microphone, camcorder, and VCR hooked up to a cable TV outlet. Whether complex or simple, the TV studio is where much of the TV production work is done and where live TV shows originate. Your school's TV studio may include some elements of the complex TV studio and some elements of the simple TV studio. This chapter will help you plan your own TV studio. A simple TV studio is not necessarily found in elementary schools and complex TV studios in high schools. Plenty of elementary schools have complex studios and plenty of high schools have simple ones. What type of studio should you set up? It may have some complex and some simple elements. Obviously, you need a bigger budget for the complex studio. The more complex the studio, the more things can go wrong. Perhaps you'll want to select some elements of the complex and some elements of the "simple" in designing your own TV studio. This chapter will also discuss what you'll need to create a TV news show.

## Things In Common for Simple and Complex TV Studios

Where should the TV studio be situated? A location in the library media center is needed. You don't have time to be running all over the building producing videos. If your TV studio is not in the library area, it's unwise to have a TV studio. If you had a TV studio in another part of the school building, you'd be unable to keep tabs on what's happening in the library and the TV studio at the same time. You must be able to supervise both areas, since you are responsible for their operation.

Since video equipment and tapes are sensitive to temperature, an air-conditioned environment is ideal. The temperature in the TV studio and control room should constantly be set at 72° F.

The equipment set up for the TV studio should stay intact. The equipment used in the studio should not be moved to other locations when teachers or students need to do video projects in other parts of the building. Dedicate other equipment for that purpose. It takes a great deal of time and effort to set up the studio the way you want it. When someone comes into your studio and takes out equipment or changes they way the cables are set up, it causes unbelievable headaches for you. Don't let that happen!

A backdrop is needed for every TV studio. The backdrop is simply the background for your talent. You don't want the typical dull looking cinder block walls of a classroom or school library for a backdrop. Instead purchase a drop cloth from a painting store.

In either the simple or complex TV studio, a VCR with an S VIDEO input is not needed. VCRs without S VIDEO are considerably cheaper than VCRs with S VIDEO capability. Be sure your VCR is set to the LINE or AUX position, not the TUNER position when you are recording your news show. In either the simple or complex TV studio always run cables from a VIDEO OUT to a VIDEO IN and an AUDIO OUT to an AUDIO IN. The TV picture quality of a VCR with S VIDEO is better than the TV picture quality of a VCR that has only Video In and VIDEO OUT. However, excellent video production work in a complex TV studio can be done without using S VIDEO.

A computer can enhance any production. Hook up a computer with a presentation program like *PowerPoint* or HyperStudio to a TV device that will convert the computer signal to a video signal. (See Chapter 6, "Linking Computer and Video," page 57, and Figure 6.1, "All-in-Wonder Pro' Video Input/Output Computer Device," page 58.) Macintosh computers use a different computer to TV device. Any computer presentation can go from the VIDEO OUT of the computer to the VIDEO IN of the in school cable TV system. That way, a *PowerPoint* presentation can be shown on the TV show presented through the in-school cable TV system. This process will also work with a simple video switcher.

In both the simple and complex TV studio, you'll need music and/or sound effects for specific situations. Have a CD player available. Obtain music on CD that can be used for theme music, background music for sports features, or music for holidays.

All equipment in any TV studio should be attached to surge protectors. This will protect all the TV studio equipment in case there is a sudden power surge in the building, which could destroy the equipment. Surge protectors can save you thousands of dollars in replacement equipment.

## Simple TV Studio

### Cable Hook Ups

For the basic hook ups for the simple TV studio, consult Figure 10.1 "Simple TV Studio Connections Diagram," page 98. In the simple TV studio, the TV picture is going from the VIDEO OUT jack on the camcorder to the VIDEO IN jack on the recorder VCR while the sound is going from the AUDIO OUT jack on the camcorder to the AUDIO IN jack on the recorder VCR. A cable from the VIDEO OUT jack of the recorder VCR connects to the VIDEO IN jack of your in-school cable TV system. A cable from the AUDIO OUT jack of your recorder VCR connects to the AUDIO IN jack of your in school cable TV system. In the simple TV studio only one TV receiver is needed. This TV receiver is hooked up to the VCR that is sending your video and audio signals into the in-school cable TV system.

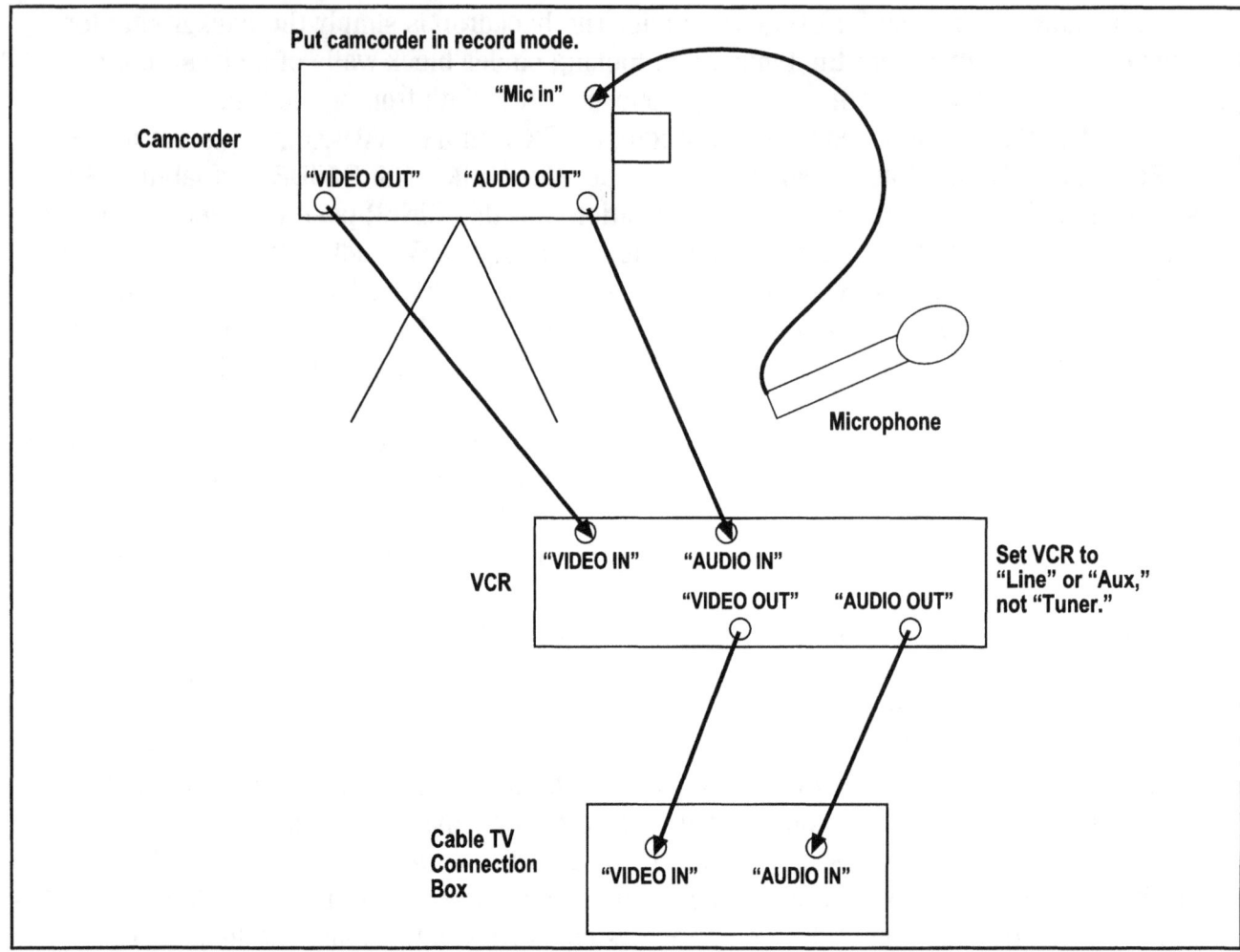

*Figure 10.1 Simple TV Studio Connections Diagram*

## Live and Taped Elements

In the simple TV studio, you can play a prerecorded tape as part of a TV show. To do this in the simple TV studio, simply press the FADE button on the camcorder and switch the camcorder from the CAMERA to the VCR setting. Then insert the prerecorded tape in the camcorder, and press PLAY on the camcorder. It's difficult to get live and videotaped segments at the same volume level. Try to use the same microphone in both your live and videotaped segments. Encourage the talent to talk equally loud in both live and taped segments. Keep the microphone the same distance from the talent in both live and taped segments.

## Room Considerations

For a simple TV studio, the backdrop should be 10' high x 13' wide. A simple TV studio needs a much smaller room, about 22' wide x 16' deep x 10' high. No control room is necessary. In a simple TV studio, the director communicates with camera operators or talent with hand signals because the microphone would pick up voices. The director needs to be located where he can be seen by the camera operator and talent. Maybe pointing a finger means, "start the show" and a hand in the air means, "end the show."

In the simple TV studio you do not need a lighting kit. If your TV studio is as well lit as a typical school library, your TV picture will be adequate. However, your TV picture will look brighter and sharper if you do use a lighting kit. Lighting adjustment and lighting safety can cause you problems. The lights get very hot and could easily burn a student's hand. Lighting adjustments can also be time consuming. Many school librarians who do school TV news shows view lighting as one more thing that can go wrong.

**Microphones**

For the simple TV studio you need one microphone that hooks into a camcorder. A low impedance microphone is ideal for this. When hooking a low impedance microphone into a camcorder, be sure to obtain a special cable that will have an XLR jack on one end and a mini plug on the other. The mini plug hooks into the camcorder. Adapters that go from an XLR jack to a mini plug are available, but don't use them. The weight of the mini plug adapter makes the connection between the microphone and the microphone jack of the camcorder unreliable. Generally, low impedance microphones don't have ON/OFF switches. That's a good thing because a student can switch some microphones off at the last minute, causing you to have to shoot a scene over.

On the other hand, high impedance microphones often do have ON/OFF switches. That's another good reason to buy low, not high impedance microphones. However, a high impedance microphone will work. The sound will not be as loud as the sound from a low impedance microphone but if the volume is turned up in the classroom TV receivers, the TV program will be audible. A high impedance microphone usually has a shorter cable than a low impedance microphone. Thus, if you use a high impedance microphone in your studio, the talent has to be closer to the camcorder. High impedance microphones are much cheaper than low impedance microphones. In the simple TV studio the microphone may not function unless the camcorder is set to CAMCORDER, not VCR. The camcorder needs to have a videotape in it and be recording to activate the microphone. To pick up sound from a CD/audiocassette player, hold the microphone attached to the camcorder near the speaker of the CD/audiocassette player.

## Simple TV Studio Equipment Needed Checklist

_____ 1. Camcorder with VIDEO OUT and AUDIO OUT.

_____ 2. Tripod for camcorder.

_____ 3. VCR with AUX or LINE.

_____ 4. TV receiver or TV monitor.

_____ 5. Microphone stand.

_____ 6. Microphone with mini plug.

_____ 7. CD/audio cassette player.

# Complex TV Studio

## Room Dimensions

For a complex TV studio, the room where the talent will perform in front of the cameras should be at least 21' wide x 30' long x 15' high. This room is called the floor of the TV studio. An adjacent room called the control room should be at least 8' deep x 18' long x 8' high. Equipment such as a video switcher, a/v digital mixer, audio mixer, recorder VCR, playback VCR, and computer are found in the control room. There should be a window at least 3' high x 11' long between the control room and the floor of the studio.

## Cable Hook Ups

For basic cable hook ups of a complex TV studio, consult Figure 10.2, "Complex TV Studio Connections Diagram," page 99. A typical complex TV studio requires six male 25' RCA (phono) cables, five male 6' RCA phono cables, two male 6' S Video cables, one 6' male RF cable, one 25' male RF cable, three 25' male XLR cables, one 6' male phone cable, and one 6' male phone to RCA (phono) cable. Plastic molded cables work much better than cables with metal adapters. The cables with metal adapters slip out of place from time to time causing temporary loss of audio.

In the complex TV studio you need a recorder VCR that can record your show as it broadcasts over the in-school cable TV system. In the complex TV studio, the recorder VCR will receive the picture from the video switcher or a/v digital mixer at the VIDEO IN jack and the sound from the audio mixer through the AUDIO IN jack. A cable from the VIDEO OUT jack of the recorder VCR connects to the VIDEO IN jack of your in-school cable TV system. A cable from the AUDIO OUT jack of your recorder VCR connects to the AUDIO IN jack of your in-school cable TV system.

## Mixing Multiple Video Sources

In the complex TV studio you will be using more than one camera, so you need the ability to switch between cameras. A simple video switcher is an inexpensive item that allows for simple switching between cameras without special effects. (See Figure 7.1, "A Simple and Inexpensive Video Switcher," page 66, and Chapter 7, "Switchers and Mixers," page 65.) An a/v digital mixer provides you with more features when you switch from one camera to another. (See Figure 7.2, "Panasonic A/V Digital Mixer," page 66.) An S VIDEO or RCA (phono) cable from the computer to TV device goes into one of the a/v digital mixer's video inputs allowing computer presentations to be used in your shows.

The TV picture from the playback VCR is easier to deal with than the audio in the complex TV studio. You run your cable from VIDEO OUT on the playback VCR to one of the VIDEO IN inputs on the a/v digital mixer or video switcher. (To get more video inputs, the video switcher can be hooked up to the a/v digital mixer.) Run a cable from the VIDEO OUT or S VIDEO OUT on the video switcher or a/v digital mixer to the VIDEO IN or S VIDEO IN on the recorder VCR. In this way, the TV picture from a videotape playing on the playback VCR can be selected by the a/v digital mixer or video switcher just as you would select the TV picture from a TV camera. (See Figure 10.2.)

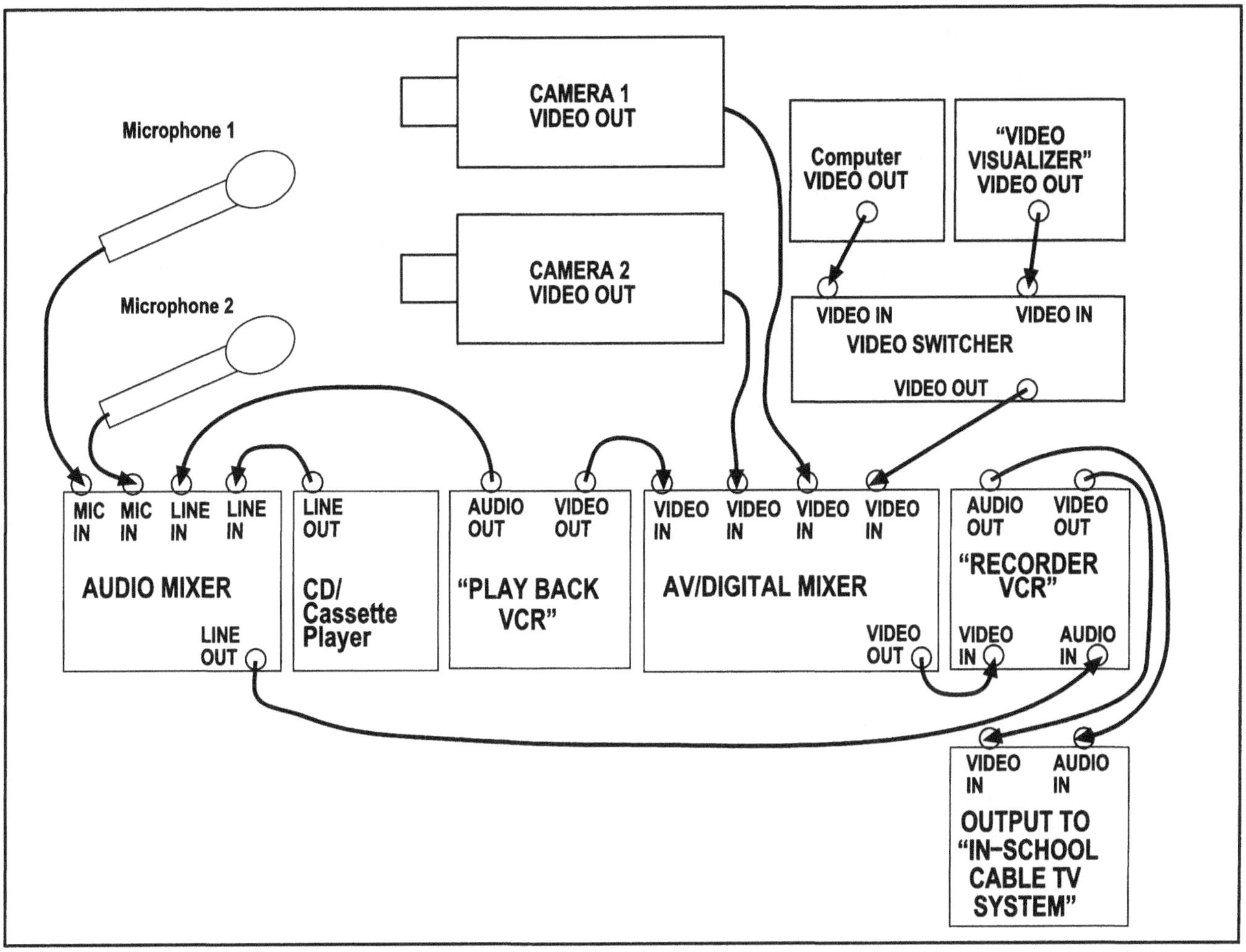

*Figure 10.2 Complex TV Studio Connections Diagram*

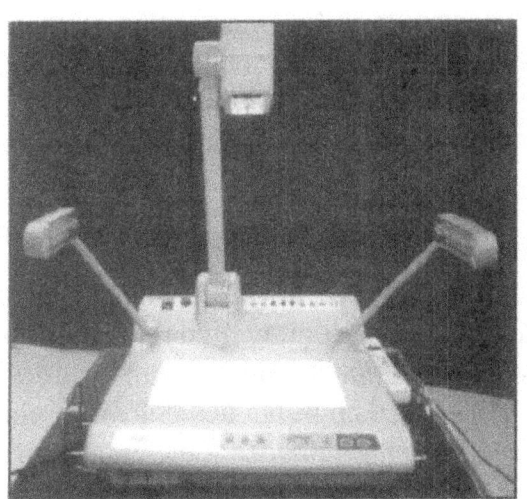

*Figure 10.3 JVC Visual Presenter*

### Visual Presenter

One important piece of equipment in the complex TV studio is a visual presenter. This device looks like a camera copy stand. The camera shoots down to get pictures or text from a piece of paper or book. Visual presenters can zoom in or out, so the picture or text from one portion of a page can be shot to fill the entire TV screen. The daily class schedule or the school lunch menu can be typed on an 8 1/2" x 11" sheet of paper and shown on the visual presenter. The visual presenter magnifies the image, so it can be easily seen by students watching a TV in the back of the classroom. (See Figure 10.3.)

If you can't afford the cost of the visual presenter, you can use the macro attachment on most camcorders. The macro lens will achieve the same effect of enlarging text or a picture from a book or handout, so it can fill the entire TV screen and be readily visible to all the students watching the TV.

## Receivers and Monitors

In the complex TV studio, at least two TV receivers are needed: one for the recorder VCR and one for the floor of the TV studio so the talent can see the TV picture being sent out on the cable TV system. At least two TV monitors are also needed: one for the visual presenter out on the floor of the TV studio so the visual presenter operator can see how the picture looks on that camera and one TV monitor for the a/v digital mixer that allows the tech director to preview a special effect before it is sent to the recorder VCR. An ideal complex TV studio would also have a TV monitor in the control room for each camera. This is an area where you can cut corners in purchasing equipment for a TV studio. The preview TV monitor for the a/v digital mixer can be used to see what the picture looks like on any camera. This helps the tech director a great deal. For example, before the tech director switches to a shot on camera two, the tech director can preview what that shot looks like on the a/v digital mixer's preview TV monitor.

## Mixing Multiple Audio Sources

The sound from your live talent may often be louder than the sound from a prerecorded videotape. To solve this problem in the complex TV studio, hook up the audio cable from the AUDIO OUT of the playback VCR to the LINE IN of the audio mixer. Another audio cable goes from LINE OUT on the audio mixer to AUDIO IN on the recorder VCR. This set up will allow you to make the sound from the prerecorded videotape as loud as the sound for the live segment of the TV news show. You do this by adjusting the audio mixer's volume levels. You bring up the volume level of the LINE IN on the audio mixer for the input from the playback VCR. You also bring up the LINE OUT on the audio mixer. This method solves the biggest problem on a TV news show—going from a live segment of the TV news show to a prerecorded segment of the show and maintaining the same level of volume for the audio. So many things can cause the level of sound to be uneven between live and videotaped segments of the show—microphones of different quality, voices of different strength, and acoustics of different rooms. The audio mixer is vital to balance the sound between the live microphone inputs and the videotaped LINE inputs. **There is no substitute for this piece of equipment in the complex TV studio.**

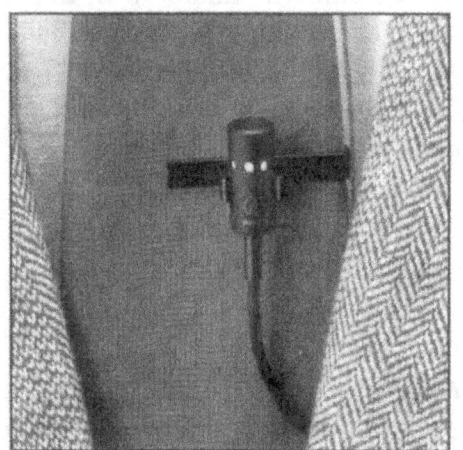

*Figure 10.4 Low Impedance Lavaliere Microphones Improve Sound Quality*

## Microphones, CDs, and Audiocassettes

For the complex TV studio, use three low impedance lavaliere microphones that hook into an audio mixer. These microphones enhance sound quality. This is a top priority item. Low impedance lavaliere microphones deliver better sound than high impedance microphones. Low impedance microphones will make your video presentations more audible. (See Figure 10.4.)

In the complex TV studio, you will want to use music from CDs and audiocassettes. This requires a LINE input in your audio mixer and a LINE output in your CD/audiocassette player. LINE inputs and LINE outputs may also be labeled AUX inputs and AUX outputs on your equipment. Many CD/audiocassette players do not have a LINE output. Instead, these CD/audiocassette players probably have a SPEAKER OUT or a PHONE OUT. You will need to feed the sound from the CD/audiocassette player's SPEAKER OUT or PHONE OUT into the LINE IN of another audio device. You may want to use an old audiocassette recorder that has LINE IN and LINE OUT jacks as your other audio device. Attach the appropriate audio cable from the LINE OUT of the old audiocassette recorder into the audio mixer's LINE IN input. This only works when the old audiocassette recorder is in the RECORD mode. Put an audiocassette tape in the old audiocassette recorder and place the old audiocassette recorder in the RECORD/PAUSE mode. You'll have to adjust the recording level of the old audiocassette player to get the correct volume level coming into your audio mixer. It's a good idea to have a counter on your CD/audiocassette player so cassette tapes can be easily cued. (See Figure 10.5.)

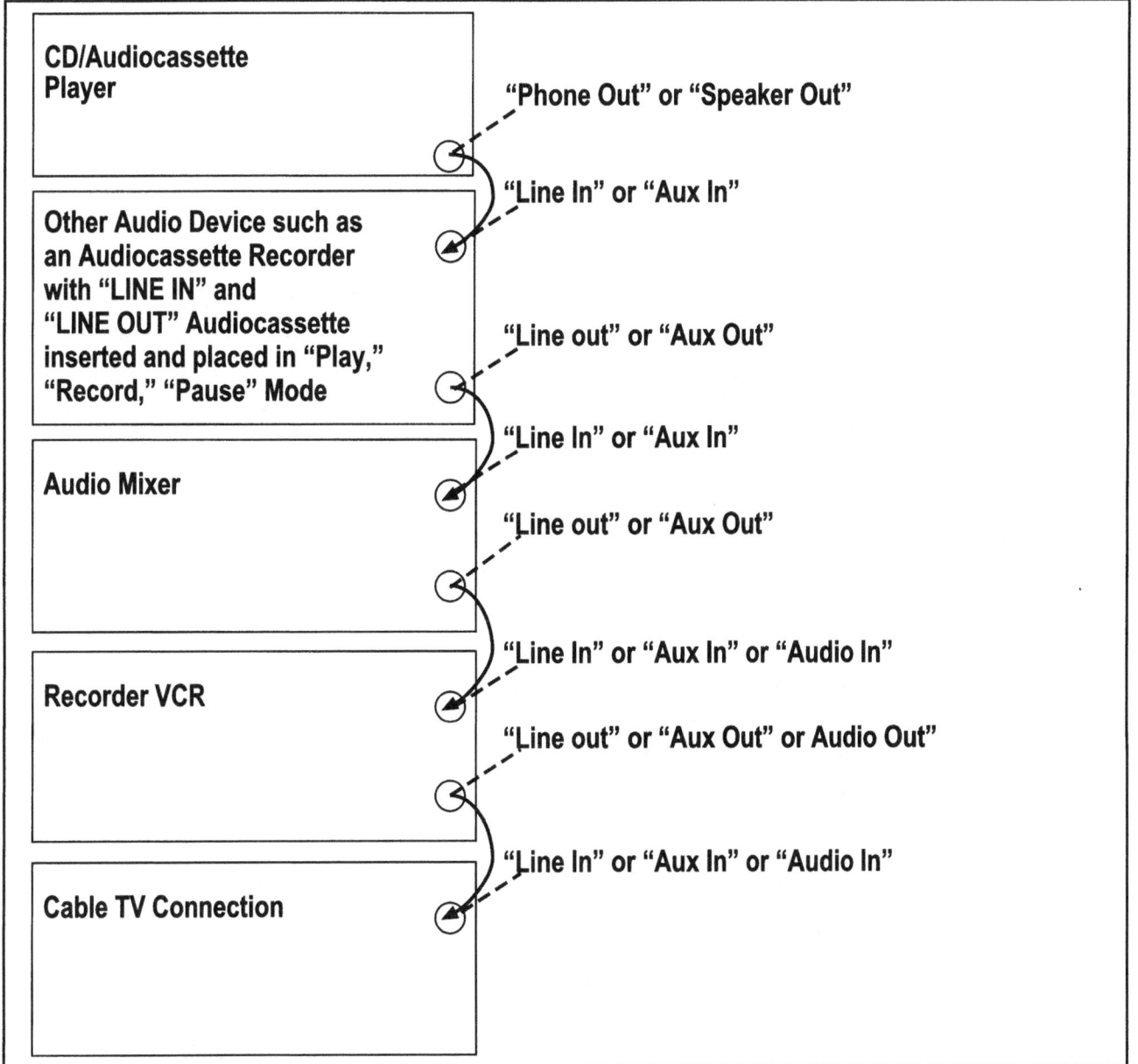

*Figure 10.5 Hooking Up a CD/Audiocassette Player Without LINE OUT Into an Audio Mixer*

## Acoustics

Don't ignore the acoustics of the TV studio room. Sound travels in waves. Those sound waves are scattered as they hit the walls, ceiling, floor, and objects in the room, or they may be absorbed by objects in the room. For a sound source to sound "real," some of the sound waves need to be absorbed in the room and some need to be scattered. A backdrop made out of cloth is not only an excellent background for talent, it's also an excellent source for absorbing sound waves. Other good sources for absorbing sound waves are a chair made with fabric or a rug. Sound is scattered by the metal and plastic in TV studio equipment, the cinderblocks in the walls, and the tiles in the floor. To get ideal acoustics in your TV studio, experiment by adding or taking away more fabric elements such as cloth backdrops or padded chairs. The goal is for the sound to seem natural. With too much fabric, the sound seems dead. With too many hard surfaces, the sound seems like it needs more bass and less treble.

## Headset Communication

In the complex TV studio, you may want to use a two-way headset communication system. This system enables the tech director in the control room to talk to the camera operators on the floor of the TV studio and for the camera operators to communicate back to the tech director. This is especially necessary when planning camera shots. For example, the tech director may tell the camera two operator to set up a close-up shot while the audience is watching a medium shot from the camera one operator. When the camera two operator has correctly focused and framed the shot, the tech director will use a video switcher or a/v digital mixer to switch from camera one to camera two. The audience now sees the close-up from camera two. (See Figure 10.6.)

*Figure 10.6 Portacom Head Set and Power Supply*

## Backdrops

For a complex TV studio, purchase a drop cloth or two large enough to cover a wall area 17' long x 8' high. This will be your backdrop. The talent will stand or sit in front of it. If you can't find a drop cloth large enough, two king size sheets will cover the same area. First, paint these sheets or the drop cloth. A simple latex water-based paint will do. Your students will enjoy doing the painting. Light blue is an excellent color to use. You may want to use your school color. That's OK but the color should be

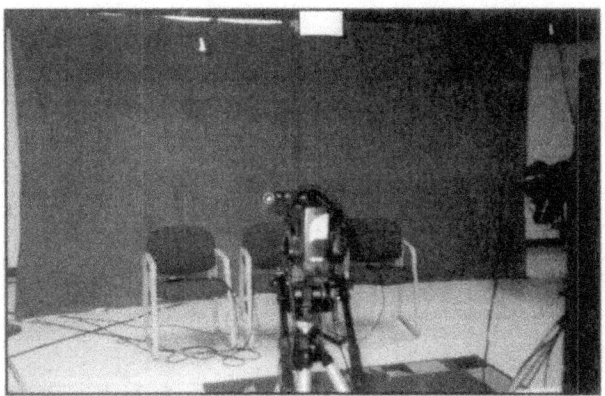

*Figure 10.7 Painted Backdrop Using Two King Size Sheets*

light. If you are planning to do special effects from a digital mixer, use "Digital Video Chroma Key Blue, Roscoe Ultimate TM Paints 5720 Ultimate TM Blue." (See Chapter 25, "Buying Video Production Equipment," page 201, for order information.) Punch holes in the sheet or drop cloth and tie them with string to the support beam above the ceiling tile in your TV studio room. You will have to take out the ceiling tile in the area of the studio where you hang the backdrop. (See Figure 10.7.)

### Flat in the Back of Your Set

You can put a "flat" in the back of your set. A flat is a background that covers the area in back of where the talent sits. A flat is a wood frame covered by muslin cloth or canvas. The frame of the flat consists of five pieces of 1" x 4" wood, usually white pine. It should be about 7' high x 15' wide. First, build the frame. Then stretch the canvas or muslin over the frame as tightly as possible, and attach with nails or a staple gun. This will avoid wrinkles. Apply a few coats of latex paint over the flat with a roller before painting the desired color or design on the flat. Flats can really improve the look of your set.

### Platforms and Gobos

Some TV studios use platforms to mount their sets. To construct a platform, first build the frame. Nails at least 3" long should be used to build the frame, made up of 2" x 4" wood. The size of the frame is 4' width x 8' length x 16' high. Nail 8' plywood boards to the frame with 2" nails. You'll probably need four platforms in all. Attach the platforms together with bolts.

Another item for the TV studio set is a gobo. A gobo is a prop in a foreground that gives the illusion of a specific location. Using a window frame as a gobo on a TV set gives the viewers the illusion that they are looking through a window into a house. (See Figure 10.8.)

*Figure 10.8 A Gobo*
*From "Looking Great with Video Production" by Augie Beasley*

## Anchor Desk

An anchor desk is nice for a TV set but not essential. To make an anchor desk quickly, take a library table and cover the area where the table legs are with corrugated cardboard or paper. This type of cardboard comes in a roll and is usually used for bulletin boards. You may already have some in a supply room.

To make it easy on yourself, forget about the anchor desk. Find four stools about 24 inches high. Your announcers can sit on these stools for general announcements. If you use medium shots, the stools will never be seen by the audience.

If you want a more elaborate set, you can build a professional looking anchor desk. Here is a good plan for one. Make it about 30" high with wood in front so you can't see the "talent's" legs. With some 2" x 4" pieces of wood, strip molding, plywood and paint, you can make an attractive set. The set construction crew of a high school drama department would be a good resource for advice and help in set construction. By making a call to a local TV studio, you might find an old anchor desk the TV studio was planning to discard.

## Lighting

For the complex TV studio, additional lighting is a necessity. In the complex TV studio, use a lighting kit that allows you to do key, back, and fill lighting. How do you hang lights in a TV studio? The lights are mounted to the metal grid with C clamps. There will be no need for ceiling tiles. Having a high ceiling allows you to place your lights higher so the lights can shoot at a downward angle, eliminating shadows to some extent. Plan for a few pipes running across the ceiling. (See Figure 10.9.)

*Figure 10.9 Pipes Running Across Studio Ceiling*

How do you place lights in a TV studio? The simple solution is to use the tripods that come with the lights in a lighting kit. If the talent will be sitting down, the lights mounted on tripods should be elevated 10'-12.' If the talent will be standing, the lights should be 15' high. Plastic filters can be placed over lights to create certain effects. A red filter on a back light helps separate the talent from the background.

# The Future for School TV News Shows

The school TV news show is the wave of the future and "the future is now!" It allows the school librarian and the students to deliver important communication to the student body every day. It is one of the most exciting and promising developments in the history of school libraries. Whether you have a complex or simple TV studio, the method by which you deliver your show may change. New cable wiring configurations for schools will have cable TV, the

Internet, and e-mail all running on the same cable. Perhaps someday, a new technology currently referred to as "streaming technology" will be used for school news shows. In streaming, your news show could be delivered on an Intranet, an online network for your school building. Using streaming technology, the videotape of your daily TV news show, both audio and video, becomes a digitized file on your computer and can be accessed by other teachers at your school on their classroom computers.

To find out more about streaming technology, go to Microsoft's Web site <www.msn.com>. For other good sources on the Web, go to Realimpact <www.realimpact.net>, and Apple Computer <www.publicsource.apple.com/projects/streaming/>. Streaming technology on the Internet today has a few limitations. The picture is not full screen and picture quality is not the best. Perhaps, these problems will be solved in the near future.

## Complex TV Studio for School News Show Checklist

_____ 1. A location in the library media center is needed. The room should be at least 21' wide x 30' long x 15' high with an adjacent control room at least 8' deep by 18' long x 8' high. There should be a window at least 3' high x 11' long between the control room and the studio.

_____ 2. An in-school cable TV system with a cable drop and TV receiver in every classroom is needed.

_____ 3. At least two color TV cameras or camcorders with VIDEO OUT output jacks are needed.

_____ 4. A TV video visualizer camera for TV graphics that shows 8 1/2" x 11" pictures or signs is a valuable addition. A color TV camera with a macro lens capability will also work.

_____ 5. At least three low impedance lavaliere microphones that hook into an audio mixer help enhance sound quality.

_____ 6. A CD/cassette player that hooks into the sound mixer is a requirement.

_____ 7. To do a multi camera program a video switcher and/or a/v digital mixer is needed.

_____ 8. You need a recorder VCR that can record your show as it broadcasts over the in-school cable TV system.

_____ 9. A playback VCR that hooks into the audio mixer for sound and into the a/v digital mixer or video switcher for the TV picture is vital. This enables you to play prerecorded tapes on your TV news show.

_____ 10. Hook up a computer with a presentation program to your video switcher or a/v digital mixer.

_____ 11. A head-set communication system between tech director and camera operators is very desirable.

_____ 12. A TV receiver for the recorder VCR is needed. This TV receiver shows you what is going into the cable TV system from the studio.

_____ 13. A TV receiver on the TV studio floor is required for the talent, so they can provide narration for the TV picture coming from the playback VCR, display camera, or computer *PowerPoint* presentation.

_____ 14. A TV monitor for the video visualizer is needed, so the picture can be positioned correctly.

_____ 15. A TV monitor for the a/v digital mixer is helpful, so the tech director can preview a special effect or a shot from a specific camera before it is seen by the audience.

_____ 16. A backdrop on the wall in back of where the talent will perform is necessary.

_____ 17. A lighting kit consisting of three incandescent lights with tripods, screens (scrims), focus knobs, and barn doors is essential.

## TV Studio Safety Checklist

_____ 1. Tape down extension cords to floor, so no one trips over them.

_____ 2. After lighting has been set up, tape down lighting tripods to floor with duct tape. (A hot light and tripod falling on a student could cause serious injury.)

_____ 3. Unplug a light's AC power before changing lamps.

_____ 4. Do not change lamps with bare hands. Oil from hands causes lamps to burn out faster.

_____ 5. Be sure the light can handle the wattage of the lamp you're using. Using a lamp with too much wattage could start a fire.

_____ 6. Never touch hot lamps with your bare hands. Use leather work gloves, instead.

_____ 7. Use heavy-duty extension cords, not household-weight cords.

_____ 8. Be sure the building's electric circuit breaker can handle the amount of electricity used in the TV studio.

_____ 9. Allow lights time to cool before moving them.

_____ 10. Be sure all TV equipment is plugged into surge protectors

# Complex TV Studio Equipment Needed Checklist

_____  1. At least two camcorders with VIDEO OUT and AUDIO OUT.

_____  2. Tripods for each camcorder.

_____  3. Playback VCR.

_____  4. Recorder VCR with LINE or AUX.

_____  5. Video switcher and/or a/v digital mixer.

_____  6. Audio mixer with MIC and LINE inputs.

_____  7. Character generator.

_____  8. Video visualizer for graphics.

_____  9. TV monitor for video visualizer.

_____ 10. Preview TV monitor for a/v digital mixer.

_____ 11. TV monitor or receiver for recorder VCR.

_____ 12. TV monitor or receiver for TV studio floor.

_____ 13. CD/audio cassette player with LINE OUT.

_____ 14. At least two, low-impedance microphones.

_____ 15. If microphones are not lavaliere, two microphone stands.

_____ 16. One computer with VIDEO OUT device.

# Video Production Troubleshooting

At the last minute, when you've got another commitment, the panic call comes. Mr. Jones is having a problem with his video presentation set up. You've got to fix the problem fast, because everyone in the audience is twiddling their thumbs. This checklist is designed to help you solve video production equipment problems quickly.

## Video Production Troubleshooting Checklist

1. **The camcorder's recording light won't come on.**

   _____ A. Be sure CAMERA/VCR switch is in camera position.

   _____ B. Be sure videotape is in camcorder.

   _____ C. Be sure tab on the videotape has not been pulled off.

2. **The camcorder's power light won't come on.**

   _____ A. Be sure the battery is charged.

   _____ B. Be sure the battery can still hold a charge. If you recharge the battery, and it still won't work, throw it away.

   _____ C. Be sure the AC adapter is hooked up to camcorder if you're not using the battery.

   _____ D. Take battery out of camcorder if you are using AC power.

3. **After playing back tape on a TV receiver/VCR that was recorded on the camcorder, all you see is snow.**

   _____ A. Be sure the RF cable goes from RF out on the VCR to the RF jack on the TV. Be sure the TV receiver is tuned to the same channel that the VCR's signal is set.

   _____ B. Be sure you rewind tape to the point where you started recording.

   _____ C. Clean the heads on the camcorder using a tape head-cleaning cassette.

   _____ D. Clean the heads on the playback VCR using a tape head-cleaning cassette.

4. **The tape you recorded on the camcorder using a handheld microphone does not have sound.**

   _____ A. Check the microphone. Was the ON/OFF switch left in the OFF position?

   _____ B. Is the microphone plug only partially inserted into the microphone jack?

   _____ C. Is the microphone plug inserted into the headphone jack instead of the microphone jack? Record again. This time insert the microphone plug completely and loop the microphone cable, around the camcorder, so the microphone plug does not fall out.

   _____ D. Is there a short in the microphone cable or is the microphone broken? Record again with a different microphone.

   _____ E. If you have not solved the problem yet, the problem maybe in the sound recording mechanism inside the camcorder. Send the camcorder to the repair shop.

5. **A just-recorded show cannot be seen or heard when you play it back on your VCR.**

   _____ A. Check to see if the TV/Video switch on the TV receiver/monitor is on Video setting. Make sure you are using an RF cable to hook up the VCR to the TV. Switch the TV receiver/monitor to the TV setting. On many TV receiver/monitors, you need a remote unit to do this. Press the TV/Video button on the remote unit.

   _____ B. If the VCR is set in the back to channel three, and the TV receiver is tuned to channel four, set the TV Receiver to channel three.

   _____ C. If you have the TV and VCR both set to channel three, and you still have no picture, go into the TV's menu and be sure channel three has been selected. You'll see a check next to the channel in the channel summary section of the TV's menu on many models.

   _____ D. If the RF cable connected to the TV receiver is attached to the TV IN or RF IN jack on the VCR, connect the RF cable to the TV OUT or RF OUT jack on the back of the VCR.

   _____ E. If all the connections and setting for the TV and VCR are correct, and you still have no picture, check the cable itself. The wire in the middle of the cable may be bent or too short to reach the TV receiver or VCR jack even though the cable is connected to the TV and VCR. Get a new RF cable to attach to TV and VCR. Give the broken cable to the TV repairperson.

   _____ F. If the cables and connections are correct, and still you have no picture or sound on the TV, screw the cable in more at the TV jack and VCR's RF OUT jack.

6. **The just-recorded show cannot be seen when it is played on the VCR; only the sound can be heard.**

   _____ A. Check the back of the VCR to see what channel has been selected. Be sure the TV receiver is tuned to that channel.

   _____ B. If the TV receiver and VCR are tuned to the same channel and still you get sound but no picture, the heads on the VCR need cleaning. Use a video head cleaner tape to clean the VCR heads.

7. **When playing back a videotape, using two TV receivers connected to a VCR via a two output splitter, you are not getting a picture.**

   _____ A. Be sure the RF cable goes from RF OUT on the VCR to the IN jack on the splitter. Then run an RF cable from each of the OUT jacks of the splitter to the two TV receivers.

8. **There isn't a picture from the computer screen on the data projector's screen when the computer is connected to the data projector, even though you've tried each input option from the input select button on the data projector.**

   _____ A. If the 15 pin cable from the computer is inserted into the RGB OUT jack, connect this cable from the computer to the RGB IN jack.

9. **The pictures from cameras one and two are running through your a/v digital mixer into your recorder VCR. The digital mixer is set correctly, yet you don't see the picture from either camera on the TV receiver hooked up to the recorder VCR.**

   _____ A. The recorder VCR has an S VIDEO/LINE switch. If the cable connecting from the a/v digital mixer is an S VIDEO cable, be sure the S VIDEO/LINE switch is set on S VIDEO. If the cable connecting the a/v digital mixer to the recorder VCR is an RCA (phono) cable, be sure the S VIDEO/LINE switch is set to LINE.

10. **The VU meter on the microphone mixer is not registering when the talent speaks into the low-impedance, lavaliere microphone.**

    _____ A. Be sure the microphone is set to the ON position.

    _____ B. Be sure the microphone is plugged into the microphone mixer.

    _____ C. Be sure you know into which input the talent's microphone is plugged. Turn up the volume of that input on the audio mixer. Turn off the other microphones connected to the audio mixer. Test another microphone in the same input. Do you now get a reading on the VU meter? The other microphone may be broken.

11. **The TV in a classroom cannot receive the school TV news show on cable channel 6, even though you selected channel 6 in the TV receiver's menu. The RF cables are set up correctly from the cable drop on the wall to the VCR and then to the TV receiver.**

   _____ A. Turn the power OFF on the VCR.

   _____ B. If you still don't receive a good TV picture, check other channels.

   _____ C. If you're not receiving a good TV picture on any channels, check the connections of all your cables. Be sure the RF cables are screwed in tightly.

   _____ D. If you still don't receive a good TV picture, contact the TV repairperson. The problem lies in the cable TV system, not your VCR, TV receiver, or related cables.

12. **You are playing back a tape from a VCR to a TV monitor and get no picture or sound.**

   _____ A. Be sure the TV monitor is set to VIDEO or LINE, not TV.

   _____ B. Be sure the RCA (phono) cable goes from VIDEO OUT on the back of the VCR to VIDEO IN on the back of the TV monitor.

   _____ C. Be sure the RCA (phono) cables go from AUDIO OUT on the back of the VCR to AUDIO IN on the back of the TV monitor.

13. **Two or more TV receiver/monitors are connected together to show a videotape program. You are using RCA (phono) jacks and cables from VCR to TV receiver/monitor and from one TV receiver/monitor to the next. You get no picture when playing the tape.**

   _____ A. Be sure the TV receiver/monitors are set to AV, VIDEO, or LINE, not to TV or ANTENNAE.

   _____ B. Be sure your RCA (phono) cable for video is going from VIDEO OUT on the first TV receiver/monitor to VIDEO IN on the second TV receiver/monitor.

   _____ C. Be sure your RCA (phono) cable for audio is going from AUDIO OUT on the first TV receiver/monitor to AUDIO IN on the second TV receiver/monitor.

   _____ D. Be sure your RCA (phono) cable for VIDEO OUT from the VCR is going to VIDEO IN on the first TV receiver/monitor.

   _____ E. Be sure your RCA (phono) cable for AUDIO OUT from the VCR is going to AUDIO IN on the first TV receiver/monitor.

14. **The in-school TV news show live segments are always much louder than taped segments.**

   _____ A. If you are using low-impedance microphones for the live talent, use low-impedance microphones for the taped segments as well.

   _____ B. When you play a videotape as part of your otherwise live news show, run the sound cable from the AUDIO OUT of the playback VCR to a "line input" on the audio mixer. The person operating the audio mixer can turn up the volume on the "line input" and the master "audio output" to make the sound from the videotape as loud as the sound from the live microphones.

# Great Communication and Great Instruction with Video Production in School Libraries

# Learning, Instructional Design, Research, and Video Production

Why plan video production into your learning activities in the first place? First, video production is an all-purpose, inexpensive medium that can fit many learning purposes. In the 1960s, things were different. If vocational teachers wanted still shots for a physical activity like the steps in doing the wiring for an AC outlet, they *wished they could* shoot a series of photographic slides without paying for film development. If biology instructors wanted to present different attributes of mammals, *they wished they could* easily add color pictures to their overhead thermographic transparencies. If tennis instructors wanted to correct the flaws in the swings of tennis players, these instructors *wished they could* shoot 8-mm films of their tennis players' strokes and play them back immediately. If sociology teachers wanted to show the effects of racism, they *wished they could* interview a victim of racism. They'd have wanted to shoot their interview in color with close-ups and audible sound. They'd have needed a 16-mm film camera to do this.

Today, biology instructors create *PowerPoint* presentations with clip art pictures of mammals and transfer the presentations to video if their classrooms have TV and VCRs. Tennis coaches use camcorders to videotape their players' swings and play the tapes back on TVs and VCRs. Vocational teachers produce *PowerPoint* slides detailing the steps involved in electric wiring, first videotaping close-up someone doing a wiring job, then adding these video shots to the *PowerPoint* presentation. Sociology teachers use a camcorder with a handheld microphone to produce videotapes of interviews about racism.

In the 1960s, none of these projects would have been possible in a typical school. There were no camcorders, computers, or 16mm cameras in school libraries then, just 16 mm projectors. Today, most school libraries in the United States have the camcorders, videotapes, VCRs, TVs, computers and disks needed to do all these instructional projects without spending additional money. They can also be done quickly, with no wait for film to be developed, because these projects all use the same medium—the VHS videotape.

The question today is not only what medium will you use to complete your instructional project, but how will you use this medium of video production to meet your needs? Do you need stills? Do you need graphics? Do you need full motion? Do you need close-ups and a handheld microphone for dramatization? You, the video producer of today in a school library, need to be aware of the many types of video productions you can create.

What type of video production can best serve your needs? A series of still shots or a *PowerPoint* presentation? Perhaps, but keep in mind that the biggest advantage of video production is that it captures movement and sound simultaneously. Thus, many important school events, such as a speech by a guest speaker, a teaching performance of a student teacher, or a field trip, can be easily documented on video. The physical analysis of any visible activity can be videotaped. No one loves video production more than coaches. They can review team members' tackling techniques or tennis serves a hundred times, point out mistakes, and model proper technique. Speech instructors can videotape their students' speeches to correct mistakes in delivery, word choice, and body language. History teachers can assign their students to interview older people in the community to create an oral history. English teachers can assign students to write and produce TV advertisements, and in doing so, teach techniques of persuasion. These are some of the many ways video production can enhance learning.

# Instructional Design

Instructional design is a big part of the school library media specialist's job. Instructional design for the school library media specialist is based on the idea that activities that encourage students to read, research, write scripts, create video presentations, and present them to classmates are going to enhance learning. These activities need to be designed into the instruction. It's the job of the library media specialist to initiate that design.

Generally, classroom teachers are expected to design instruction alone. Generally, the classroom teacher is isolated and does not plan projects with other teachers. You, the school librarian, can change that expectation by working collaboratively with teachers to design instruction.

What is instructional design? To understand instructional design, look to the masters in the field, Heinich, Molenda, Russell and Smaldino. In their book, *Instructional Media and Technologies for Learning,* 6th ed., they provide the ultimate instructional design model, the "ASSURE Model." This method calls for analysis of the learner, stating of objectives, selection of methods, media and materials, utilization of such with learner participation required, and evaluation and revision of the entire process.

The problem is that the ASSURE Model does not talk specifically about a school librarian's role in instructional design. Instead, the ASSURE model is designed for all educators using instructional media. In *Video Production for School Library Media Specialists: Communication and Production Techniques,* the focus is on what you, the school librarian, will do to facilitate the instructional design process. Our book is written for library media specialists working with students in elementary, middle, and secondary schools. We accept and assume all the elements of the ASSURE model, but we've simplified it as a tool for library media specialists in public schools doing video production products.

# The P.I.E. Model for Instructional Design

First, as a library media specialist, you've got to **plan** with the teachers for a **product** (P). You go to a teacher you suspect might enjoy doing a video or video/computer production project. Don't wait for that teacher to come to you. The product that you and the teacher decide on could be a *PowerPoint* presentation on video, an ad for the school TV news show, a computer/video research presentation, or video book talk. The point is that you initiate the collaborative planning process with the teacher. In fact, according to A.A.S.L. and A.E.C.T. in *Information Power Building Partnerships for Learning*, you ought to initiate projects with teachers so often and so effectively that your effort "encourages a culture of collaboration throughout the school" (51). Together you and the classroom teacher define what product the students will create.

Second, you've got to **implement** your plan (I). *In Information Power Building Partnerships for Learning*, you can look to "Indicator 4" of the "Information Literacy Standards" for a sample plan for students to implement. "Grades 6-8 (Foreign Language)—A French class plans an imaginary trip to Paris. Each student researches information about a particular part of the city to present to the class. Students find historical facts, descriptions of important sites, and information on costs. The class produces the videotape, with narrative in French, as a travel guide to Paris" (20-21) Part of the (I) in P.I.E. is setting deadlines for each phase of the production, doing research, scriptwriting, and a presentation deadline. Another part of the (I) is dividing up the workload and responsibilities for video production. How many students will be in a group? Who is going to research what? How will scriptwriting duties be divided among students? Who will operate the camera? Who will be the announcer? Who will train and supervise the students? Will deadline dates be staggered so the library media specialist isn't overwhelmed with five groups wanting to finish their projects on the same afternoon? How many periods a day can the library media center staff assist students with their video productions? (See "Instructional Design for a Video Production Project Checklist," page 120.)

Third, **evaluate** your results and make necessary revisions, (E). Did the students succeed in implementing the assignment? Were all the objectives of this unit met? Did the students enjoy the project? Were student directions clear? Did the audience enjoy and learn effectively from the students' presentation? Would you do this unit again? How would you change the unit? Did you, the library media specialist, do too much of the work? How can the burden be shifted more equitably among teacher, student, and library media specialist? (See "Video Product Evaluation Form," page 122, and "Video Project Evaluation Form," page 123.)

It's the P.I.E. model not because it's easy as pie. In fact, you may get pie in your face a few times while doing it! It's a new paradigm in education that focuses on students reading, researching, writing, and producing video presentations. That's a lot more complicated than preparing students to do multiple choice tests. It's the way that you'll ensure the library media center program in your school shares a big piece of the instructional pie.

You also make the pie taste better. You improve it. You change it. When you, the school library media specialist, create an instructional design unit that includes researching, writing, scripting, and producing videos, you do something awesome. You become, as Susan Dowling points out in her *School Library Journal* article of May 1997, "Brooklyn Cinderella or The True Story of Transforming P.S. 3," a teacher on the cutting edge of the "Library Power" movement. Your instructional design model becomes "a catalyst for schoolwide reform and takes the school librarian beyond the role of library administrator and guardian of books to one of teacher, curriculum consultant, mentor, technology expert, publicist, and lobbyist for enlightened change" (25).

# Research Findings to Justify the Use of Student Video and Multimedia Production

There is evidence that when students research, script, and produce visual presentations about some phase of the curriculum using technology, they learn more effectively. Richard Lehrer, in the book, *Computers as Cognitive Tools,* writes about a study he did with eighth graders who worked in groups to create visual computer presentations about the Civil War. The students who created visual presentations about the Civil War were compared with other students who learned about the Civil War by listening to classroom teacher presentations. Both groups were tested on the Civil War material. Both groups did equally well, and Lehrer was very discouraged. It seemed that students creating visual presentations hadn't proved a more effective way of learning as opposed to student learning by listening to teacher presentations. A year later, these same students were tested on the Civil War material again. The students who had created visual computer presentations still scored well while the students who had listened to teacher presentations scored very poorly.

Lehrer's research points to the likelihood that when students use computer and video production together to present information, they learn better and retain the information longer. For those reasons alone, projects where students create visual presentations using video and computers should be designed into the instruction. (See Chapter 19, "The Computer/Video Research Project," page 163.)

When students write scripts for video and multimedia projects they are doing some very effective learning. The SWEET process, discussed in Chapter 3, was inspired by the research of Dr. Susan Rich Sheridan. Sheridan has discovered that when students draw an object before writing about it, their writing improves. Sheridan writes in her book, *Drawing/Writing and the New Literacy Where Verbal Meets Visual* that "Once the brain of the child cracks the visual/spatial code, it is prepared to crack the verbal/linguistic code. Through extensive practice with drawing as a visual code, the brain learns to write and calculate more easily" (46). Sheridan has countless case histories to site as evidence of the efficacy of this approach. The success of Sheridan's approach may have applications for scriptwriting. In the SWEET process students first sketch each scene in the "Simple Script Sheet," Figure 2.12, page 20. Then after sketching a scene, the student writes the appropriate narration or dialogue for that scene. Using the SWEET method of scriptwriting may be a powerful way to improve student writing. The possibility of improving a student's writing in this way may be the best reason for students to design and produce video and multimedia presentations.

When students design their own multimedia or video presentations, it's important to let them use computers in the design process. When students write on a computer, Valeri-Gold and Deming have found there is evidence that they write more effectively (61).

Getting students to present what they've learned to others using multimedia and video production is an important teaching strategy. It's a cornerstone of educational reform. The teaching staff at Christopher Columbus Middle School in Union City, New Jersey, produced a tremendous boost in standardized test scores in 1996. It was true that Bell Atlantic had supplied the school with many computers. In his article, Jay Mathews writes that the teachers at Christopher Columbus felt the improvement in test scores was mainly due to the way they taught. "Margarita De Candia, an English and social studies teacher at Christopher Columbus, found students enjoyed lessons and remembered more when she let them explore textbooks and encyclopedias for the answers rather than force-feed them a lecture or an assigned reading of just one book. Students were encouraged to work together on projects and present their findings to the class" (A1).

This is the type of instructional design that we advocate. When students research, script, and produce presentations using video and computers, they learn more effectively. Something else happens as well. Research shows many students become very productive in that kind of environment. These students become motivated by a sense of self-confidence from producing a video, not by achieving a high grade in a class. These students become confident in their ability to create a presentation. Video productions help build student self-confidence. This is backed up by an article by Liu and Rutlege, "The effect of a 'learner as multimedia designer' environment on at-risk high school students' motivation and learning of design knowledge," found in the 1999 *Research Report on the Effectiveness of Technology in Schools, 6th Edition*.

Liu and Rutledge did research on the effect of "Providing a learner as multimedia-designer environment." The kind of video production described in this book involves creating computer multimedia presentations and incorporating them in video presentations. In the Liu and Rutledge experiment, one group of high school students engaged in creating multimedia projects. The students in the experimental group produced segments for a local Children's Museum. The students in the control group in the experiment attended a computer class in the same school where various computer applications were taught.

The results of this experiment: "Following students' involvement in the program, the researchers reported significant gains in intrinsic goal orientation (finding tasks rewarding for their own sake, rather than because of external reward or pressure); task value (interest in the tasks students were performing); and self-efficacy for learning (students' confidence in their own ability to accomplish learning tasks). In contrast, scores for the control group-a computer class at the same high school in which students were taught the use of various computing tools-remained about the same over the course of the semester and in the case of task value, actually decreased" (70).

Another important aspect of involving students in researching, scripting, and creating computer/video or video productions is cooperative learning. Student video production projects are usually done cooperatively, in groups. It usually takes a group of at least four people doing many tasks to produce a video—researcher, scriptwriter, camera person, an announcer. That group must work together effectively to get a video production completed successfully. This effective cooperative learning model encourages the students to give each other feedback and to have each student in the group assigned to a specific role. Heinich, Molenda, Russell, and Smaldino point out in *Instructional Media and Technologies for Learning* that, "Research by Robert Slavin, Spencer Kagan, and David and Roger Johnson has revealed that not only does cooperative learning yield better acquisition and retention of lesson content, but it also promotes better interpersonal and thinking skills" (315). The biggest pitfall in cooperative learning is structuring the assignment so all students do their share of the work.

## It's Time for P.I.E.

Use the P.I.E. model for instructional design with your teachers and students. **Plan, implement,** and **evaluate** projects with them. Get students involved in researching, scriptwriting, producing, and presenting their own video productions to their classmates. Be aware of the many advantages these projects have for your students. The students will remember the material better after going through the process of creating the presentation. The students will learn more effectively because they worked together cooperatively. The students will gain in self-confidence because they were able to present to others a real product—a video or computer video presentation. That is real educational reform based on real educational research. This approach makes it more likely that students will achieve better learning results in school.

So get started! Let the instructional design process involving student video production start in the library media center. Are all the teachers going to buy into this idea? Of course not! If one third of the teachers in any school participate, the library media specialist will be swamped with projects.

## Instructional Design for a Video Production Project Checklist

_____ 1. Plan with a specific teacher. Ask if the teacher is interested in a project using video production equipment and computer presentation software where students research, script, produce, and present information to their classmates.

_____ 2. Ask the teacher if students would react favorably to such a project at this time.

_____ 3. Define the instructional goals of the project. For example, "Each student project will have nine visuals explained by factual information. The presentation will reflect effective writing with an introduction, transitions, and a conclusion."

_____ 4. Before beginning the project, determine how much training the students will need in research, scriptwriting, computer presentation equipment, and video production equipment.

_____ 5. When can the activity be scheduled in the library media center calendar?

_____ 6. How many of the teacher's classes will be scheduled to do this project?

_____ 7. How many class periods in the library media center will be required to complete this project?

_____ 8. How many students will be in each group?

_____ 9. What will the job responsibilities be for each group member?

_____ 10. What topic will each group be assigned?

_____ 11. How will subtopics be divided within each group?

_____ 12. Will each student in each group research and script a section of the presentation?

_____ 13. Within each group, how will job assignments for computer software presentation, camera operation, announcer, and cue-card holder be made?

_____ 14. How many groups can produce their video computer presentations at the same time?

_____ 15. Where will the production work take place? TV studio? Library? Classroom?

_____ 16. Who will monitor the students as they produce their productions?

_____ 17. Will there be separate deadlines for research, scriptwriting, and production?

_____ 18. Will all final productions be due at one time or will the deadlines be staggered?

_____ 19. Can the library staff handle supervising the number of video productions being done and still handle their other library responsibilities?

_____ 20. When will all the finished productions be shown to the class?

_____ 21. Should the finished productions be shown to other classes or groups?

_____ 22. How will the finished productions be evaluated?

_____ 23. Who will evaluate the finished productions?

_____ 24. After the productions have been presented, meet with the teacher involved to determine if instructional goals were achieved.

_____ 25. Discuss with teacher what changes should be made in the project for next year.

# Video Project Evaluation Form

To: Everyone involved in the _____ video project. Read statements 1-6 below and score as follows: (4) strongly agree, (3) agree, (2) disagree, (1) strongly disagree.

_____ 1. The students involved succeeded in implementing this assignment.

_____ 2. The students met all the objectives of this assignment.

_____ 3. The students involved seemed to enjoy doing this project.

_____ 4. The student objectives, assignments, and directions were clearly stated.

_____ 5. The work of the project was shared equally among the students.

_____ 6. What changes would you suggest in this video project the next time it is assigned?

| Quick Check Evaluation | Student | Teacher |
| --- | --- | --- |
| Objectives of assignment met? | Yes/No | Yes/No |
| Project was enjoyable? | Yes/No | Yes/No |

**Comments:** _____

_____

_____

_____

_____

_____

_____

_____

_____

_____

_____

_____

_____

_____

# Video Product Evaluation Form

Title of video production:
_____

Names of student producers:
_____
_____
_____
_____
_____
_____
_____
_____

Score each question from 0-10 points.

_____ 1. The videotape communicates its message effectively.

_____ 2. The picture is in focus.

_____ 3. The lighting seems natural and appropriate.

_____ 4. The sound is clearly audible and even.

_____ 5. The camera work demonstrates good picture composition.

_____ 6. The narration/dialogue/music/sound effects are effective and appropriate.

_____ 7. The information appears to be factual, if this is a nonfiction piece.

_____ 8. The story seems believable to the audience, if this is a fiction piece

_____ 9. Titles are readable from the back of the classroom or viewing area.

_____ 10. The videotape maintains the interest of the audience.

_____ **Total**

# Training Students for Video Production

## How to Select the Students Who Will Produce the Video

How do you recruit students for video production? One option is to note some students who are successful in their class work. You might pick a few students who speak well or write well. You might pick a few students with aptitude for working with computers and video equipment. You might pick only students with a 3.0 academic average or spotless school citizenship records. In some schools, students who want to work in a video production program fill out an application. (See Figure 13.1)

You could also announce a meeting to be held one day in early September right after school. The students who show up will be your crew. Choose a method of video crew selection that is comfortable for you.

In elementary schools, you may want to work with one class at a time. That class will do all your video production work. Every few months, however, you may want to train another class to give more students the opportunity to learn video production.

In secondary schools, you might want to form a video production club and work with your students one day a week after school. You may find another good time to train students is at lunch or when a teacher sends them from a class.

# APPLICATION FOR
## WBRN MORNING NEWS SHOW

Name of Applicant: _____

Teacher's Name: _____

State the reason(s) why you feel you would like to be a member of the morning news team.

_____
_____
_____
_____

What part of the news team is of most interest to you and why? (Anchor, Weatherperson, Video Coordinator, Music Coordinator, Cue-Card Person, Production of Opening and Closing Credits)

_____
_____
_____
_____

If you are chosen, you must arrive at the TV studio no later than 8:20 a.m,. or as soon as your bus arrives if it is later than 8:20. Failure to arrive promptly will result in a substitute being chosen for your duty that day. If you are absent on a day you have been scheduled to be in the studio please call the school and leave a message for _____.
This will help the crew to obtain a substitute in a timely fashion.

*Figure 13.1 Application for WBRN Morning News Show*

# Develop a Video Production Training System

Training students in video production is always surprising! The video production program in an elementary school may be much more sophisticated than a high school program. A group of third graders may produce a better show than a group of twelfth graders. The third graders may have more sophisticated equipment with which to work.

Whether you work in an elementary or a secondary school, you'll develop a training system that is effective for you. You may end up training students in large groups, small groups, or individually. Perhaps you'll delegate the training to another staff member or a capable student. The bottom line is reach out to your students. Motivate them. You'll find some of your students are already excited about video production. A well-trained student video production team will help you implement your entire program.

Train the students with a practical goal in mind like producing a news show for the student body or producing a show to be entered in a video production contest. Tell the students who show up at your meeting what the video production club will do, what the rewards are, and what the requirements are. If your school gives out letters, arrange with school administration to award letters for video production. Students need a sense of purpose when being trained. Otherwise, the students will wonder why they are producing a video. One of the biggest thrills for educators is to witness the improvement in the academic and social life of a student who has found something like video production to focus on. Create special training seminars for your students. Invite community people with a video background to help you do the training. When you provide an audience and a deadline for your students' work, you motivate your students to learn more and produce more.

Encourage the students to come after school, on days when you don't have meetings, to provide them with training. Lunchtime is another excellent opportunity to train students. The time you spend training students is time well spent. Going through the training checklists in this book with students helps them build confidence. The training process helps build positive relationships with students. That relationship you build with students is one of trust and encouragement. You become their mentor. The relationship with each student is the glue that holds the school news show together.

# Set Standards, Rewards, and Expectations

You can post video training checklists that each of your students has completed on one wall of your TV studio or some other place in the library. On the same list, each student keeps track of the number of video productions completed. Keep a record for the number of hours of participation for each club member. To get your students committed to working on a daily school news show, set up a contract for each student, and have them sign it. Set a number of video productions each student must produce. If your school gives out letter awards, give out a school letter award to the students who meet your requirements. Here are some suggested letter requirements: (1) complete checklists in areas such as camera operation, lighting, talent, editing, switchers and mixers, and scriptwriting, (2) complete four video features that require no editing, such as an interview, (3) complete two edited video features using one of the methods of editing described in Chapter 8.

Training your students is an exciting process. Meet with your students after they've produced some video segments. Critique these segments, and validate everything that's good about them. Also talk about areas for improvement. Students love to talk about their video production work.

## Let the Students Train You

It's important to let the students experiment. If you have mixers or editors, let the students experiment with special effects. The students love to be creative, to try something new. Go along with some of this experimenting! The end result of training students in video production is that the students take ownership of video production.

School library media specialists today must learn about the many types of equipment and software—computers, Windows, Microsoft Internet Explorer, *PowerPoint*, HyperStudio, CD-ROM, e-mail, computer card catalog, circulation system, and video equipment. Who has to know more technologies than you? You don't necessarily have to be an expert in all phases of video production. When you start training the students, some of them realize that they know more than you. If you're smart, that's when you let the students train you. When a student trains you on how to operate equipment consider that a magic moment. Write it down, type it up, and put it in a training notebook.

## Create Training Partnerships

Your students are not the only people who can train you. Your principal, an instructional aide, the TV repairperson, a custodian, or a parent can train you, too. Just ask for help. It's amazing how many people are willing to spend 10 minutes showing you how to master some phase of technology. It might take you hours to learn the same information another way. Your openness to learning from others may lead you to a sense of interdependence with your students and colleagues which leads to a desire to create partnerships. Those partnerships define your effectiveness as a school librarian. Without partnerships, you would be sitting in the library media center alone. By establishing partnerships with the students and teachers, you're functioning at the heart of the instructional process. You can initiate this process by training students and teachers. Some of the checklists in this book will help you do that. But the checklists are only a start. In the training process, you'll learn at least as much as you teach.

# Working with Student Talent

## CHAPTER 14

## Terms

- **on location**
- **production crew**
- **talent**

The key to a successful video shoot is the teamwork between the talent (announcers and actors) and the production crew (camera operator, tech director, sound person). It takes some rehearsing before the entire video production team can successfully produce a news show or a scene in a dramatic video. Allow an adequate amount of rehearsal time for planning for a video shoot; it often takes longer than you think.

## Selecting the Talent

One of the toughest jobs in the video production process is deciding who will be the talent. To decide who your announcers or actors will be in the production, conduct a talent tryout. Create a situation similar to the actual video production, and place prospective actors or announcers in that situation. Videotape the tryout. Get some faculty members from your school to help do the judging, using a judging criteria sheet. (See Figure 14.1.) Students with a strong voice, good diction, a positive attitude, a friendly manner, and appropriate dress and grooming will enhance the TV production a great deal. You may find that many students want to be in the video production. Obviously, not everyone can be the anchorperson on the news show or the lead role in a dramatic video production. If you are doing a news show, you may want to select a few students who show promise in the talent tryout to be news anchors for your show. In a live news show situation, some of your students will rise to the occasion, others won't. The students who do well can be your news anchors.

# Talent Tryout Sheet

Name _____

Score each category from 1-10. 10 is highest score and 1 is lowest score.

_____ 1. The talent conveys interest.

_____ 2. The talent makes eye contact with camera.

_____ 3. The talent's speech is easily understood.

_____ 4. The talent makes good transitions to next speaker.

_____ 5. The talent reads the word of the day effectively.

_____ 6. The talent effectively operates cue card scroll.

_____ 7. The talent speaks at an appropriate speed.

_____ 8. The talent reads the announcements smoothly.

_____ 9. The talent adjusts emotional tone as needed.

_____ 10. The talent handles tech. problems effectively.

_____ **Total**

*Figure 14.1 Talent Tryout Sheet*

Find another role for the students who are not effective as news anchors. Some of these students may excel at being an interviewer in a taped segment of the show. For taped segments, students have more opportunity to rehearse. If the student makes a mistake, the segment can be shot over. In a live show the anchorperson does not have a second chance to deliver the news segment. You may want to have a news show where some segments are live and some are on videotape. This will allow more of your students to perform as talent on your show.

Getting the appropriate sound level for the talent is vital for a successful video production. When a dramatic production is shot outside, there is a problem of getting quality sound. Actors can't hold the microphone in their hands. Put the microphone on a broom or long stick for a situation like this. Hold the microphone a little above and in front of the talent so that the microphone can't be seen on camera. This is similar to the boom microphone used on Hollywood sets, but we call it a broom microphone. For this type of shoot, you need the best possible microphone. We suggest using a low impedance microphone.

# Cueing the Talent

*Figure 14.2 Student Using Scrolling Cue Card*

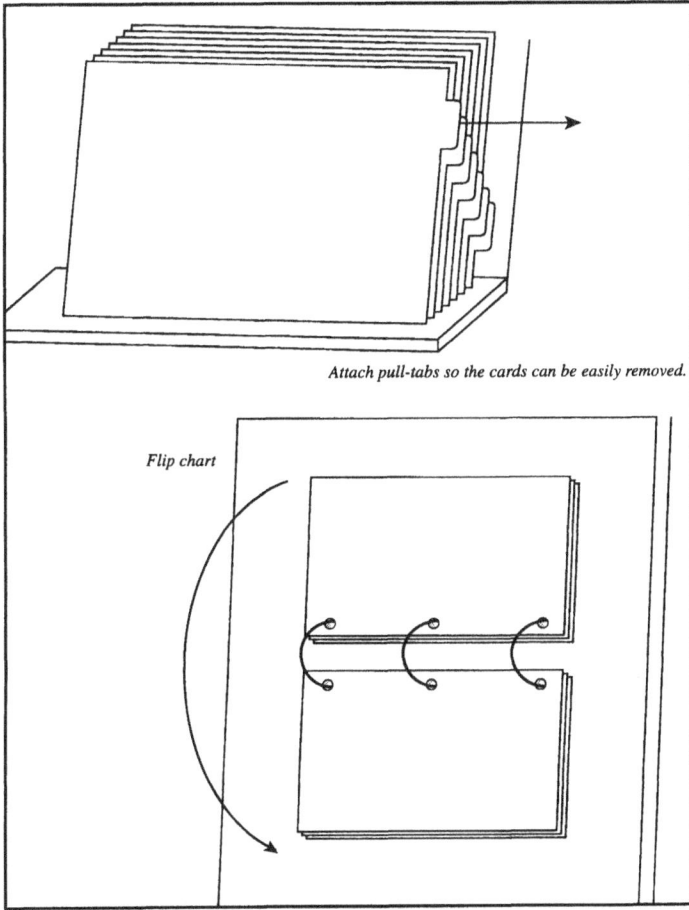

*Figure 14.3 Manipulating Cue Cards From "Looking Great with Video Production" by Augie Beasley*

Cue cards are often necessary for the talent to read during a production. Holding up a series of cue cards for the talent to read can be a cumbersome affair. A cue card gets stuck in your hand and the talent stares at the camera until you hold the right cue card up. Here are a few solutions to the cumbersome cue card problem. Use a "scrolling cue card," a series of cue cards taped together and wound around a tin can around 10" in diameter. The cue card holder holds the cue card directly above and in back of the camera. The cue cards are wound up around the tin can after they've been read. The large tin can for the scrolling cue card must be rotated at a speed comfortable for the talent. Otherwise, the talent will be talking too fast or too slow. When this job is done poorly, it causes the announcer to make mistakes on the air. (See Figure 14.2, "Student Using Scrolling Cue Card," for some other effective cue card ideas.) (See Figure 14.3.)

It's a good idea to let the announcers and actors do the job of cue card operator. They can appreciate more than any one how important the job of cue card holder really is. If you have a daily TV news show with two announcer positions, use four regular announcers. Let them alternate so that each day during the show, two run cue cards while the other two announce.

A teleprompter is still a very expensive item for a TV studio. However, a computer software program for teleprompting called "Easy Prompter" is available. It sells for about $100 and is available from <www.schooltv.com>. It can be used with almost any PC, but it does not work with Macintosh computers. The computer screen is positioned on a cart right next to the camera so the talent can read the narration off the computer while looking at the camera.

## Things Talent Must Know

If the interviewer and interviewee stand at a 90° angle from each other, it's easier for the camera operator to zoom in on the interviewee during the interview. (See Chapter 4, "The Camera," p. 34.) The talent needs to be trained to hold the microphone 6" and at a 45° angle from the mouth of the person speaking, to never tap on the microphone, and to always leave the microphone's ON/OFF switch in the ON position while recording. Also, they need to be instructed never to chew gum while talking on camera and to make eye contact with the camera and the other people with whom they are talking on camera.

## Talent Checklist

_____ 1. On location, place the microphone in the camcorder microphone jack. Verify that microphone is in the ON position. Instruct the announcer not to tap on microphone.

_____ 2. In the TV studio, attach the microphone to the talents' shirts or blouses if using a lavaliere microphone. If using a handheld microphone, attach the microphone mike stand. Verify that the microphones are turned on. Verify that sound levels for talents' voices are acceptable.

_____ 3. Create cue cards. We use 8 1/2" x 11" sheets of paper with text in 48-point font size. Verify that cue cards are correct. Verify that the talent can read and understand the cue cards. Hold cue cards directly in back of the camera above the lens. Never have cue cards on both sides of a page.

_____ 4. Instruct the camera operator to cue the talent 10 seconds after recording begins.

_____ 5. Verify that the talent assumes the attitude required for the situation, speaks up sufficiently, and maintains eye contact with the camera.

_____ 6. For an on-location interview, be sure the interviewer stands at a right angle to the interviewee. Be sure the interviewer always holds microphone 6" and at a 45° angle from the mouth of the person speaking and moves the microphone near the interviewee's mouth as needed.

_____ 7. For an on-location interview, be sure the camera person begins the shot as a medium shot of the interviewer and interviewee, zooms in to close-up of interviewee during the interview, and gets both eyes of interviewee in the shot.

_____ 8. If an on-location interview is done outside, be sure the microphone has a foam covering to act as a windscreen.

_____ 9. Verify that the talent is wearing appropriate clothing—no checks or plaids and no blue clothes when using a blue screen chroma key effect.

_____ 10. In a dramatic production, create a "broom microphone." Attach a microphone to the end of a broom with masking tape. Verify that the "broom microphone" isn't seen on camera and that the talent speaks louder when using it.

_____ 11. Instruct the talent to never turn their backs to the camera.

_____ 12. Instruct the talent to never chew gum during a video shoot.

## Interviewing Techniques Checklist

_____ 1. Find out the full name of the person you will interview.

_____ 2. Find out some information about your guest before the interview.

_____ 3. Write down some interview questions based on what you know about your guest. Use questions that begin with "why, what, when, or how." Avoid questions that can be answered with a simple "yes or no."

_____ 4. Memorize your introduction and the questions you will ask or make cue cards.

_____ 5. Select an interview location with good lighting and an interesting background.

_____ 6. Rehearse the interview ahead of time by yourself.

_____ 7. Before the interview, discuss the questions and interview location with your guest.

_____ 8. Take gum or candy out of your mouth. Relax and make your guest feel comfortable.

_____ 9. Position your guest six to ten feet in front of the camera.

_____ 10. Position yourself at a 90° angle from your guest.

_____ 11. Don't move your feet. Turn your neck to look at the camera.

_____ 12. Always hold the microphone.

_____ 13. Hold the microphone 6" below your mouth at a 45° angle when you talk. When your guest talks, hold the microphone the same way in front of your guest's mouth.

_____ 14. When you talk, speak up and enunciate clearly. Be sure you are using proper English.

_____ 15. When you introduce the person you are interviewing, look at the camera.

_____ 16. Look at the guest when you ask a question.

_____ 17. Listen carefully to what the guest says. You may want to change your next question based on what your guest says.

# Organizing the School TV News Show

Let's assume that your school has a TV studio and a cable system. It's time to find some student video producers and have them create an exciting news show for the student body.

## Find an Audience

Getting your video production students excited about producing the show is the first step of making the school TV news show a reality. When a real audience exists for the show, it changes the dynamics of student video production. When the students design, produce, and present video for a real audience, they become highly motivated to work hard producing the school TV news show.

Without an audience, the attitude and motivation of your students are quite different. In some video production programs, the emphasis is on the academic study of the medium of television. In vocational video production programs, the emphasis is producing videos for clients. These types of video production programs require a full-time teacher.

You've laid the groundwork and done the organizing. Now you're ready to produce a show. You have some decisions to make about the type of show you want.

## Taped, Live, or a Combination of Both

One option in producing the show is to edit each show the day before it is shown. This enables the producers to edit out mistakes. Editing is a time-consuming process, but a good editor can learn to edit quickly and effectively. At one high school, the library staff person in charge of the show reports that the show is finished by 3:30 PM each day, ready to air the next morning.

Another option is to have a live show with edited feature segments on videotape each day. This approach results in more mistakes. A live mistake cannot be edited out. You, the show's sponsor, are more vulnerable in a live show. The audience will become familiar with your mistakes. One advantage of the live show is that it can be more up to date. Last minute news can easily be incorporated into the show. An exciting sports event from the evening before can be discussed in the show using video highlights.

Another option is the totally live show with no videotaped highlights. Less will go wrong in a show like this. You do not have to worry about the videotape not being cued correctly or the difference in sound level between a live and a taped segment. Live, videotaped, or a combination of the two, you must pick the type of show with which you feel most comfortable.

## Daily, Weekly, or Monthly

Another question to consider is whether the show is to be daily, weekly, or monthly. Without the pressure of producing a show each day, you can focus more on in-depth features and your expectations for quality of production can be higher. You may want to start with a monthly show before you do a daily show. The daily show requires a TV in every classroom. If you do a monthly show, you can move TVs around, combine classes in larger viewing areas, or present your show many times during the day so all the students can see it. When you're presenting the show more than once, you'll most likely want to always videotape the show.

## Organize a Video Production Club to Produce Your Show

You, the school librarian, already have a job. It's a mistake for you to get bogged down in teaching a class every day. Your focus ought to be on producing a product, the news show for the school, not teaching a class. At many elementary, middle, and high schools today, library media specialists are producing school TV news shows with the help of students organized as either a video production club or as a regular classroom activity. We visited a primary school where third graders produce a wonderful daily news show. You can do it too!

Have meetings with the video production club once a week after school or during lunch. The other option is to work with a class for a period of time. In one school, the librarian selects a different class to produce the news show every six weeks. Whichever option you choose, tell your students they are being prepared to produce a school TV news show. Concentrate on training the students in video production. Start with the "Camcorder Checklist" in Chapter 4 and the "Basic Scriptwriting Checklist" and the "Advanced Scriptwriting Checklist" in Chapter 2. Select other checklists in the book that fit your program. Then get your students involved in producing video productions that can be used later in your news show.

Another good project is to create a computer animation introduction for your show. You might want to have your school seal, symbol, or mascot in your animation. One good software program for computer animation when animating a symbol for use on your news show is *Ray Dream 3D M/W*. It will work with Macintosh or Windows computers.

The type of student who is going to join your club to produce the school news show is a highly motivated individual. You can easily find 10 or 15 such students in your school, and they will do the bulk of the work producing the show.

## Find Another Teacher to Teach a Video Production Class

The type of students who take a video production class may be just as motivated. It would not be a good idea for you to teach a video production class every day. With all your other library media center duties, you may not have time. Recruit another teacher to do the teaching. If you're in a high school, a journalism, speech, drama, or technology teacher may be interested. It would probably end up being one of the five classes per day that such a teacher is expected to teach.

## Work with Different Classes and Teachers to Produce the Show

In an elementary school you may want to work with one class for a month or a grading period. That class could incorporate video production in all phases of their curriculum. For science, students could produce a daily segment for the news show on the weather. For English, students could produce an interview with the author of a book the students had just read. Have a student reporter interview a student playing the role of the author, Mark Twain. In math the students could work on a fraction problem showing what fraction of a student's allowance could be spent on milkshakes at McDonald's after school. For social studies, have the students survey the school regarding what candidate is most popular for U.S. President or other public office. Interviews and survey results can be presented on the news show. Train each student in the class to write a script, be an announcer, handle cue cards, and operate the camcorder, the VCR and the computer. Be sure you rotate jobs so each student learns each phase of video production.

## Schedule the News Show into the School Day

Arrange with the principal to schedule one class period 5-10 minutes longer than the others for the next school year. This will be the class period when the school TV news show can be shown during the last 10 minutes of the class. Teachers hate to lose teaching time for any reason. Adding 10 minutes for the news show to the daily school schedule ensures that this will not happen. Teachers are an important part of the viewing audience. You don't want to alienate them.

# Simple TV Studio Jobs

If you have a simple TV studio, you need one **camera operator**. You also need a **tech director** who gives hand signals for the start of the show and also coordinates use of videotaped segments with live action. You'll need one microphone that will be shared between two **anchor people**. Since you only have one camera, you will need only one **cue card operator.** (See Figure 15.1) Also, remember one of your most important tasks is selecting students for the news show's anchor positions.

---

**Simple News Show Jobs List**

Anchor Person: _____

Anchor Person: _____

Cue Card Operator: _____

Tech Director: _____

Camera Operator: _____

---

*Figure 15.1 Simple News Show Jobs List*

# Complex TV Studio Jobs

More student jobs are needed for the news show in a complex TV studio. The **producer** oversees all aspects of the daily news show and checks to be sure all the equipment is working and turned on. The producer makes sure that each person is present and ready to perform their duties. If the announcer or a camera operator fails to show up for a show, the producer needs to quickly find someone else to do that job.

The **tech director** runs the a/v digital mixer or camera switcher, communicates with the camera operators from the control room over the head set system or with hand signals, coordinates live and videotaped segments of the show and records the entire program each day.

The **audio director** ensures that all microphones are set to the right level and ensures that CDs and tapes are played at the right time. The audio director is always watching the VU meter on the audio mixer and the recorder VCR and adjusting the dials on the audio mixer and CD/cassette player. It's the audio director's job to be sure that the audio going out to the TV receivers throughout the school on the cable system is loud enough and even. If the VU meter is bouncing between +4 and +10 decibels consistently throughout the show, the audio should be even and easily heard on classroom TVs. It's the audio director's responsibility to ensure that the videotaped segments are as loud as the live segments. Before and after the daily news show, the audio director unplugs the audio cable hooking up to the cable system so that the audience does not get to hear what the news team members say before and after the show.

The **camera operator** makes sure that the camera is always in focus, sets up the necessary close-up, medium, and long shots for the news show, and follows the camera directions of the tech director. Often, a new show will have two or three camera operators, each operating a camera. If one of the cameras is a visual presenter, that camera operator ensures that the appropriate graphics are zoomed in and focused when needed. Before the show begins, each camera operator shooting the talent zooms in for an extreme close-up of the talent. Then the camera operator sets the manual focus with the camera's focus ring. The camera operator then zooms out and sets up a medium close-up shot of the talent following the rule of thirds. In this way, when the show begins the talent will be in focus and there will be no distracting camera movements.

The **cue card operator** manipulates the cue cards, which are taped together in the correct sequence on a large tin can. The tin can is placed next to the camera. The cue card operator rotates the tin can so the talent can see and read the right cue card at the right time.

The **anchorperson** is the on-camera talent who delivers the news live to the student body during the news show. A strong voice, enthusiasm, and a pleasant and engaging demeanor are the traits of a capable anchorperson. The anchor has to be quick thinking since mistakes can't be edited out of a live TV show.

The **lighting director** turns on and adjusts the TV lights before each show. It is the lighting director's job to ensure that each talent is well lit. Because the skin shade of each talent may be different, this is a challenging job. A good understanding of bounce, key, fill, and back lighting is required for this job.

The **floor director** checks with the talent to be sure their microphones are turned on and checks the cue card scrolls to be sure they are accurate. The floor director also checks with the talent to be sure they can pronounce all words on the cue card scroll. The floor director helps the tech director and producer communicate to talent, camera operators, the lighting director, and cue card operators and makes sure that only the necessary video producers are in the studio when the show is being produced. Extra people in the studio may cause distracting noise.

**Videotape feature producers** are vital for the creation of an interesting TV news show. A typical news show is part live and part on videotape. The videotaped segments feature producers or announcers who are often not the regular anchors. Some announcers do better when they can produce their segment on videotape. They have more time to practice and can tape their segment over again if they make mistakes. Videotape feature producers create segments of the show that could not be aired live. Usually the videotape feature producer writes the script, does the announcing, and gets another student to do the camera work. For example, a videotape feature producer can oversee the shooting and editing of a contest, interview, or sports event held after school. He or she would probably do the editing.

**Videotape camera operators** work with video feature producers to shoot and possibly edit videotaped segments for use on the news show.

You'll need to develop your own system to organize your students as they produce the news show. (See Figure 15.2)

---

### TV News Show Job Description Sheet

Locations-control room and TV studio floor, known as "floor"

Talent/cue card operator_____
Talent/cue card operator_____
Talent/cue card operator_____
Talent/cue card operator_____
Talent/cue card operator_____
Talent/cue card operator_____
Talent/cue card operator_____
Talent/cue card operator_____

There are 8 slots in all. Both jobs take place on "floor." 3 students serve as talent each day. 3 students serve as cue card holders each day. All talent alternates as a cue card holder some days and "on camera" talent other days.

Camera operator/lighting operator_____
Camera operator/lighting operator_____
Camera operator/lighting operator_____
Camera operator/lighting operator_____
Camera operator/lighting operator_____
Camera operator/lighting operator_____

---

*Figure 15.2 TV News Show Job Description Sheet*

There are 6 slots in all. Both jobs take place on "floor." 3 students serve as camera operators each day. They run either a camcorder (camera 1 or 2) or the display camera (camera 3). Each camera operator works as camera operator one day and lighting operator the next day.

Scriptwriter/floor director_____
Scriptwriter/floor director_____

There are 2 slots in all, both located on "floor." The scriptwriter writes the script for the show in consultation with the library media specialist. Then the scriptwriter prints out copies on the computer for the production crew. The floor director handles last minute changes in the show such as special bulletins or last minute emergencies. The floor director checks off each news announcement on the script as it is announced to verify that all announcements get made. The students doing these two jobs switch jobs each day.

Tech director/VCR operator_____
Tech director/VCR operator_____

There are 2 slots in all, both located in control room. The tech director runs the digital video mixer (video switcher) and gives instructions to camera operators, audio operator, VCR operator, computer operator and floor manager. He or she communicates to camera operators using the mike/headsets system. The VCR operator checks that all videotapes to be used on the show are cued. He/she plays tapes at the tech director's signal and records the entire show. The students doing these two jobs switch jobs each day.

microphone operator/audio operator_____
microphone operator/audio operator_____

There are 2 slots in all. The microphone operator works on the "floor" and audio operator works in control room. The microphone director verifies that all microphones in use are functioning. Part of this job is to see that microphones are turned off before the show begins and turned on when needed. The audio operator verifies that all microphones and other audio inputs are at the right sound levels. The audio operator makes sure all music is cued and follows tech director's signal for music. The students doing these two jobs switch jobs each day.

Computer operator/computer print out person_____
Computer operator/computer print out person_____

There are 2 slots. The computer operator works in the control room and the computer print out person works mainly on the "floor." The computer operator makes sure that all *PowerPoint* presentations to be used for the show are available on the hard drive of the computer and brings up the appropriate *PowerPoint* presentation at the tech director's signal. The computer print out operator makes a print out of the "vocabulary word of the day" feature and goes over it with the talent doing "vocabulary word of the day" to be sure the talent can pronounce the word and knows its meaning. The students doing these two jobs switch jobs each day.

*Figure 15.2 TV News Show Job Description Sheet continued*

# Create a Spreadsheet for Job Assignments

Create a weekly spreadsheet with a schedule of job assignments. Distribute this to all the students each week. (See Figure 15.3)

The students need to know they are expected to do certain jobs on certain days. Require all students attend meetings once a week. Assign jobs like anchorperson, tech director, and camera operator to the students who actually show up for the weekly meeting. At the weekly meeting, train students on the different phases of video production.

## Sample Job Assignment Spreadsheet

| *JOBS | Thurs., 12-16 odd | Fri., 12-17 even | Mon., 12-20 odd | Tue., 12-21 even | Wed., 12-22 odd |
|---|---|---|---|---|---|
| TALENT 1 | SANDY | AZMEE | AMETHYST | KYM | CHRIS |
| TALENT 2 | AMETHYST | CHARLENE | CHRIS | KRISTY | APRIL |
| TALENT 3 | EDWARD | DANIEL | MIGUEL | AZMEE | CHARLENE |
| CUE CARDS 1 | MIGUEL | TYPHANIE | TYPHANIE | MIGUEL | TYFFANIE |
| CUE CARDS 2 | SHADARA | MIKE | JEFF | JEFF | MIGUEL |
| CUE CARDS 3 | DANIEL | CHARLENE | SHADARA | CHRIS | DAVID |
| P. A. | TYPHANIE | CJ | CJ | TYPHANIE | BREE |
| COMPUTER | TONY/NGHIA | TONY/NGHIA | TONY/NGHIA | TONY/NGHIA | TONY/NGHIA |
| CAMERA 1 | JOANNA | JOANNA | JOANNA | JOANNA | JOANNA |
| CAMERA 2 | MIKE | SHADARA | DAVID | SHADARA | MIKE |
| CAMERA 3 | BREE | JACKIE | BREE | JACKIE | BREE |
| SOUND | TRAVIS | TRAVIS | TRAVIS | TRAVIS | TRAVIS |
| LIGHTS | JUAN | JUAN | JUAN | JUAN | JUAN |
| PRODUCER | SENDY | SENDY | SENDY | SENDY | SENDY |
| TECH DIRECTOR | JOHN | BRANDON | JOHN | BRANDON | JOHN |
| FLOOR DIRECTOR | CHRIS | DANIEL | CHRIS | DANIEL | CHRIS |
| ASS'T TECH DIRECTOR | TOM | TOM | TOM | TOM | TOM |
| ASS'T FLOOR DIRECTOR | REBECCA | REBECCA | REBECCA | REBECCA | REBECCA |

\* ALL JOBS ARE SUBJECT TO CHANGE

*Figure 15.3 Sample Job Assignment Spreadsheet*

## Prepare for No Shows

For sure, you will address the issue of student dependability. Sometimes, the anchorperson will not show up when needed for a show. Perhaps the student was sick or had a test and could not be released early for the show. It's a good idea to encourage all your students to show up to produce the news show every day. That way, you'll have someone if you need a last minute replacement.

## Help Teachers Hook Up to Your Show

It's not guaranteed that all the teachers will figure out how to receive your school TV news show on the TV receivers in their classrooms. First, send out a checklist for teachers on how to access your show, such as the one in Figure 15.4, "How to Get Mt. Vernon Morning News on Channel 6." Then, on your in-school cable TV system transmit a TV graphic for your news show and some theme music from a CD for sound. Tell the teachers to practice picking up the signal you are transmitting on a specific channel via the in-school cable TV system. Be sure your teachers are receiving both sound and picture. Send out a survey to find out which teachers are having a hard time picking up your TV signal. You'll probably have to visit some classrooms to train teachers how to pick up your show.

---

**How to Get "Mt. Vernon Morning News" on Channel 6. This show airs beginning Mon. May 3 and replaces the morning announcements.**

1. Turn on your TV using your gray JVC remote unit. Press the "POWER" button on the upper left of the remote unit.

2. If the TV won't turn on, replace the batteries in the remote unit. You probably need two AAA batteries.

3. Once your TV is on, turn off your VCR.

4. Press the up or down arrow at the lower front section of the remote unit until the arrow on the TV screen is next to "Channel Summary." (If your screen comes up in Spanish, move the screen arrow to "Lista de Canales.")

5. Press the right arrow at the lower front section of the remote unit. You will see the channel numbers. You want channels 2-8 to have a check next to them under "MEM" on the screen. Move the up or down arrow on the remote unit so that the blue rectangle on the screen is next to the channel on the screen you want checked. Press the right arrow on the remote unit to get the channel checked.

6. When channels 2-8 are checked, press the "EXIT" button on the lower front section of the remote unit.

7. Press the channel up down button on the remote unit. You should see programs on channels 2-8. Channel 6 should display the "Mt. Vernon Morning News" logo.

8. If you don't see the "Mt. Vernon Morning News" logo on channel 6, check your TV cables. Be sure the cable is connected from the wall at the "TV" jack to the back of the VCR at the "ANT IN" jack. Be sure another cable goes from the "RF OUT" jack to the "75 VHF/UHF" jack on the TV.

9. For each cable connection be sure the wire in the middle of the cable fits into the hole in the middle of the jack.

10. If you still don't see the "Mt. Vernon Morning News" logo, contact the Media Center. There may be a problem with the cable system leading into your classroom.

---

*Figure 15.4 How To Get Mt. Vernon Morning News Show on Channel 6*

## Have a Camcorder Lending Policy for Students

You may want your show to have highlights of things happening in the local community. For a high school that could be a sporting event. For elementary school it could be a parade held on Saturday. The students are going to need a camcorder to tape these events. You'll need to set a camcorder lending policy. You may want to demand that the student return the camcorder before class starts the next morning. You may want to have a parent notification and responsibility slip. The parent signs the slip acknowledging that their child will take responsibility for the camcorder and return it in a timely fashion. Students need to be carefully coached when given a camcorder to take home. They need to understand that they have to monitor the camcorder at all times. Would you lend out a camcorder overnight to a first grader? Would you lend out a camcorder overnight to a sixth grader? How many camcorders do you have? Do you have good repair service? Do you have a budget to replace equipment? This is a tough decision that only you can make? If you're willing to lend out a camcorder, lend it only to the students in your video production club or the class you are currently training. If the student breaks a camcorder due to negligence, what will you do? Your policy for that should be in place before camcorders are loaned to students for overnight use. The students who are borrowing your camcorder and their parents need to know what your policy is about camcorder negligence.

## Sample Policy for Checking out Camcorders to Students

1. The student borrowing the camcorder and his or her parent sign the following note: "I am borrowing a camcorder from the school library for a school project. I will pick up the camcorder on the following date _____. I am aware that only (student's name) _____ and no one else is authorized to operate this camcorder. I will treat the camcorder with great care, lock it up in a secure area when not using it, and return it on the following date _____ to the school library by 7:20 AM.

   Parent's signature_____

   Student's signature_____

2. All students borrowing a camcorder for use outside school must take a half-hour course in camcorder operation taught by school library staff.

# Sample Camcorder Check-Out Sheet

**Camcorder # 6 Check Out**

Name of student: _____

   Student's phone number and address: _____

   Supervising teacher: _____

   Accessories borrowed (battery, microphone, videotape): _____

   _____

   Date borrowed: _____

   Date due: _____

# Organizing the School TV News Show Checklist

_____ 1. Inventory the TV equipment you have. Determine if you have enough for a simple or complex TV studio.

_____ 2. Get the agreement from your school administration to replace the daily morning announcements with a school TV news show.

_____ 3. Decide on a start date for the show.

_____ 4. Organize a student TV production club in your school or make arrangements to work with a specific class.

_____ 5. Plan features for your news show before you begin.

_____ 6. Arrange with your school administration to give your students a letter award or other recognition for participation in your school TV news show.

_____ 7. Contact a professional video production person to mentor your students.

_____ 8. Set a target date for your first show. Prepare your first show based on what equipment you currently have.

_____ 9. Decide what production jobs your students will do during each show.

_____ 10. Conduct tryouts for each job.

_____ 11. Make job assignments for each student involved.

_____ 12. Begin rehearsing your first school TV news show. Allow five rehearsals before attempting your first live show.

_____ 13. Give each student a production assignment for the show.

_____ 14. Provide teachers with a checklist on how to operate their TV to receive the news show on the classroom TV.

_____ 15. Send out a sample signal of sound and picture from your studio to all the classrooms, allowing your teachers to practice accessing your show.

_____ 16. Post pictures along with names and job titles of the members of your school's TV news team on a bulletin board somewhere in the library media center.

_____ 17. After the show has been produced for six months, survey the students and staff on how they like it.

_____ 18. Review survey results with your students and make appropriate changes.

## Daily Production Checklist

_____ 1. Are the "30 seconds to show," "20 seconds to show," and "10 seconds to show" signs in place on camera 3?

_____ 2. Are all announcements taped to the cue-card scrolling device? Are announcements referring to taped segments of the show attached to cue-card scrolling device?

_____ 3. Can the talent correctly pronounce the "Word of the Day?"

_____ 4. Does the talent know how to pronounce every word on their cue cards?

_____ 5. Are all videotapes cued?

_____ 6. Are all TV production jobs on today's "Jobs List" filled?

_____ 7. Has the audio director done a sound check on each talent?

_____ 8. Is sound getting from the audio mixer to the recorder VCR?

_____ 9. Has the tech director been told when to play taped segments?

_____ 10. Does each talent look well lit?

_____ 11. Is the assistant producer writing up a list of all announcements and checking them off as they are made?

_____ 12. Is the intro music cued in the CD player? Is the audio-taped intro cassette cued in the cassette player?

_____13. Is the red RCA (phono) cable in the video jack of the cable systems so the school can see the show?

_____14. Did the audio director insert the white RCA (phono) audio cable in the audio jack of the cable system right before the show begins, so the school can hear the show?

_____15. Is the microphone available at the tech director's chair, so the tech director can say, "Stand for the pledge!"

_____16. Did the tech director remember to take his microphone out of the microphone jack after saying "Stand for the pledge?"

_____17. Is the show being videotaped, so it can be shown again later in the day?

_____18. Is the tech director playing a taped segment made with a high-impedance microphone? If so, did tech director increase volume on "Hi-Fi Rec. Level" on the recorder VCR from 5 to 10?

_____19. Is the production crew being quiet once the show is running?

_____20. Is sound level coming through the VU meter on the recorder VCR between +4 and +10 decibels?

_____21. Are camera operators listening to the tech director and following directions with their head sets on?

_____22. When the show is over, is the white audio cable pulled out of the cable system audio jack, so the producer can talk to the crew without the entire school hearing it?

_____23. Has the videotape of the day's show been labeled with the correct date?

# The Instructional Value of the School TV News Show

CHAPTER 16

You've laid the groundwork and done the organizing, and now your news show is up and running. What's the instructional value of a school TV news show?

## The News Show Should Promote the School Library

Whether you work with a class or a club, you'll find the students to run your news show. You are building the most powerful tool imaginable for a school librarian. With your daily news show, you obtain the right to influence the students, faculty, and staff.

You can promote books in the TV news show. In your news show you may want to have some kind of book talk or book promotion every week. To promote your summer reading contest, you could impersonate celebrities. Some of the students could put on black suits, black hats, sunglasses and be the "The Books Brothers." If you do that on your school news show, every student at your school will know about your reading contest.

Promoting reading is the first priority for the school librarian. Pam Spencer, a prominent writer in the field of school libraries, feels that reading promotion has been put on the "back burner" in the '90s and replaced with the emphasis on technology. Why not use technology, especially video production technology in your school TV news show, to put reading promotion on the "front burner"?

However, students don't do enough research either. The school TV news show can be used to promote student research. You could begin to do this by promoting career-related research. How about a "Career of the Week" feature? (See Figure 16.1.) Students can take current information on any career and use it in a 30-second *PowerPoint* presentation to be shown on the school TV news show.

Another possibility is an "Academics of the Week" feature where a student does research on an interesting phase of an academic class and presents his findings to the school in a 30-second *PowerPoint* feature on the show.

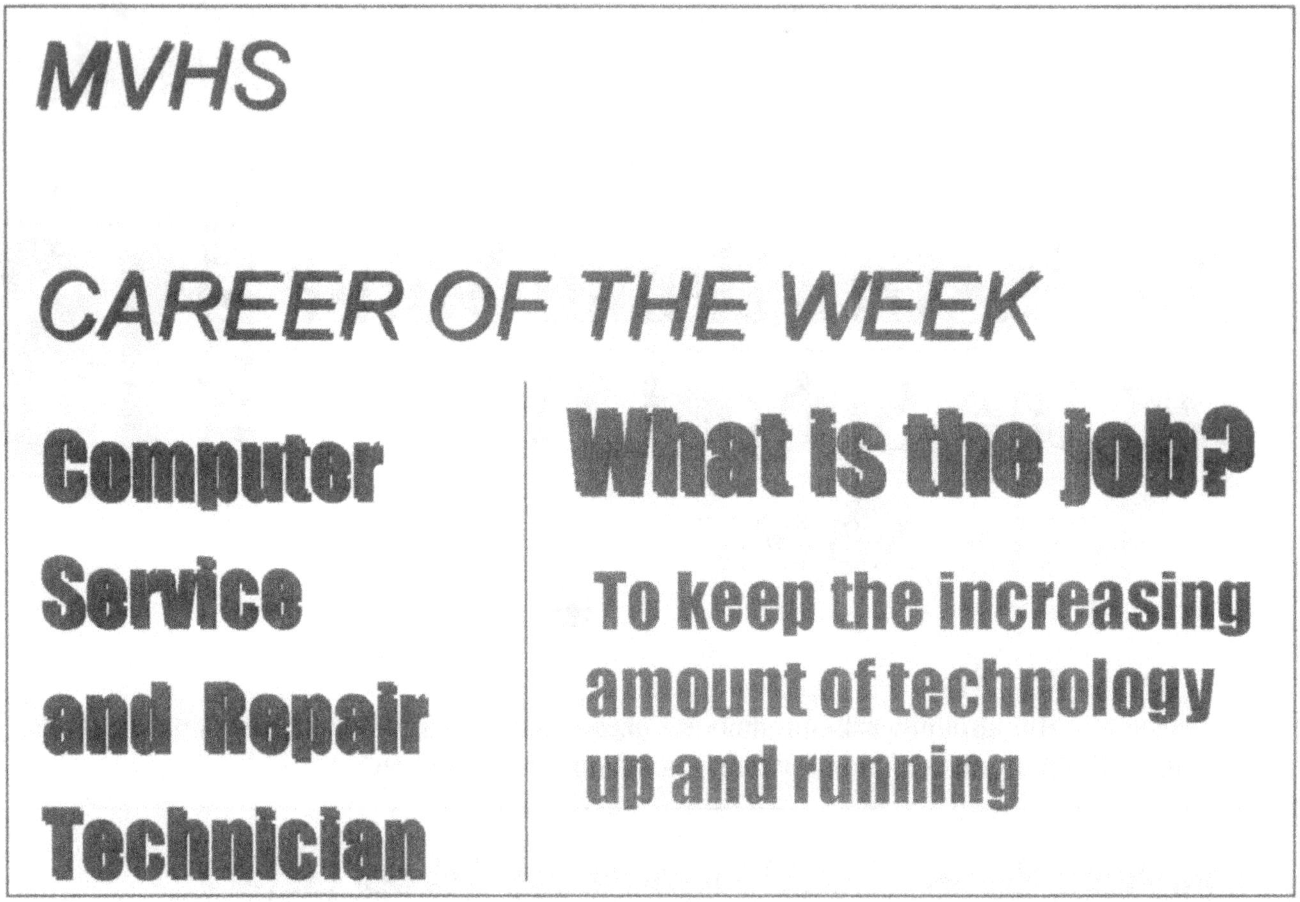

> # MVHS
>
> ## CAREER OF THE WEEK
>
> | **Computer Service and Repair Technician** | **What is the job?** To keep the increasing amount of technology up and running |

*Figure 16.1 The Career of the Week*

Another popular element of your TV news show could be the "word of the day." You could show the word, its definition, and a sentence using that word. Again this is easily done on *PowerPoint*. While the *PowerPoint* slides are shown on the TV screen, the talent reads the slides aloud into the microphone. One good source for the "word of the day" is the "Princeton Review." They could provide excellent words that would help students preparing for the SAT test. To obtain the word list, call 1-800-REVIEW, or visit their Web site at <www.review.com>.

In one elementary school, the students come to school early every day for breakfast. While eating breakfast, the students write the copy for the news show. One student is the weatherman and gets the local newspaper and finds out the weather forecast for the day. Then the "weather" student writes a script for the day's weather and presents it during the news show. Another student does the same thing for sports. That student gets the sports page and finds out which local teams have won their games. Then, the sportscaster writes a script and presents the sports news. Other students have different responsibilities like presenting school activities and community news. The entire news team eats, reads, writes, rehearses, and presents the news show each day as school begins. At that elementary school the news show is an educational and tasty treat!

When you unleash the school news show, you are unleashing something powerful. Just remember, it's the students' show. You set the agenda collaboratively with the students, the teachers and the administrators. Don't forget that part of the agenda comes from you, the school librarian.

## Producing the Show Benefits Students

Whatever type of show you choose, the bottom line is that you give a student an assignment to create a feature for the news show. Whether you're working with a video production club or a class, you are out on a limb. The show airs tomorrow. Will the students come through? Will the students produce a show that they can be proud to call their own? Surprisingly, the answer will usually be "yes." Some of your students are going to just love to do video productions. With a little encouragement from you, many excellent student features will get produced. You're creating a multimedia/video design environment.

The research of Lui and Rutledge (Software and Information Association 70) shows that many students become very productive in that kind of environment. These students become motivated by the joy of producing a video, not by achieving a high grade in a class. These students become confident in their ability to create a presentation.

By producing a school TV news show for an audience, you are creating an environment that your students are going to find very rewarding. Students will gain a sense of self-confidence in their abilities in this environment that they may not gain elsewhere. For this reason alone, creating a TV studio for the school news show is a very worthwhile endeavor.

Students will begin to take ownership of the TV news show they are producing. As much as possible, allow this to happen. The "Daily Production Checklist," p. 146, may enable your student producer to run the show independently.

## Keep the News Show Brief

Video features for the school news show don't need to be more than a minute or two in length. School time is precious, and it's unlikely school administration would want your show going over 10 minutes each day. Examples of features for your show could be edited footage of a school sporting event, edited highlights of the school play or an unedited interview with the "student of the month." Ask teachers if they would like a school activity or class promoted on the school TV news show. Talk to the teachers who have your video production club members in their classes. You may be able to set up a situation where your video production club members get class credit for video productions they create for the school news show.

## Create Partnerships with Teachers

Think about the school TV news show as a means of creating partnerships with teachers. Class projects teachers assign their students can be shown on the school TV news show. One possible project is the career of the day. Students in a class can do research in the library media center on a specific career and create a short *PowerPoint* presentation about that career. That *PowerPoint* presentation can be shown on the TV news show using the computer to video technology described in Chapter 6.

## Introduce the Notion of Service

Introduce the notion of service to your student video producers. It's a service to the school to produce the TV news show on a daily, weekly, or monthly basis. Other service opportunities will present themselves. Encourage the students to get involved with them. For example, the school marching band may hold a special competition where school bands from across the state perform to a large audience. The students in your video production club can videotape this event as a service to the school band. A certain class or organization in your school may need a videotape about their group for publicity purposes. Assign one of your video production students to the teacher in charge of that class or group. Encourage the student to write for the publicity videotape. Then encourage the student to produce the video.

Introduce the notion of service to adults in your community with a TV production background. These people will be role models for your students. These people can show your students that video production can be a viable career. They may have a wealth of information on video production techniques.

## Strive for Excellence, but Expect Mistakes

Keep in mind that producing a TV news show, especially a live show, is a challenging task. The more complex your TV studio, the more things can and will go wrong. You will come to appreciate the local 6 o'clock evening news show in your town. You'll begin to notice every mistake the professionals make. Strive for excellence with your school TV news crew, but don't expect perfection right away. (See the "Commitment to Excellence Evaluation Checklist," p. 153, at the end of this chapter to evaluate each show.)

## Get Feedback

You need feedback from students, staff, and administrators to make the show better. What do students want on the show? A survey of the students and staff every few months can help you effectively plan the direction of your school TV news show. (See "Survey Question for Students and Staff Regarding the School TV News Show," p. 154.)

The student video producers need feedback too. Score each news show from one to 100. Tell the students their score every day immediately after the show. Identify to the students the areas of weakness and strength in the show each day. Watch the smiles on their faces when a show scores 100%.

# Commitment to Excellence Evaluation Checklist

Date of Show_____

_____ 1. 30 sec., 20 sec., 10 sec. to show signs displayed. (1-5)

_____ 2. Music was played for 30 seconds before show. (1-5)

_____ 3. Producer said, "Stand for the Pledge of Allegiance." (1-5)

_____ 4. Talent 1 said, "Hello." (1-5)

_____ 5. Talent 2 said, "Now, for more news." (1-5)

_____ 6. Word of day was done correctly by talent. (1-5)

_____ 7. Talent 3 said, "Good bye." (1-5)

_____ 8. Sound was even throughout show. (1-5)

_____ 9. Camera shots reflected good camera work. (1-5)

_____ 10. Computer segments came on at right time. (1-5)

_____ 11. Lighting for talent was appropriate. (1-5)

_____ 12. Talent had good eye contact and a friendly manner. (1-5)

_____ 13. Cue cards didn't block camera, were easily seen. (1-5)

_____ 14. Camera operators followed directions. (1-5)

_____ 15. Switching between cameras was effective. (1-5)

_____ 16. Production crew was quiet while show was on. (1-5)

_____ 17. Names were pronounced correctly by talent. (1-5)

_____ 18. Tapes were cued correctly. (1-5)

_____ 19. Show was completed before bell rang. (1-5)

_____ 20. Show taped for play back later. (1-5)

_____ Total score out of 100 possible points

# Survey Questions for Students and Staff Regarding School TV News Show

1. Rate the following questions below regarding the school TV news show:
   4 strongly agree, 3 agree, 2 disagree, 1 strongly disagree.

   _____ A. I can hear what people say on the show.
   _____ B. I can see the TV picture clearly.
   _____ C. Usually, the show is boring.
   _____ D. Usually, the show is interesting.
   _____ E. The show keeps me up to date on what is happening in school.
   _____ F. The show increases my enjoyment of school.
   _____ G. I sometimes learn something from the show.
   _____ H. I look forward to the show.

2. What part of school life would you like to see more features on?
   _____ A. sports
   _____ B. fashion
   _____ C. music
   _____ D. student opinions
   _____ E. other _____

3. What do you like best about the show?
   _____
   _____
   _____

4. What do you like the least about the show?
   _____
   _____
   _____

5. How do you think the show can be improved?
   _____
   _____
   _____

# The Library Media Center Orientation Video

This is one of the most important video projects for any library media center. With new technology coming into the school library every day, some teachers feel more and more intimidated to be in the library media center. Five years ago some of these teachers might have complained about the disappearance of the wooden card catalog drawers or the *Reader's Guide to Periodical Literature*. Today, some may not bring their classes to the library anymore. To counter this, a school librarian might set aside the first two weeks of the school year for orientation or plan library training for teachers after school. Some of the teachers are going to say, "I'd love to come but I don't have time." This can be translated as, "I can't figure out just what our school library does anymore."

The library media center orientation video can help solve this problem. Teachers want to come to the library on their timetable, not the school librarian's. They want to understand what's happening in the school library *before* they get there.

## What Do Teachers Want in the Library Orientation Video?

Get input from many teachers regarding what they want in the library orientation video. The teachers will be showing this videotape to their students in the classroom before they come to the library. Some ideas for things to include in the orientation video are: library rules, directions on use of the computer card catalog, and directions for accessing a database on the Internet. Use the macro lens of the camcorder to get close-up shots of where to click on the computer screen in order to show, step by step, how to access a database or find a book.

In *Instructional Media and Technologies for Learning*, Heinich, Molenda, Russell, and Smaldino emphasize the importance of feedback in the communication model. Feedback from staff is vital in the production of the library orientation video. When you start planning it, ask teachers who use the library what they'd like to see in the video. The more teacher input you receive, the better chance that the teachers will be able to use it effectively to teach their students how to use the library media center. If you create your orientation video on *PowerPoint* and then convert it to videotape, you can take advantage of still video shots, clip art, and text to deliver your message. You may want to use still shots instead of motion video to show how to operate the Internet or the computer card catalog, but videotaping a computer screen causes flicker problems. Still shots can eliminate that problem. The still shots can break down the steps of how to find a book in the computer card catalog and how to access information on the Electric Library database. (See Figure 17.1.)

*Figure 17.1 A* PowerPoint *Slide from a High School Library Orientation Video*

## Show the Orientation Video Before a Class Comes to the Library

The purpose of the orientation video isn't for one showing in September. Instead, make this video available for teachers to show their classes for review purposes right before the class comes to the library. You may want to design a different orientation video for students in kindergarten through third grade and another for fourth through sixth graders. On a secondary level, you could use one for science classes, one for English classes, and one for social studies classes. Remember that the editing of an orientation video about your library takes time. It also takes a lot of time to run through your library orientation for all the students in your school. The library orientation video may save you some time in the long run.

# Library Orientation Video Checklist

_____ 1. Meet with the teachers who use the library. Share with them your concerns and ideas about training students and teachers with an orientation video.

_____ 2. Make an outline. Some suggested topics are, (A) book checkout and fine policy, (B) using the computer card catalog to find a book, (C) finding a magazine using an online service such as EBSCO, Electric Library, or Bell and Howell Information and Learning (ProQuest), (D) finding information on a social studies topic using *S.I.R.S. Researcher* or *S.I.R.S. Government Reporter* on CD-ROM or online, (E) finding author information using the Gale *Contemporary Authors or Dictionary of Literary Biography* database on CD-ROM or online, (F) rules for printing off of the computer screen, (G) simple word processing and copy and paste skills, (H) photocopy machine rules and procedures, and (I) library passes and behavior requirements.

_____ 3. Write a script.

_____ 4. Produce the video using *PowerPoint* on a Windows or Macintosh computer. Create *PowerPoint* slides about each phase of your orientation.

_____ 5. Then go around the library and get shots that will add to your presentation using a camcorder or digital camera. Add these shots to your *PowerPoint* slides, and use many close-up shots that show the steps concerning how to get to a specific Internet location. Still shots work well for this purpose.

_____ 6. Once the *PowerPoint* presentation is complete, convert it to a videotape. Then on the videotape create an audio narration and/or musical background to accompany your *PowerPoint* slides. You could edit in a live action speech recorded on videotape. For example, you might want to use short speeches from students explaining how they successfully used the library media center to do a report. Keep your orientation video short and to the point, yet cover what you consider important.

_____ 7. Make the library orientation videotape available to all the teachers at your school. Have plenty of duplicate copies on hand.

_____ 8. Insist that all teachers review the orientation video with their classes before coming to the library media center for the first time or for review purposes.

# Student-Produced Video Book Talks

CHAPTER 18

What librarian doesn't want to get students reading more books? Traditionally, one way to do this has been book talks. Why not get students to produce their own book talks on videotape? Students can produce video book talks to make library books more visible to the students. This is the **Great Books** unit.

The video book talk unit may be especially important for high school library media specialists. Sadly, high school students are not reading as many books as they should. Pam Spencer writes in *What Do Young Adults Read Next? A Readers Guide to Fiction for Young Adults, Volume 2,* "The Hart survey found 86 percent of nine-year-olds read a book at least a few times a week while only 42 percent of 17-year-olds do" (xiii).

## Work with a Teacher to Identify Book Titles

Whether you are an elementary, middle, or secondary level school library, your job is to get students to read more. Develop a partnership with a teacher to encourage your students to read more library books on the subject of social studies. Work with this teacher to identify fiction and nonfiction book titles that fit the curriculum. If the subject is American history, identify 15-20 historical fiction and nonfiction book titles that relate to the American history teacher's program. Purchase five copies of each title from your library materials budget. Use book reviews in *The Book Report* and *School Library Journal*. Also Spencer's book, *What Do Young Adults Read Next? A Reader's Guide to Fiction for Young Adults: Volume 2*, is very helpful.

Here is a sample list of books to purchase for secondary students in American history: *Across Five Aprils* by Irene Hunt, *Amistad* by Alexs Pate, *Beyond the Burning Time* by Kathryn Lasky, *The Bomb* by Theodore Taylor, *Cesar Chavez, A Triumph of Spirit* by Richard G. Delcastillo and Richard A. Garcia, *Four Perfect Pebbles, A Holocaust Story* by Lila Perl and Marion B. Lazan, *Geronimo, His Own Story* edited by Frederick Turner, *Hard Drive* (Bill Gates) by James Wallace and Jim Erickson, *I Never Had It Made, The Autobiography of Jackie Robinson, In Country* by Bobbie Ann Mason, *Last Train North* by Clifton Taulbert, *Narrative of the Life of Frederick Douglass, an American Slave* by himself, *Red-Tail Angels: The Story of the Tuskeegee Airmen of World War II* by Patricia and Frederick McKissack, *The Road Home* by Ellen Emerson White, *Silver Rights* by Constance Curry, *Soldier Boy* by Brian Burks, *SOS Titanic* by Eve Bunting and *True North* by Kathryn Lasky.

These are books that students at many different reading levels enjoy and do not find too difficult. Make a list of your own to meet the reading level, subject area, and needs of your students. If you are making it a requirement that a student reads one of the books on your list, select titles carefully. Between your library staff, teachers you're working with, and volunteers, read all the books on your list. *Heart of a Woman* by Maya Angelou was taken off our list because certain scenes were too sexually explicit. *Cold Mountain* was deleted from our list mainly because the reading level was too high. *Amistad* by David Pecsi had too much strong language. Instead, *Amistad* by Alexs Pate was used because it is very readable for teens and doesn't have any strong language.

All the books weeded out of the **Great Books** unit are excellent books that are available in the school library for all students to read. But the **Great Books** unit is not about just making books available. Instead, the **Great Books** unit is about promoting certain books and demanding that each student involved reads at least one from the list. Don't have your students' enthusiasm for reading quelled by teacher or parent complaints about book content.

# Book Talk Statement

After all the books on the list have been read by either you, your staff, or the teacher involved, have everyone who read a book on the list write a book talk statement about the book. A book talk statement is a one- to two-minute statement written from the viewpoint of a character in the book. A student in your school's drama program can act out the book talk statement. In an elementary school, there would be no drama class so the acting would probably be done by students who had read the books. The purpose of the book talk statement is to get the students interested in a character in the book and what problem that character faces. Of course, the book talk statement would not reveal how the character resolves the problem. The students have to read the book to find that out.

### Make the Book Talk a Video Production

In a secondary school, a member of your video production club could videotape the drama student performing the book talk statement. In an elementary school, students in a certain class would be the actors and the video producers. When possible, the students performing the book talks should dress in costume. Use many close-up and medium shots. Use a broom microphone, described in Chapter 14. Frederick Douglass, Geronimo, or a Colonial farmer from the Massachusetts Colony would look funny holding a microphone.

### Edit the Book Talks

Once all the book talk statements have been performed and videotaped, they can be edited together. *PowerPoint* titles can be created on a computer that will introduce each book. If a scanner is available, you can scan in the book title into the *PowerPoint* slide. The *PowerPoint* presentation can be converted into videotape. Then the appropriate *PowerPoint* slides can be edited together with the video book talks.

Take the edited book talk videotape and the books to the classroom. This edited videotape is played back to the students right before they select the book they are to read in the **Great Books** unit. Have each student make a first, second, and third choice. The students are divided into groups of two to five students based on the book they have chosen. Attempt to give students their first choice. Bring the students to the library to check out their books. That's easier than asking the teacher to keep a record of the books each student has chosen. There will be fewer mix-ups if you hold the students responsible for the books they check out.

The students will spend some time in class reading the books. Then they will plan a presentation to the class about the book they read.(See Figure 18.1.)

Your **Great Books** unit can be used year after year. You may want to add or delete a few titles each year. Because the book talks introducing the unit are on videotape, the videotape can be used over and over to motivate students. (See Chapter 8, "Video Editing," p. 73, to add new video book talk statements or delete old ones.)

## Great Books Group Presentation Guide

Names of group members _____

Title of book _____

Number of pages_____ Author of book _____

Type of book   Circle one.     Fiction     Non-Fiction     Biography

Describe the setting of the book. _____

If fiction, describe the plot. _____

If non-fiction or biography, describe a problem people in the book faced and how they solved it _____

Tell something about the book you enjoyed. _____

What aides will you use in your presentation?   Circle one
Video Tape     *PowerPoint* Slide     Poster     Handouts     Guest Speaker
Music on CD or Cassette     Other (Describe.) _____

*Figure 18.1 Great Books Group Presentation Guide*

# Student-Produced Video Book Talks Checklist

_____ 1. Work with a teacher to select 15-20 book titles you will use in your **Great Books** unit. Order five copies of each book.

_____ 2. Begin reading the books. Ask everyone on your library staff and your teacher partner to read at least one book.

_____ 3. For each book, write a short one- to two-minute book talk statement written from the viewpoint of one of the characters in the book.

_____ 4. Collect all the book talk statements and give them to the drama teacher.

_____ 5. Have the drama teacher assign each student the job of acting out the book talk statement.

_____ 6. Get your video production club students to videotape each drama student making the book talk presentation.

_____ 7. Have one of your video production club students create a *PowerPoint* slide for each book.

_____ 8. Transfer the *PowerPoint* slides to videotape.

_____ 9. Have your video production club create an edited video that contains the *PowerPoint* slide and book talk for each book.

_____ 10. Play the book talk video to the class and let the students select the book he/she wants to read.

_____ 11. Check out all the books to the students.

_____ 12. Allow the students to read their books during part of each class period.

_____ 13. Have the students meet in groups based on the book they read to plan a presentation about their book.

_____ 14. Have the students create presentations to the class about their books.

_____ 15. Have each group make a presentation to the class about their book.

_____ 16. Evaluate the effectiveness of the project. (See the "Video Project Evaluation Form," p. 122)

# The Computer/Video Research Project

## CHAPTER 19

One of the library media specialist's main goals is to encourage more student library research. It's a challenge to encourage teachers to assign research projects. Another challenge is encouraging teachers to assign a bibliography. Often, teachers don't demand a bibliography with the papers they assign. When the students go to college or junior college, they'll need to know how to create a bibliography for their research paper.

## Teach Research Skills without Doing a Research Paper

The Computer/Video Research Project is a way to teach many of the skills required to do a research paper without having the students do one. This project requires note taking, outlining, scriptwriting, bibliography, cooperative learning, *PowerPoint* or HyperStudio, and video production skills. That's the technical "heart and soul" of this project. In the past we referred to this project as a "multimedia" project. Since it's a fusion of video and computer technologies, we presently refer to it here as the Computer/Video Research Project.

## Start a Partnership with a Teacher

Before the project begins, a partnership needs to be created between the library media specialist and the teacher. With the teacher decide what classroom topics would work well for student group presentations. Be sure each group picks a different topic that would be suitable for review for state standardized tests at the end of the school year.

## Student-Produced Videos Are Visible Outcomes of Teaching and Learning

A major role of the library media specialist is to work with teachers to enable students to create presentations on areas of the curriculum that students are required to learn. The library media specialist becomes a visible catalyst for the improvement of student learning. The video/computer presentations that the students create are visible outcomes of the teaching and learning process. These videotapes can be shown to other students, teachers, and parents. These videotapes help everyone understand just what the library media program can do.

*Information Power: Building Partnerships for Learning*, published by A.A.S.L. and A.E.C.T., emphasizes the importance of student produced learning products. "The student is able both to understand and enjoy creative works presented in all formats and to create products that capitalize on each format's particular strengths." (26). Video production is definitely one of those formats. Projects that get students to research, write, and then create video/computer presentations are sanctioned by the groups that speak for the professional school librarian. These activities are vital for school library media specialists who want to offer a complete library media program to their students and teachers.

The Computer/Video Research Project is described here as a *PowerPoint* project. The computer side of the project could be done just as easily with HyperStudio. *PowerPoint* is recommended for two reasons. First, *PowerPoint* is used widely in the business world. Second, *PowerPoint* is available in both Windows or Macintosh computer format. Thus, *PowerPoint* presentations can be produced on computers in most school libraries today.

## Provide Structure for Groups

There is a lot of structure in the group work students do for this project. In each group, students receive a handout describing their duties in detail. (See Figures 19.1-19.6, pp. 166-171.) Don't try the Computer/Video Research Project without these handouts. Elementary, middle, and secondary students require a great deal of structure when doing a collaborative computer/video presentation project. The handouts give the students a sense of purpose. The students know what is expected of them and for what they are accountable. Your students will know what the final product will resemble if you create a sample computer/video presentation for them to see on Day One. Deadlines for each step of the process also need to be established and enforced.

This need for structure in cooperative learning with computers is backed up by educational research. In 1993, Judi Repman completed a study on the importance of providing structure for 7th grade social studies student groups doing computer-related tasks. She found that student groups that received structured guidance while doing computer-related group work achieved at a significantly higher level than student groups that received no such guidance.

**Graph Maker**

The Graph Maker job description sheet (Figure 19.3, "Graph Maker," p. 168) is different from the other job description sheets. The other sheets are generic. You could use them with many different topics. The Graph Maker sheet has to be specific to the subject on which students are working. We've found that you can't tell a high school student, "Go find some facts on your subject and make a *PowerPoint* graph." As Repman points out, initially students need structured guidance to complete computer-related projects. The Graph Maker handout forces the student to look up specific factual information in specific sources. Once the student has some relevant statistical information, the student can then select the data to use in a *PowerPoint* graph. Of course, each time a new subject is selected for a Computer/ Video Research Project, the questions on the Graph Maker job assignment need to be changed. Is the Graph Maker job really that important? Knowing how to present statistical information is vital in the business world today.

## Creating the Final Presentation

To create the final presentation, it only takes two students, the "Tech Director" and the "So What?" Statement/Announcer." The other students in each group don't need to be involved during this day of work.

The "So What?" Statement/Announcer" reads the script into the microphone for the entire presentation. At the end of the presentation, the conclusion, the "So What? Statement" is read into the microphone. While this statement (approximately 30 seconds in length) is read, it's effective to have a picture of the student who is reading it on screen along with a caption that says "Conclusion" or "So What?" To do this you need to know how to take an image from the camcorder and add it to the *PowerPoint* or HyperStudio presentation.

We did this unit producing two computer/video productions at a time using two VCRs and two computers. This configuration may not be convenient for you. One group at a time may be easier on your nerves. Only you know how much time and energy you have to give to this activity. We tried three and four groups creating projects at one time. It was a disaster. Too much was going on at one time. It was very confusing.

# Multimedia Job Assignments

Name_____Script Writer: Your job is to write a script. Write it out by hand first using the "Simple Script Sheet." Then type it on the computer using the "Simple Script Sheet" template. Save it to your disk on the "A:" drive. Save it to the "C:" drive. Print out a copy to be kept in the folder.

Name_____Graph Maker: Your job is to create a graph on *PowerPoint* using some statistics you found. Save it to your disk on the "A:" drive. Save it to the "C:" drive. Print out a copy to be kept in the folder.

Name_____Bibliography Maker: Your job is to create a bibliography on *PowerPoint*. Write it out by hand first. Follow the sample bibliography format in the book, Write Inc. Be sure you put the bibliographic entries in alphabetical order. Type it up using a large size font on *PowerPoint* and save it to your disk on the "A:" drive. Then save it to the "C:" drive. Print out a copy to be kept in the folder.

Name_____So What? Statement Writer/Announcer: Your job is to write a statement in 3 or 4 sentences about why your topic is important. Write it out by hand. Then type it on a computer using a large font. Save it to your disc on the "A:" drive and to the "C:" drive. Print out a copy to be kept in the folder. Practice reading the audio sections of the script in the folder. You will be the narrator of the multimedia presentation. At the end of the multimedia presentation you will present your So What? Statement on camera. You will use your typed So What? Statement as a cue card.

Name_____Tech Director: Your job is to create *PowerPoint* and Gallery2 clip art title graphics. Save your title graphics to your disk on the "A:" drive and to the "C:" drive. Print out a copy for the folder. Your other job is to learn how to record the sound and picture of your multimedia presentation on to the editor VCR. You and the So What? Statement Writer/Announcer will work together to record your multimedia presentation on videotape.

*Figure 19.1 Multimedia Job Assignments*

# Script Writer

Your job is to find four visuals you will include in your script. One could come from a CD-ROM like <u>National Geographic</u>. One could come from the <u>American History</u>, <u>World History</u> or <u>Western Civilization</u> video disk. One could come from a book. After you fill out 1-4, start writing your script using the "Simple Script Sheets." Then type your script on computer using the "Simple Script Sheet" template. Save the script to the "A:" drive and "C:" drive. Put the script and the disk in the folder.

1. Describe visual_____author_____. title of article_____

    title (book, CD-ROM, video disc, circle one) _____.

    date of article_____. city_____: publisher_____, date_____.

    page (book)_____ code # (video disc)_____

2. Describe visual_____author_____. title of article_____.

    title (book, CD-ROM, video disc, circle one) _____.

    date of article_____. city_____: publisher_____, date_____.

    page (book)_____ code # (video disc)_____

3. Describe visual_____author_____. title of article_____.

    title (book, CD-ROM, video disc, circle one) _____.

    date of article_____. city_____: publisher_____, date_____.

    page (book)_____ code # (video disc)_____

4. Describe visual_____author_____. title of article_____.

    title (book, CD-ROM, video disc, circle one) _____.

    date of article_____. city_____: publisher_____, date_____.

    page (book)_____ code # (video disc)_____

*Figure 19.2 Script Writer*

# Graph Maker

Your job is to find statistics about your subject. You will present these statistics in a *Powerpoint* bar graph. Use <u>The World Almanac and Book of Facts</u> or other reference book as your source.

1. Look up "World War I" in the index and find the number of black troops who served in World War I_____, World War II_____ and the Vietnam War_____.

2. How many battle deaths did American troops suffer in World War I? _____

3. How many battle deaths did American troops suffer in World War II?_____

4. How many battle deaths did American troops suffer in Korea?_____

5. How many battle deaths did American troops suffer in Vietnam?_____

6. How many battle deaths did American troops suffer in the Persian Gulf War? _____

7. How much money did the U.S. spend on World War I? _____

8. How much money did the U.S. spend on World War II? _____

9. How much money did the U.S. spend on the Korean War?_____

10. How much money did the U.S. spend on the Vietnam War? _____

11. Source. title of article_____. title of book _____

    city_____: publisher_____, date_____.

12. You will also use *Powerpoint* to create a graph. This graph will show some of the information you gathered in your research questions 1-11.

13. Statement for announcer to read: "This graph shows."
    _____

What will be the title of this graph?_____

14. Save graph to floppy disk on "A:" drive and to "C:" drive. Use your first name as filename. Type on computer and print out statements for announcer to read. Put print outs and disk in your group's folder.

*Figure 19.3 Graph Maker*

# Bibliography Maker

Collect the sources used in making this presentation. Refer to the "Bibliography" section of the "Research Helper" note-taking sheet. Consult with the other members of your group to compile all sources used. You should have at least four sources.

1. author_____. title of article_____.

    title (book, CD-ROM, video disc, circle one) _____.

    date of article_____. city_____: publisher_____, date_____.

2. author_____. title of article_____.

    title (book, CD-ROM, video disc, circle one) _____.

    date of article_____. city_____: publisher_____, date_____.

3. author_____. title of article_____.

    title (book, CD-ROM, video disc, circle one) _____.

    date of article_____. city_____: publisher_____, date_____.

4. author_____. title of article_____.

    title (book, CD-ROM, video disc, circle one) _____.

    date of article_____. city_____: publisher_____, date_____.

Now type up your bibliography on the computer. Use the format contained in the book, Write, Inc. Be sure to put the entries in alphabetical order. Save to a floppy disk on the "A:" drive and to the "C:" drive. Use your first name for a filename. Print out your bibliography and place it in your folder with the disk.

*Figure 19.4 Bibliography Maker*

# "So What?" Statement Writer/Announcer

You will be the announcer of your multimedia presentation. You will read the script, the summary of the graphs and the "So What?" Statement into the microphone.

1. List the most important fact you learned about the subject you reported on.
   _____
   _____

2. State why you think this fact is important for your classmates to know.
   (Limit your remarks to 3 or 4 sentences.)
   _____
   _____
   _____
   _____
   _____

3. List the source where your fact came from.

   author_____. title of article _____

   title (book, CD-ROM, video disc, circle one)
   _____

   date of article_____. city_____: publisher_____, date_____.

4. Now type your "So What?" Statement on a computer. Save to a floppy disk on the "A:" drive, save to the "C:" drive and print out your "So What?" Statement. Put the disk and the print out in your folder.

5. Now create a *PowerPoint* slide that says "So What?" Statement by _____ (your name). Use the "VIDEO IN" computer card software and a video camera to add your picture to this *Powerpoint* slide. Save your "So What?" Statement on the "C:" drive. Use the "So What?" Statement you printed out as a cue card.

*Figure 19.5 "So What?" Statement Writer/Announcer*

# Tech Director

Your first job is to find a piece of clip art in the Corel Gallery II clip art book. You will use this piece of clip art in your title.

1. Look in the table of contents in the clip art book to find a picture for the subject you are presenting.

    What is the category?_____

    What is the filename?_____

2. Use a library reference source to find out three facts regarding your subject.

    _____    _____    _____

3. Source: title _____. city_____:

    publisher_____, date_____, page_____.

4. Create your title in *Powerpoint* on the computer. Add the clip art piece you've chosen. Create a "Credits" *PowerPoint* slide. Include the first and last names of your group members. Save the title and credits to a floppy disk on the "A:" drive and to the "C:" drive. Use your first name for a filename. Put the floppy disk in your folder.

5. Now transfer your *Powerpoint* title and credits to videotape. As you do this, use the microphone to add narration, music and sound effects. Label the videotape and place it in the folder.

*Figure 19.6 Tech Director*

# Computer/Video Research Project Checklist

_____ 1. The library media specialist envisions a partnership with a specific teacher doing the Computer/Video Research Project.

_____ 2. The library media specialist becomes aware of what curriculum that teacher must cover.

_____ 3. The library media specialist meets with teacher and plans appropriate subjects for the Computer/Video Research Project.

_____ 4. The library media specialist schedules library time for teacher's classes that will be involved in the project.

## Day 1

The entire class comes to library. Students are divided in groups of five. Sample Computer/Video Research Project demonstration is made by library media specialist. The different jobs are explained to the students. Students do research and take notes. Deadlines are assigned for each group. Each group member is assigned a specific job. (See Figures 19.1-19.6, pp. 166-171.) Job description sheets are filled out and placed in a folder. After each day of work all assignments are placed in the group's folder.

## Day 2

Entire class comes to library. Research is completed. Research note taking sheets from all students are due.

## Day 3 and Day 4

Most of the class will be in the classroom doing the regular class work the teacher has assigned for that day. Only scriptwriters from each group come to the library media center. Handwritten scripts are due at end of Day 3 and computer printouts of scripts are due at the end of Day 4. Some students will want to start writing their scripts on the computer. Other students will need to write the script out longhand first and then type it on to the computer. Be sensitive to the fact that many students need to write down their ideas in longhand before they type them on a computer. Some students will become very frustrated if you force them to start writing a script on the computer. A template can be made on the computer of one of the script formats. (See Figure 2.11, "TV/ Computer Presentation Script," page 19, or Figure 2.12, "Simple Script Sheet," page 20.) With the template on the computer, the student can type the script using the appropriate script format.

## Day 5

Only Graph Makers from each group come to library. These students fill out Graph Maker sheet. Graphs are saved to floppy disks and computer hard drives.

## Day 6

Only Bibliography Makers from each group come to library. Printouts of bibliographies are due. Bibliographies are saved to floppy disks and computer hard drives.

## Day 7

Only "So What?" Statement Writer/Announcers from each group come to library. Their "So What?" Statements and "So What?" *PowerPoint* slides are due.

## Day 8

Only Tech Directors from each group come to library. Printouts of *PowerPoint* title slides and credits slides are due. Title and credits slides are saved to floppy disks and computer hard drives. Tech Directors practice video-recording techniques on editor VCRs.

## Day 9

Assignments from Days 1-7 must be completed before final steps of the Computer/Video Research Projects begin. These projects are produced at two stations in different parts of the library. Only Tech Directors and "So What?" Statement/Announcers from first two groups come to library to produce their presentations.

## Day 10

Next two groups produce their presentations.

## Day 11

Last groups produce their presentations.

## Day 12

The entire class views all their Computer/Video Research Projects in class using a TV/VCR. Have the students and teachers involved fill out the "Video Project Evaluation Form," p. 122. Have popcorn. Invite the principal. Make this a celebration!

## Day 13

With the teachers involved, review survey results and consider future changes in this project.

# Video Animation Projects

## Terms

- **animation**
- **cut out**

There are four main types of video animation projects: (1) those done entirely on a computer animation software computer program and then transferred to videotape, (2) projects done using a VHS video camera and edited with a video editor, (3) those done with a digital camera or camcorder and a computer program such as *PowerPoint*, and (4) projects done with a digital camera and then edited with a video editor.

## Computer Animation Software

Some excellent computer animation software programs are *Autodesk Multimedia Explorer*, *Microsoft 3D Movie Maker*, and *Ray Dream 3D*. Once the animation is completed in the computer, it is converted to videotape. Once the animation is in a video format, sound can easily be audio dubbed using an analog or digital video editor.

## VHS or Digital Camera to Analog Video Editor

The animation will not be very convincing using this system of VHS or digital camera to analog video editor. A typical VHS camcorder or VHS analog editor with flying erase heads allows for primitive animation. Each scene is shown for about one second. The problem is that each scene is too long and the finished product looks very awkward. The motion does not flow. The earlier models of VHS analog video editors in the late 1980s and early 1990s allowed for a better animation effect. This effect could be created using pause control on the editor. Each scene was about 1/5 of a second long. Sadly, in later models, the animation capability wasn't as good. The motion was more awkward, less flowing. Each scene was about one second.

## VHS or Digital Camera to Computer

The third option, using a VHS camcorder or digital camera with a computer *PowerPoint* program, produces excellent results. Any camcorder with a VIDEO OUT jack will do. The computer should have 64 or 128 or more MB of RAM (random access memory.) This will allow more frames of animation to be stored in the computer at one time. The computer should have more than a one-gigabyte hard drive and a Pentium processor. This will allow each animation frame to be added quickly. It takes more memory, a faster processor, and more gigabytes of hard drive to animate shots from a camcorder or a photograph than a piece of clip art.

## Digital Camera with Animation Setting

Some digital cameras have built in animation controls. These controls will capture each frame for one fifth of a second. Each scene in the animation can be captured on the digital camera and then added to the next animation scene on an analog video editor.

## Animation Using Drawings or Cut-Outs and Claymation

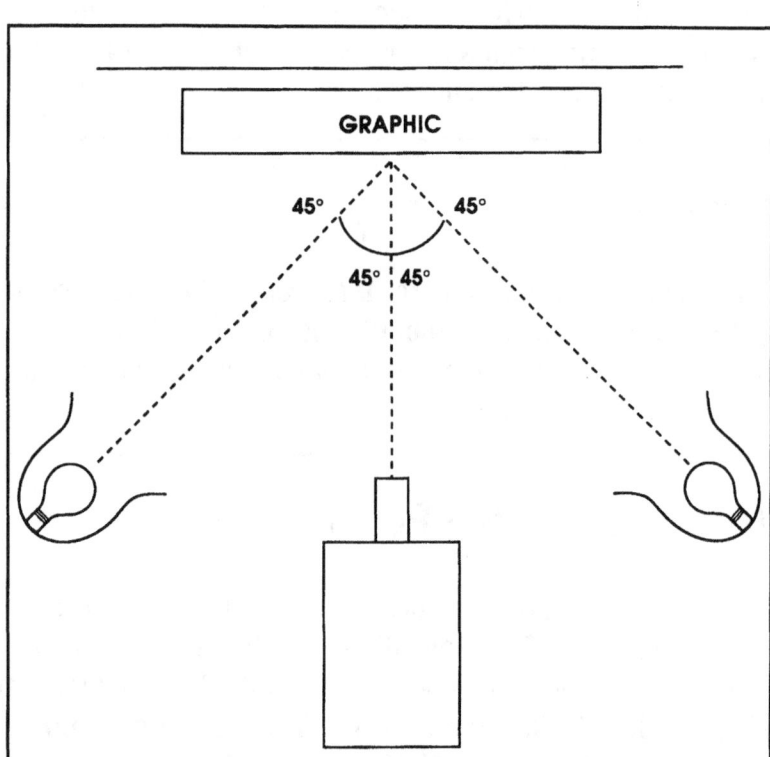

*Figure 20.1 Lights On Each Side of the Camera Improve Picture Quality From "Looking Great with Video Production" by Augie Beasley*

For an animation using drawings or cut-outs, a display camera would be ideal. A visual presenter would do well also. If you are using a regular camera, it's a good idea to mount it on a copy stand. (See Figure 20.1.) If you do not have a copy stand, put the camera on a tripod and put your artwork on a music stand. Some tripods allow you to shoot straight down on your subject. Whichever method you choose, the camera is zoomed in or out to the desired setting and focused. Then, of course, the camera is not moved while each scene in a sequence is created. If the background is moved, the effect of the animation will be lost. Each scene is placed on the display area and captured as a *PowerPoint*

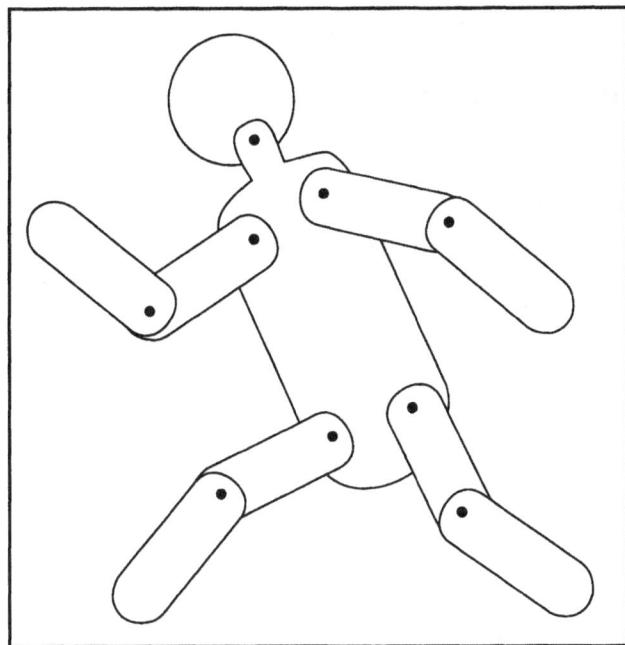

*Figure 20.2 Cut Out Figure With Moveable Arms and Legs for Animation* From *"Looking Great with Video Production"* by Augie Beasley

scene in the computer. In a simple animation project, you could get by with one background scene. You could show a cut-out figure with movable arms and legs walking across your background. A good example of an animation using cut-out figures is "Life with Loopy." (See Figure 20.2.)

Claymation, using clay figures for animation, follows rules a bit different from the ones for drawing and cut-outs. You can't shoot claymation on a copy stand or visual presenter. Instead of shooting down on the subject, you'd shoot from the side, probably on a table. You'd need a backdrop that you could place on the table. To shoot the clay figures on a camcorder, the macro lens setting would be used. You'd place the claymation figures near the edge of the table, next to the camcorder. As in the animation scenes using drawings or cut outs, once you begin an animation sequence, you don't change the position of the camera. A famous claymation is "Gumby."

## VHS Camcorder to *PowerPoint* to Video Editor Animation Checklist

_____ 1. Set up VHS camcorder on a tripod.

_____ 2. Use the zoom in, zoom out, macro, and focus to set up a scene. You may have many shots in that scene, but the camera and camera lens will always be in the same position for each shot. This is how you create the animation effect.

_____ 3. Hook up the RCA (phono) cable from the camera to the VIDEO IN jack on the VIDEO IN card or other VIDEO IN device.

_____ 4. Let's say you are going to animate a rock moving across a room by itself. In the first scene, the rock is in the far-left side of the picture. Save or capture that scene to your computer hard drive using your Video In attachment to the computer. You'd give it a filename like "rock 1."

_____ 5 Open your *PowerPoint* software and add your animation frame using choices such as INSERT, PICTURE, C: DRIVE and SNAPPY. Another way to go on some computers would be ADD or COPY and PASTE. You would add the picture, "rock 1" to the first *PowerPoint* slide.

_____ 6. Click on picture of "rock 1." Enlarge it to cover the entire *PowerPoint* slide

_____ 7. Save your *PowerPoint* presentation on the hard drive of the computer. You'd give the presentation a filename like "moving rock."

_____ 8. "Without moving the camera, move the rock a little bit more toward the far right side of the picture." Save or capture this scene as you did in Step 4. You'd give it a filename like "rock 2."

_____ 9. Repeat Step 5. This time you'll be adding the "rock 2" picture to the second *PowerPoint* slide in your presentation.

_____ 10. Repeat step #6 for "rock 2." Save the presentation again using the same filename.

_____ 11. Keep repeating Steps 4-7. Each time you move the rock a bit more toward the far right side of the picture.

_____ 12. Your last *PowerPoint* slide will have the rock on the far right side of the screen. Save your *PowerPoint* presentation for the last time.

_____ 13. For a Windows or Macintosh computer, hook up the VIDEO OUT device to the VIDEO IN of the VCR.

_____ 14. Open your *PowerPoint* presentation (in this case under filename "moving rock.") Open it so that the picture takes up the full computer screen.

_____ 15. Start recording on the VCR.

_____ 16. Wait 10 seconds. Then start your *PowerPoint* presentation.

_____ 17. The first sequence of your animation video, the scenes of a rock moving across a table, is complete.

_____ 18. Once the first sequence has been captured on videotape and you're are pleased with it, you may need to delete the animation *PowerPoint* slides you've just used. Otherwise, your computer may not be able to capture any more video images. Video images take up a great deal of RAM memory. If you had 30 video animation *PowerPoint* slides you used an enormous amount of RAM memory. If your computer has a zip drive, you could save all your animation images on the zip drive and free the hard drive space for other uses.

_____ 19. Continue doing Steps 2-18 until all animation sequences have been added to videotape.

_____ 20. Edit your video animation sequences on a video editor.

_____ 21. Add music, narration, and sound effects using the audio dub on a video editor.

# Digital Camera to Video Editor Checklist

_____ 1. Mount the digital camera on tripod.

_____ 2. Use the zoom in, zoom out, macro, and focus to set up a scene. You may have many shots in that scene but the camera and camera lens will always be in the same position for each shot. This is how you create the animation effect.

_____ 3. Put your digital camera in the animation mode. Refer to the manual of the digital camera for instructions. The digital camera should be able to shoot a shot in less than one second. Some digital cameras with animation settings shoot a shot in 1/8th of a second. Not all digital cameras have an animation mode.

_____ 4. Let's say you are going to animate a rock moving across a table by itself. In the first scene, the rock is in the far-left side of the picture. Record the first shot with the digital camera. Keep moving the rock a bit and shoot another shot.

_____ 5. Repeat this process until you've moved the rock entirely through the screen in the camera's viewfinder.

_____ 6. Play back the tape in the digital camera. If the action is too jerky, try moving the rock less between shots.

_____ 7. When you like the way your first animation sequence looks, record it to your video editor. You'll be going from VIDEO OUT on your digital camera to VIDEO IN on the video editor.

_____ 8. Repeat Steps 4-7 for the next animation sequence.

_____ 9. When all your animation sequences are shot, edit them together in the video editor.

_____ 10. Add sound effects, music and/or narration using the audio dub function of the video editor.

# Part IV: Organizing for Great Communication with Video Production in School Libraries

# Copyright and Other Permission

Every school librarian needs to have a good understanding of how copyright laws effects the use of copyrighted materials in student video productions. The American Library Association's Web site, <www.ala.org/library/fact7.html>, is an excellent resource for learning about copyright laws and the use of copyrighted materials.

## Face-to-Face Instruction

One key area to understand is "face to face" instruction. In some cases, there are no problems using copyrighted materials in the video or computer presentation when they are used in face-to-face instruction in a classroom in your school building. According to the American Library Association's Web page, "Video and Copyright," "Classroom use of a copyrighted video is permissible only when all of the following conditions are met: The performance must be by instructors or pupils. The performance is in connection with face-to-face teaching activities. The entire audience is involved in the teaching activity. The entire audience is in the same room or same general area. The teaching activities are conducted by a non-profit educational institution. The performance takes place in a classroom or similar place devoted to instruction. The person responsible for the performance has no reason to believe that the videotape was unlawfully made" (2).

Note the sentence in the ALA copyright guidelines, "The entire audience is in the same room or same general area." Would the audience of a school TV news show, which goes out to each classroom in the school, be considered "in the same room or general area?" No, it would not. All the classes see the school news show. The face-to-face instruction that allows for the use of copyrighted materials in the classroom does not pertain to more than one classroom. It pertains to the class of an individual teacher. Carol Simpson, educational copyright expert, sheds more light on this topic in an e-mail message to Terry McConnell, stating, "I personally asked noted copyright attorney Ivan Bender if using a video distribution system to send curricular video to multiple classrooms was permitted and he replied that if the showing went to a single campus (only to the classrooms studying the topic) that this was permissible use" (1).

# Guidelines for Using Copyrighted Materials in a Multimedia or Video Production

New legislation involving copyrights has yet to be passed into law by the U.S. Congress. However, professionals in the media field have created a set of guidelines to follow when incorporating copyrighted work into a student-produced media production. These guidelines are as follows:

(1) Students may use portions of copyrighted works in their multimedia presentations.

(2) Teachers may use portions of copyrighted works in their multimedia presentations that involve face-to-face instruction with students.

(3) These multimedia productions may be retained by students and teachers as a part of a portfolio for learning assessment, tenure review, and job interview purposes.

(4) These multimedia presentations may be used by educators for learning purposes for only two years after their production. After two years, permission for further use must be obtained from the copyright holder.

The following may be used by educators and students in a production: 10 percent, or 3 minutes of motion media; 1,000 words of a text; 30 seconds of music and lyrics of an individual musical piece of work; up to 5 images by an artist; or 2,500 fields or cells from a database.

(5) Educators and students should credit the copyrighted sources they have used in their multimedia presentations.

# Obtain Music and Sound Effects that Grant Copyright Permission for Use in Video Productions

If the presentation is going to be shown outside your school and the audience will not be comprised of students, be sure you have copyright permission for all pictures, video clips, music, or sound effects used. Obtain music and sound effects that come with copyright permission to use in your video presentations. Such music and sound effects are available from the following sources: Fresh The Music Library, 800-545-0688, 34 South Main St., Hanover, NH, 03755, and Energetic Music, 800-323-2972, P.O. Box 84583, 645 S. Massachusetts, Seattle, WA 98124.

**Don't Set Yourself Up for a Lawsuit**

When you purchase music from sources like Fresh Produce and Energetic Music, you are not just buying the cassette or CD, you are buying the right to use the music as you wish. Music that's not from a source like this is protected by copyright, and you could be sued by the copyright owner if you used the music in your video production for a non-educational purpose. If you use the music to facilitate face-to-face instruction with your students inside your school building, it is very unlikely you would be sued since this application falls within the recent copyright agreement for multimedia. If you use the music for any purpose other than face-to-face instruction, there's a much better chance you would be sued.

**Two Types of Copyright for Music**

Permission from the songwriter and the performer must be obtained in writing in order to use copyrighted music in a video production that will be used for purposes other than face-to-face instruction in the school. ASCAP (212-595-3050) is a good source for getting in touch with recording artists regarding using their music. However, this is often a frustrating and time-consuming process. It's a much wiser course to invest in some copyright-free music and sound effects for productions that will be used outside your school.

# Copyright for Visual Materials

Usually clip art software programs grant you the right to use the images in any way you choose, but still pictures, photographs, and video clips are often copyrighted. As with musicians, photographers and video producers may not want their work to be used by you. Many times it's hard to track down the copyright holder of a visual. As with music, obtaining the rights for visual material is a long and frustrating process.

There isn't any law requiring the copyright holder to respond to your letter, fax, e-mail, or phone call. Yet, the copyright holders are within their rights to sue you if they think you are using their copyrighted material without permission. For further questions on copyrights, refer to Carol Simpson's excellent book, *Copyright for School Libraries: A Practical Guide* (Professional Growth Series, Linworth Publishing).

# Family Permission for a Student to Appear in a Video

It is often necessary to get permission for a child to be in a video. Many school districts have policies on this. A typical policy would be as follows: If a parent signs a certain form to be kept on file in the school, the parents' child may not appear in a video production shown in a school in that system. So if a letter is not on file stating that the student cannot appear in a videotape production, the student may appear in a production produced in that school system. This policy varies from school district to school district. Know what your district's policy is on this matter.

# Video Production Outside School—Media Festivals and Cable TV

CHAPTER 22

It's easy to get wrapped up in doing video production at your school. Don't forget about the world of student video production outside of your school—the world of student media festivals and cable TV.

## Media Festivals

Most state educational media, library, or technology associations sponsor media festivals with video production categories. Such festivals are also sponsored by school districts, private corporations, trade associations, or TV stations. If you can't locate a media festival in your area, go to an Internet search engine and type in "student media festival" or "student video production contest." You'll probably find one you can enter. When you get the entry forms for any media festival, read the directions very carefully. Encourage your students to read the entry forms carefully, too. Deadlines are very specific. Late entries are usually not accepted. Many festivals impose time limits for the video productions. Usually those time limits fall within 5-10 minutes. There is usually a place where the library media specialist signs to authenticate the work produced as being totally the work of the students involved.

### Copyright Laws

In most cases, if any copyrighted materials are used in these video productions, a copyright permission letter from the copyright owner must be supplied along with the videotape entry. For the productions that you'll be sending to contests, be aware of copyright laws. Be sure you have the permission to use the music in your video productions for contests. When you purchase music on CD or cassette from sources such as Energetic Music or Fresh Produce, you also are purchasing the rights to use this music in your students' productions. See Chapter 25, "Buying Video Production Equipment" for addresses and phone numbers of sources of music for which you can purchase copyrights. Save the copyright agreement forms that come with this music. You may need to send copies of these copyright agreement forms when you send in your entries.

**Stiff Competition**

Media festivals are usually very competitive. You may want to enter a video production that your students produced that you think is excellent work. Prepare your students for a disappointment. What you think is excellent may get only "Third Place," "Honorable Mention," or worse yet, "Certificate of Participation." Often the judges for these media festivals are professional video producers. The standards of excellence for such a judge may be quite different than your own. It's inevitable that someone's feeling get hurt at a student media festival. No matter how you slice it, all the video entries will not get the recognition the producers think they deserve. Generally, if you and your students were not very proud of your production, you would not go through the time and trouble of entering. If you think your students have done a great job on a video production, take the risk of entering it in a local or state media festival! Teach your students to focus on the challenge of being evaluated by a panel of critical judges. Make the students' entry into a media festival a learning experience. Discuss the process with the students. Did your students think the best video production won first place? If the judges allowed you to see their criticisms of your students' video production, do your students agree with those criticisms? People often miss a very simple truth about video production. The group that entered their project in the media festival probably met a deadline, achieved a set of requirements, and felt good about their finished product. That is quite an achievement for the students and you, their sponsor. Validate your students and yourself for that because that is more important than what any judge thinks.

# Local Cable TV Stations

The winning video productions from media festivals are sometimes shown on a local educational cable TV stations. The same copyright restrictions that apply to student media festivals apply to student video productions on cable TV. Be sure you have written documentation of copyright permission to use copyrighted materials. Showing your students' video productions on cable TV gives your video production program and your school publicity and recognition. Encourage your local cable TV provider to establish a TV show where the video productions of local students are highlighted.

# Student Media Festivals Checklist

_____ 1. Inquire to your statewide library media or educational technology association regarding entry forms for student media festivals.

_____ 2. Inquire to school district library media services regarding entry forms for student media festivals.

_____ 3. Search on an Internet search engine for "student media festival" or "student video production contest."

_____ 4. Carefully read entry forms and encourage your video production students to do likewise.

_____ 5. Write entry deadlines for media festivals on your calendar.

_____ 6. Plan with student groups for video productions to be entered in media festivals. Keep contest rules in mind during planning.

_____ 7. Contact copyright holders to obtain written copyright permission as soon as possible.

_____ 8. To simplify the production process, use music in your production that you already have copyright permission to use.

_____ 9. After the video is produced, have students involved fill out and sign entry form.

_____ 10. Sign the entry form yourself.

_____ 11. Package and label the entry according to contest rules. Be sure all necessary forms are included.

_____ 12. Photocopy all entry forms for your records and make a duplicate copy of the video production being entered.

_____ 13. Mail or deliver your entry so it arrives at the media festival address specified on the entry form before the deadline. If you mail the entry, send it certified mail and keep the receipt.

_____ 14. Make travel arrangements with students so they can attend the media festival.

_____ 15. Encourage students' parents and school administrators to attend the media festival.

_____ 16. If your students win any awards at the media festival, publicize results in the school newspaper, PTA newsletter, school TV news show, and local community press.

_____ 17. Express thanks to media festival directors and sponsors.

_____ 18. Discuss the entire process of producing a video and entering it in a media festival with your students. What did they learn from the experience?

# The Video Production Hall of Fame

You've spent many hours helping students create high-quality video productions, you've developed relationships with those students. The process of creating videos with students is a rewarding process. It creates a bond with students, one of the greatest rewards of being a school library media specialist. It is a good feeling when one of your students wins an award for excellence in a video production contest. Having students create quality video productions is rewarding, regardless of any awards they may receive.

## Careers in Video and Multimedia Production

What can you do to help the students who have become talented video producers? You can guide them toward a career in video production. According to *Bridges*, an online career information source, the future outlook for TV news video producers is bright. Hazel MacClement and Keri-Lynn Smith write on the *Bridges* Web site, <www.usa.cx.bridges.com>, that, "A 1999 trend suggests about 86 percent of stations are making money (with their local TV news shows.) ...The Bureau of Labor Statistics says the labor market will continue to increase in this field through the year 2006 by 21 to 35 percent, and people working in the field agree with that prediction." The outlook is also bright in multimedia production. Michelle Lang and Keri-Lynn Smith write on the *Bridges* Web site that, "In the center of the multimedia world, San Francisco, the multimedia industry added 6,000 jobs- a 51 percent increase- between 1994 and 1998 reports a recent edition of the *San Francisco Chronicle*."

# Validate Former Students Who Excel in the Field of Media Production

To validate your students who have excelled in video production, establish a "Video Production Hall of Fame." Here are two criteria for inducting students in "Video Production Hall of Fame." First, the student had to be involved in video production work in your program during their time at school. Second, the student must achieve something after high school in the field of media production. For example, inductees to a hall of fame could be a former student who is a reporter on a local TV station, a former student who produces an independent film shown at local theater, or a former student who produces commercial video productions for a local video production company.

Display the pictures of your hall of fame students in a prominent spot in your library media center. Knowing some of your video production students have succeeded in the video production field will motivate your current students to learn more about video production. Use your hall of fame as a motivator. You might say something like this to one of your students. "Hey, Mary! You've written a really good script here. It's as good a script as the one written by a former student. Angela went to American University and got a degree in communication. Now you can see her on ABC News. There isn't any reason why you couldn't do something like that!"

If you work with students at a high school level, explore the possibility of setting up an internship with a local video production company. Select one of your top students to be an intern at a video production company for a few hours a week.

## Video Production Hall of Fame Checklist

_____ 1. Look through the Yellow Pages under "Video Production Services." Identify five video production companies near your school. Write letters to those companies asking them if they would have an internship opening for a talented video production student.

_____ 2. When you get a positive response from one of the companies, select your top student and visit the company with your student. Determine if the company would provide a positive work environment for your student. Do the skills of your student match the description the company gives you? Will your student get paid? Would the student's work schedule conflict with academic needs? Is transportation feasible?

_____ 3. Go through this process with any companies from which you've had a positive response. When you and the student have decided you want to set up an internship with a certain company, check the company out in the Better Business Bureau.

_____ 4. Contact the student's parents and school officials. Remember, once your internship student starts working, the student won't have as much time to devote to school projects.

_____ 5. Follow the progress of the student in the internship. If the student does a good job, the student may have a permanent position with the video production company.

_____ 6. Once your student achieves the status of a professional video producer, be sure you add that student to your "Video Production Hall of Fame."

# Funding Your Program through Grants

Grants are a way of funding your program or allowing you to get the software or hardware you need. Applying for the grant also focuses you, the school librarian, on exactly what your objectives are. Other fundraising activities tend to scatter rather than focus your energies. You can raise money selling candy, donuts, bagels or by sponsoring a dance, but that takes a lot of time that could be spent planning instructional activities to enhance the library media program. The grant writing process is a planning process. Many of the activities students do in your library media center will have their genesis in the grants you write and win.

Obtain a copy of, The *"How To" Grants Manual*, 4th ed. written by David G. Bauer. The people who are in charge of the grant you are applying for may have their own grant writing manual. Get it and read it!

Here are some sample grant ideas that have been funded in the past:

A. History projects where students use video cameras and *PowerPoint* software to present historical research.

B. Poetry videos where students write poems on *PowerPoint* and supplement the poems with video shots.

C. Math videos where students use *PowerPoint* slides to highlight the steps to solving a math problem.

Listed below are some grant sources. Don't neglect grants coordinated through your own school district. Such grants, if your win them, help publicize your program to the local community. For example, the cable TV provider in your school district may have a grant program. If you win that grant, it's likely the cable provider will highlight your library program in the cable provider's monthly guide that goes to all cable subscribers.

Don't forget the PTA or your principal's discretionary fund as possible grant sources for equipment. The chances are you won't have to spend as much time writing up this type of grant. Since you probably know the people who will be giving you the money, you'll be able to write the grant proposal in language they will understand and appreciate.

# List of Grant Sources

A. The Teachers Network-Impact II
   285 West Broadway
   New York, NY 10013
   212-966-5582
   <www.teachnet.org/docs/Funders/Welcome/index.htm>

B. Michael Jordan Fundamentals Education Grants Program for Teachers administered by the National Foundation for the Improvement of Education
   202-822-7840
   <www.nfie.org>

C. The Toshiba America Foundation
   126 E. 56th St., 28th Floor
   New York, NY 10022
   212-588-0824
   e-mail: foundation@tai.toshiba.com
   <www.toshiba.com>

D. Brinker International Charitable Committee
   6820 LBJ Freeway
   Dallas TX  75240
   972-980-4100
   <www.brinker.com/htm/006_companyinfo_framesource_communityrelations.htm>

E. Interactive Education Initiative, AOL Foundation
   22000 AOL Way
   Dulles, VA 20166
   703-265-1342
   703-265-2135 (Fax)
   e-mail: AOLGrants@AOL.com

F. A course in educational funding strategies
   Marilyn Gross
   President
   Educational Funding Strategies
   914-368-2950
   MLGross@aol.com

G. Education World © Grants For Educators Program
   <www.education-world.com/grants/>

For more grant sources go on the Internet, and use a search engine to search for "grants for educators." We predict that you'll find more grant sources than you'll ever need. The following Web site, <www.gsa.gov/fdac>, will provide a directory for federal grants. Another Web site, fdncenter.org will provide a directory for foundation grants.

## Create a Grant Writing Partnership with a Teacher

For a partner in the grant writing process, pick a teacher, someone you enjoy working with, who uses the library a great deal. You'll be spending a lot of time working with that teacher on the grant. At the start of the grant writing process decide what percentage of the money will be spent on library media center needs. Stick up for yourself here. At least half of the grant money ought to go to your school's library media center program. Keep in mind that the library media center benefits the entire school.

## Plan Your Grant to Solve an Educational Problem

Plan your grant as a solution to a specific educational problem. Cheryl C. New and James A. Quick suggest in their article, "Steering Your Way to a Winning Grant Proposal," that you "focus your creative efforts and expertise as educators on a technique, a process, or curriculum change that has a good chance of overcoming a barrier and providing at least a partial solution to the problem" (6).

## Grant Writing Is Competitive

Keep in mind that grant writing is competitive. Many grant proposals never get funded. Your first draft of the grant proposal may not be good enough to win. Focus on what the grant application says, and answer the questions in a straightforward manner. Grant evaluators complain that grant writers often fail to directly address the questions asked in the grant.

## Get Inside of the Mind of the Person Judging the Grant

Ask for budget items that the grant administrator thinks you can't get from other sources. Why would the grant officials fund your grant for 100 books and a camcorder if they knew funds from your school district were already available for those items? Attempt to get inside the mind of the grant officials who will approve your grant? What kind of proposal do they really want? It may take a few weeks of planning and revising to write a grant that will be funded. Don't start the process a week before the deadline.

## If You Don't Win, Find Out Why

If you don't win the grant, ask the grant official why you were not funded. You may be able to apply for the same grant again. The grant official may give you feedback that will help you make appropriate changes in your grant so it will eventually get funded.

## Cite Educational Research

When writing your grant proposal, use educational research results that highlight the value of your grant objectives. One excellent source for such information is the *1999 Research Report on the Effectiveness of Technology in Schools*, 6th ed., available from the Software and Information Industry Association, 1730 M Street NW, Suite 700, Washington DC 20036, 202-452-1600. We've also cited educational research on the value of student video productions in Chapter 12, page 118.

## Save Receipts

When you win your grant and spend the money, save the receipts. The grant provider may want to see them for documentation purposes. Some grant providers expect that your needs will change from the time you write the grant to the time you implement it. Thus, if you originally asked for software in the grant, the grant provider may have no objection to your using the money to help buy a new camcorder. Just tell the grant provider that your needs changed. Be sure to check with the grant provider on this issue after you win the grant.

## Grant Writing Checklist

_____ 1. Become familiar with the grant writing process.

_____ 2. Obtain grant sources.

_____ 3. Form a partnership with a teacher from another department to write the grant.

_____ 4. Brainstorm with the teacher partner about the objectives of your grant. Develop grant objectives with which you both are comfortable.

_____ 5. Design the grant as a way to solve a specific educational problem.

_____ 6. Allow time for planning and rewriting. Start writing the grant well before the due date.

_____ 7. Ask the grant provider if your grant can submitted as a word processed document. You don't want to fight with a typewriter to win a grant.

_____ 8. Answer the questions on the grant in a direct, straightforward manner.

_____ 9. When writing your grant proposal, use educational research results that highlight the value of your grant objectives.

_____ 10. When writing the grant, ask for budget items you think the grant provider will be happy to fund.

_____ 11. Avoid controversial language in your grant writing style.

_____ 12. Ask educators not involved in your grant to proofread it. It's a safe bet they'll find some mistakes, and they may have some good content suggestions too.

_____ 13. If you don't win the grant, find out why. The feedback may help you improve your grant so it wins next time.

_____ 14. Save all receipts for what you buy when you win your grant. The grant provider may want to see them.

# Buying Video Production Equipment

CHAPTER 25

You won the grant, your school is being renovated, and you have access to the renovation budget. Your school system has an equipment replacement fund, or your principal has set aside some local school money for your program. One way or another, you'll be buying TV production equipment. You need good information to make decisions about what equipment to buy.

## The Video/AV/Technology Committee

In many public school systems, a committee of teachers, administrators, and school librarians exists for that purpose. It may be called something like the video/AV/technology equipment committee. Groups like this are very careful to recommend only equipment, models, and brands that are reliable. However, since equipment ordering on a county and state level is done by a competitive bid process, the equipment that educators want on their bid list is not always what they get. However, in certain situations, if you write the specifications for the equipment you want, you can often get the equipment you want. The AV/TV bid list for Fairfax County, Virginia Public Schools can be examined on the Internet at <www.fcps.k12.va.us/DIT/TeacherOutreach>. Click on "AV Equipment Contract" when you get to this Web site for an extensive bid list for TV production equipment.

## Vendor Problems

When ordering equipment, plenty of problems can happen. At times a vendor may give you incorrect order information. Once this happened to us. After six months of weekly phone calls to the vendor we discovered that the original equipment we ordered was no longer available from the corporation. We didn't get the equipment we needed until we contacted the national office of the corporation.

# List of Sources for Video Production Equipment

**Analog Video Editor**
Panasonic Broadcast and Television Systems Company
Marketing Department
3330 Cahuenga Blvd., W.
Los Angles, CA 90068
323-436-3500
<www.panasonic.com>

**Audio Mixer**
Shure Brothers, Inc.
Customer Service Dept.
222 Hartrey Ave.
Evanston, IL 60202-3696
800-25-SHURE or 847-866-2553
Fax: 800-34-SHURE
<www.shure.com/sales.html>
email: sales@shure.com

**Camcorders, VHS**
Panasonic Broadcast and Television Systems Company
Marketing Department
3330 Cahuenga Blvd., W.
Los Angles, CA 90068
323-436-3500
<www.panasonic.com>

**Computer to TV devices, with S Video and RCA (phono) outputs and audio outputs (Macintosh and IBM-compatible)**
Focus Enhancements TView Silver
Microwarehouse
800-697-8508
<www.focusinfo.com>

**Computer to TV devices and Video to Computer devices (IBM-compatible)**
All-in-Wonder Pro
ATI Technologies
33 Commerce Valley Drive East
Thornhill, Ontario Canada L3T 7N6
905-882-2600
Fax: 905-882-2620
<www.atitech.com>

**Data Projector (for large group computer or video presentations)**
Panasonic Broadcast and Television Systems Company
Marketing Department
3330 Cahuenga Blvd., W.
Los Angles, CA 90068
323-436-3500
<www.panasonic.com>

**Digital Camera (for motion shots and animation, no floppy disk drive)**
JVC Professional Products Company
1700 Valley Rd.
Wayne, NJ 07470
973-315-5000
Fax: 1-973-315-5030
<www.jvc-pro.com>

**Digital Camera (for still shots with floppy disk drive)**
Sony Corporation
123 W. Tryon Ave.
Teaneck, New Jersey 07666
201-833-5300

**Digital Mixer (Video Mixer and Camera Switcher)**
Panasonic Broadcast and Television Systems Company
Marketing Department
3330 Cahuenga Blvd., W.
Los Angles, CA 90068
323-436-3500
<www.panasonic.com>

**Digital Video Editing Using an IBM-compatible or Macintosh Computer**
MGI Software Corporation
50 West Pearce St.
Richmond Hill, Ontario, Canada L4BIE3
888-644-7638
e-mail: sales@mgisoft.com

**Digital Video Editor**
DraCo Systems, Inc.
5485 Conestoga Court
Boulder, CO 80301
303-440-5311
Fax: 303-440-5322
<www.draco.com>

**Head Set Communication System**
Anchor Communications, Inc.
3415 W. Lomita Blvd.
Torrance, CA 90505
800-262-4671
Fax: 310-784-0066

**Lavaliere Microphone**
Audio-Technica U.S., Inc.
1221 Commerce Drive
Stow, OH 44224
330-686-2600
Fax: 330-688-3752
<www.audio-technica.com/index2.html>
e-mail: sales@atus.com

**Lighting Kit**
Lowell lighting kits available from
Kipp Visual and Security Systems, Inc.
3600 Clipper Mill Rd. #105
Baltimore, MD 21211
410-235-9900
Fax: 410-235-7122
Lowell
800-334-3426

**Microphones, Low Impedance**
Shure Brothers, Inc.
Customer Service Dept.
222 Hartrey Ave.
Evanston, IL 60202-3696
800-25-SHURE or 847-866-2553
Fax: 800-34-SHURE
<www.shure.com/sales.html>
e-mail: sales@shure.com

**Microphones, High Impedance**
Sony Corporation
123 W. Tryon Ave.
Teaneck, NJ 07666
201-833-5300

**Music and Sound Effects**
Fresh The Music Library
34 South Main St.
Hanover, NH 03755
800-545-0688
Energetic Music
P.O. Box 84583
645 S. Massachusetts
Seattle, WA 98124
800-323-2972

**Paint for TV Studio Backdrops (makes possible chroma key special effects)**
"Digital Video Chroma Key Blue, Roscoe Ultimate TM Paints 5720 Ultimate TM Blue."
Barbizon Capitol
6437-G General Green Way
Alexandria, VA 22312
703-750-3900 or 800-922-2972

**Tripods**
Bogen Photo Corp.
201-934-8500
<www.bogen.com>
e-mail: sales-reps@bogen.com

**TV Monitor/Receiver**
JVC Professional Products Company
1700 Valley Rd.
Wayne, NJ 07470
973-315-5000
Fax: 973-315-5030
<www.jvc-pro.com>

**Visual Presenter (TV Camera on Copy Stand)**
JVC Professional Products Company
1700 Valley Rd.
Wayne, NJ 07470
973-315-5000
Fax: 973-315-5030
<www.jvc-pro.com>

# TV Production Equipment Purchase Checklist

_____ 1. Prioritize your equipment needs.

_____ 2. For your top priority needs, consult with other library media specialists on the type of equipment, model, and brand they use.

_____ 3. Consult with your school district or state department of education's bid list for equipment used for instruction. The equipment on such a list is often (not always) of high quality.

_____ 4. Make a list of vendors from whom you could purchase the equipment you want. Bid lists contain the names, addresses, and phone numbers of vendors.

_____ 5. Consult professional journals regarding the models you are considering purchase of. *Videomaker* is an excellent magazine to consult for reviews on video production equipment.

_____ 6. Call vendors and ask questions. Some suggested questions are:
A. How long will it take to get this item delivered? B. Is the model you want available? C. Will the vendor accept your school's or your school system's purchase order? D. Does the vendor understand that educational institutions pay for equipment after it is received? E. Is the vendor willing and able to provide information and training on the equipment you are interested in? F. .Is the vendor easy to reach by phone or e-mail? G. Can the vendor provide you with written literature about the model and equipment you are interested in? H. What price is the vendor charging?

_____ 7. Arrange to see the piece of equipment you want in action at another school or the vendor's show room.

_____ 8. Decide on the equipment, model, brand, and vendor you want.

_____ 9. Consult with your financial officer and arrange for purchase.

_____ 10. Make a list of all the equipment/materials you purchase. When they come in, check them off, with the date of arrival next to the item.

_____ 11. Follow up with the vendor and or school system finance officer on equipment that does not come in two months after the order has been placed.

# It's a Wrap!

# Conclusion

## CHAPTER 26

Get excited about welcoming your students and teachers into "the communication age" and doing great communication with video production in your school library. Make your program visible by using video production to promote your school library program to your students, teachers, and community.

To stay visible, create instructional partnerships with teachers and students. These partnerships result in visible products like computer/video research projects. Video productions like this help tell the story of the library media program. Remember, you don't want to do it alone. In fact, you will not be able to do it alone.

Great communication with video production is a powerful strategy you possess in your library media program. And yet, too many school librarians have not given this powerful communications strategy its due credit. Too often video production has been ignored as a learning tool.

Maybe you've said "I am too busy; I don't have the time or the energy to learn how to do video production." Teaching your students video production can be a great benefit to them. Video production projects can help students learn more effectively, write more effectively, work in groups effectively, and be more self-confident. That's reason enough to begin a video production program at your school.

Many programs are already under way. Students in great numbers are doing video productions in schools today. Sophisticated TV news shows are being created in elementary, middle, and high schools. The school librarians who organize the student video producers don't fit old stereotypes. These school librarians are not just video techies and they're not just "book" oriented. Instead, they're a new breed of school librarian that values books, reading, research, writing, technology, and video production. Like Oprah Winfrey, the new breed of school librarian is equally at home sponsoring a book club or producing a TV show.

Do great communication with video production. Communicate to your school audience about books, reading, and research. Above all teach your students and staff how to communicate with video production. Get them ready for the "communication age" we're experiencing.

# Bibliography

American Association of School Librarians and Association of Educational Communications and Technology. *Information Power: Building Partnerships for Learning.* American Library Association, 1998.

American Library Association. Web page <www.ala.org/library/fact7.html>

Anderson, Ronald E., and Amy Ronnkvist. "The Presence of Computers in American Schools, 6/1/99." <www.crito.uci.edu/tlc/html/findings.html>.

Bauer, David G. *The "How To" Grants Manual.* 4th ed.: Oryx Press, 1999.

Beasley, Augie. *Looking Great with Video Production.* Worthington, Ohio: Linworth Publishing, 1994.

Blubaugh, Donelle. Telephone Interview. June 1999.

Brunner, Cornelia. "Teaching Visual Literacy." *Electronic Learning,* November 1994,16.

Card, Orson Scott. Speech made at Border's Books. Virginia: October, 1999.

Curchy, Christopher and Keith Kyker. *Educator's Survival Guide to TV Production Equipment and Setup.* Englewood, Colorado: Libraries Unlimited, Inc., 1998.

Dowling, Susan. "Brooklyn Cinderella or the True Story of Transforming P.S. 3." *School Library Journal* (May 1997): 24-25.

Facemire, Zina. Interview with school library media specialist. 1 August 2000.

Gandal. *Making Standards Matter.* American Federation of Teachers, 1997.

Glaze, Bernie. Interview with secondary social studies teacher. 1995.

Godfrey, Floyd. Interview with independent computer consultant. 25 December 1999.

Harris, Phil. Interview with video production teacher. 8 March 2000.

Heinich, Robert, Michael Molenda, James D. Russell, and Sharon Smaldino. *Instructional Media Technologies for Learning.* Prentice Hall College Division, 1999.

Kent State University. Web page <www.educ.kent.edu/vlo/literacy/index.html>

Lang, Michelle, and Keri-Lynn Smith. "Multimedia Designer." <www.usa.cx.bridges.com>.

Lehrer, R. *Computers as Cognitive Tools.* Erlbaum, 1993.

Liu, M. and K. Rutledge. "The Effect of a 'Learner as Multimedia Designer' Environment on At-risk High School Students' Motivation and Learning of Design Knowledge." Software and Information Industry Association: 70.

# Bibliography continued

MacClement, Hazel, and Keri-Lynn Smith. "TV Producer." <www.usa.cx.bridges.com>.

Marzano and Kendall. *A Comprehensive Guide to Designing Standards-Based Districts, Schools and Classrooms.* McRel, 1996.

Mathews, Jay. "N. J. School's High-Tech Myth." *The Washington Post.* 22 June 1996, A1.

Messaris, Paul. "Visual Aspects of Media Literacy." Journal of Communication (Winter 1998): 70-80.

New, Cheryl C., and James C. Quick. "Steering Your Way to a Winning Grant Proposal," *Technology and Learning* (June 1999): 6.

Oakerson, Lin. Interview with video production expert. 6 January 2000.

Oldenburg, Don. "The Teacher-Technology Gap." *The Washington Post.* 22 February 1999, A1.

Plath, Carl. Interview. 17 December 1999.

Race, Al. "A Message from the Editor." Cable in the Classroom (December 1998): 2.

Ravitz, Jason L., Yan Tien Wong, and Henry J. Becker. "Report to Participants." <www.crito.uci.edu/tlc/html/findings.html>.

Repman, Judi. "Collaborative, Computer-based Learning: Cognitive and Affective Outcomes." Software and Information Industry Association: 54-55.

Sheridan, Susan \Rich. *Drawing/Writing and the New Literacy Where Verbal Meets Visual.* Amherst, Massachusetts: Drawing/Writing Publications, 1997.

Simpson, Carol Mann. "Re: copyright issues for in-school TV news shows." Online. e-mail. directlink.net. 20 February 2000. Available: csimpson@directlink.net.

Simpson, Carol Mann. "*Copyright for School Libraries: A Practical Guide.*" Ohio: Linworth Publishing, 1994.

Software and Information Industry Association. *1999 Research Report on the Effectiveness of Technology in Schools.* Washington, D.C.: Software and Information Industry Association, 1999.

Spencer, Pam. "What Do Young Adults Read Next? A Readers Guide to Fiction for Young Adults, Volume 2." Gale, 1997.

Teaching, Learning and Computing: 1998, a National Survey of Schools and Teachers, "Snapshot # 4, Technical and Instructional Support for Teachers." www.crito.uci.edu

Valeri-Gold, M. and M. P. "Computers and Basic Writers: A Research Update." Software and Information Industry Association: 12.

# Resource List

1999 *Research Report on the Effectiveness of Technology in Schools.* Washington, D.C.: Software and Information Industry Association, 1999.
This book contains case studies that show how technology enhances the learning process.

American Association of School Librarians and Association of Educational Communications and Technology. *Information Power: Building Partnerships for Learning.* American Library Association, 1998.
This book describes what school librarians should be doing to implement successful strategies for learning in school libraries.

Bauer, David G. *The "How To" Grants Manual.* 4th ed. Oryx Press, 1999.
This book describes how to get a grant to fund an educational purpose.

Beasley, Augie. *Looking Great with Video Production.* Worthington, Ohio: Linworth Publishing, 1994.
This book for the school librarian shows how to do video production in the school library.

*Casablanca Nonlinear digital video editor System Software Version 2 Owner's* Manual. Boulder: DraCo Systems, Inc., 1998.
This is a user friendly manual for operating the Casablanca digital video editor.

Curchy, Christopher, and Keith Kyker. *Educator's Survival Guide to TV Production Equipment and Setup.* Englewood, Colorado: Libraries Unlimited, Inc., 1998.
This book describes how to use various types of video equipment in public schools.

Heinich, Robert, Michael Molenda, James D. Russell, and Sharon Smaldino. *Instructional Media Technologies for Learning.* Prentice Hall College Division, 1999.
This book is designed for all educators from kindergarten to the college level. It describes, in detail, how to utilize the instructional technologies available for optimum learning.

Marzano and Kendall. *A Comprehensive Guide to Designing Standards-Based Districts, Schools and Classrooms.* McRel, 1996.
This "how to" publication helps design district-wide standards for learning.

Sheridan, Susan Rich. *Drawing/Writing and the New Literacy Where Verbal Meets Visual.* Amherst, MA: Drawing/Writing Publications, 1997.
This book describes how to encourage students writing.

Simpson, Carol Mann. *Copyright for School Libraries: A Practical Guide.* Worthington, Ohio: Linworth Publishing, 1994.
This book gives practical explanations to educators on how to deal with copyright laws.

Wallace, Virginia, and Ramona Gorham. *School News Shows Video Production with a Focus.* Worthington, Ohio: Linworth Publishing, 1994.

Weaver, Marcia. *Visual Literacy: How to Read and Use Information in Graphic Form.* Learning Express, 1999.
This is a visual literacy book designed for the business world, not the world of TV production in schools.

Williams, Richard. *Television Production: a Vocational Approach, Third Edition.* Sandy, Utah: Vision Publishing Company, 1988.
In this book, the basic principles and techniques of TV production are defined for students in a high school vocational class.

# Glossary

**8-mm.** A smaller type of camcorder. It produces a sharper image and better sound quality than a VHS camcorder because it doesn't have iron oxide particles, which are in VHS tapes. Instead, metallic particles are used.

**A.A.S.L.** American Association of School Librarians, one of two educational associations that wrote the book, *Information Power, Building Partnerships for Learning.*

**A/B roll editing.** Editing done with two VCRs. If the edited video were of a musical performance, the original video footage shot of the performer would be A roll. The B roll consists of the shots to be edited in of the audience watching the performer. These shots are coming from a videotape being played back on another VCR.

**acoustics.** The way sound is heard in a room due to the way sound waves are either absorbed or scattered by the physical makeup of the room.

**adapter.** A device that connects two audiovisual items, making them compatible.

**A.E.C.T.** Association for Educational Communications and Technology, one of two educational associations that wrote the book, *Information Power, Building Partnerships for Learning.*

**analog.** A video image made up of iron oxide particles on a videotape. VCR heads can play and/or record on the iron oxide particles on a videotape; an analog signal must be digitized before it can be used with computer software.

**anchor desk.** A prop for a TV news show made to look like a desk. The TV news announcers sit behind it.

**anchorperson.** The anchorperson is the on-camera talent who delivers the news live to the audience during the news show. A strong voice, enthusiasm, and a pleasant and engaging demeanor are the traits of a capable anchorperson. The anchorperson has to think on his or her feet since mistakes can't be edited out of a live TV show.

**animation.** Creating an illusion of movement by combining a series of still-camera shots, drawings, or photographs. The scenes could be drawings, clay pieces, or objects. In each animation sequence, the objects are shot from the same reference point. Small incremental changes are made after each scene is shot.

**aperture.** The opening in front of a camera that lets light in.

**aspect ratio.** The ratio between horizontal and vertical units in a visual; there should be a ratio of four vertical units to three horizontal units for TV.

**assemble.** A type of editing in video production wherein the audio and video signals are copied and a control track is added.

**audio director.** Ensures that all microphones are set to the right level and that CDs and audiocassette tapes are played at the right time. Audio directors make sure that videotaped segments play at the same volume level as live segments and watch the VU (volume) meter on the audio mixer and the recorder VCR. They adjust the dials on the audio mixer and CD/cassette player to be sure the audio going out to the TVs throughout the school on the cable system is loud enough and even. Before and after the daily news show, audio directors unplug the audio cable hooking up to the cable system so the audience does not get to hear what the news team members say before and after the show.

**audio dub.** Adding new sound to a video production while keeping the same TV picture. The old sound is lost when the new sound is added.

**AUDIO IN.** The jack that accepts audio signals from another piece of equipment into a computer, VCR, TV monitor, sound mixer, or CD/cassette player.

# Glossary continued

**AUDIO LINE cable.** A cable that carries a high-level audio signal between two pieces of video, audio, or computer equipment.

**audio mixer.** A device that accepts audio inputs from microphones, CD players, and cassette recorders. As many as all or as few as one of the inputs can be selected by the audio mixer operator and sent to the recorder VCR; audio mixers often have four inputs that can be used for microphones or as line inputs for a CD/cassette player or audio input from a playback VCR. There is one audio output that is hooked up to the recorder VCR's AUDIO IN.

**AUDIO OUT.** The jack that sends out audio signals from a computer, VCR, camcorder, or television monitor, to another piece of equipment.

**a/v digital mixer.** A device that is both an audio and video mixer. It is a video switcher that has other functions, such as special effects like chroma key, fade, and still. The digital mixer works with the character generator to create titles that can be superimposed over a camera shot. A typical digital mixer has four video inputs, one video output, four audio inputs, and one audio output.

**automatic gain control (AGC).** A feature on audio and video recording equipment that boosts signal quality; AGC may be good for music but not for voices, especially when there are pauses in a narration or discussion.

**automatic iris.** A device found on many modern cameras that automatically shrinks and widens the aperture, letting the appropriate amount of light into the imaging device. Many camcorders today have an automatic iris, not a manual iris. This can cause problems in situations where there is too much back light.

**B roll.** See A/B roll editing.

**backdrop.** A dropcloth, curtain, or sheet hung from the ceiling in the TV studio. It may be painted an appropriate color for TV production work such as light blue. The talent sits in front of the backdrop when doing a TV news show or other TV production.

**back light.** (1) a function on a camcorder that allows camera operators to get a viewable shot of a subject even though they are shooting directly into a bright light; (2) a light source above and behind a subject that shines down on it, highlighting hair and giving a stronger three-dimensional appearance.

**back lighting.** A type of lighting placed over and in back of the subject. Back lighting highlights hair and gives the subject a stronger three-dimensional appearance. It creates a sense of separation between the subject and the background. The back light should be elevated so it shoots down in back of the talent at a 70° angle.

**barn doors.** Attachments on the sides of a TV studio light that can be opened or closed, either blocking the light or allowing the light to show on the subject.

**BG background.** An abbreviation in scriptwriting for the background of a scene that would appear in the visual section of the script.

**bi-directional microphone.** Absorbs sound from the left and right.

**BNC connector.** A type of video connector that twists on and off; it handles the same signals that a RCA (phono) connector does for VIDEO IN.

**BNC jack.** Handles the same signals as a VIDEO IN or VIDEO OUT jack; twisting a BNC locks it into the BNC jack.

**bounce lighting.** Pointing a light source at a low ceiling so that it bounces onto a subject.

**cable drop.** The place where a TV receiver can be connected to the in-school cable TV system. Usually, in an in-school cable TV system there is a cable drop in every classroom, large group instructional area, and office.

# Glossary continued

**cable TV.** A TV distribution system used in schools where the signal comes from a single origination point, the head end, and travels to TV receivers in offices and classrooms, via a cable. Some of the programming may originate in the school, some may come from an outside source, such as a cable company.

**camcorder.** A piece of video equipment that combines the functions of recorder and camera in one unit.

**camera angle.** The angle from which a camera is recording; See also **subjective, objective, low, high,** and **oblique.**

**camera operator.** Ensures that the camera is always in focus; sets up the necessary close-up, medium, and long shots; and follows the camera directions of the tech director. If the camera is a visual presenter the camera operator ensures that the appropriate graphics are shown when needed.

**cardioid microphone.** Absorbs sound from the front, left, and right in a heart-shaped pattern.

**CCD charged-coupled device.** A charged-coupled device changes light into electrical impulses that form the TV picture. It is more resistant to light than old video tubes. Old video tubes were large. The CCD is small, making it possible to combine the camera function and recording function in one unit, the camcorder.

**character generator.** A device that creates titles that are superimposed on a TV camera or on TV camera inputs in the a/v digital mixer. The result is that the TV picture and the title can be seen at the same time.

**chroma key.** Inserting an image from one video source into the picture of another video source. In one video source all the visual material of one color is removed; if you put a person in front of a blue background, the entire blue background is removed from the picture. Then the part of the image that remains is inserted into the other video source. If the other video source were a shot of the Eiffel Tower, the person would now be standing in front of the Eiffel Tower, not the blue background.

**claymation.** A close-up animation, using animated clay figures.

**closed circuit TV (CCTV).** A TV system that sends a signal to each TV receiver via cable. The TV signal is not broadcast.

**close-up (CU).** A camera shot showing a person's face from the top of the head to the lower part of the shoulders. Close-up shots are effective in conveying a person's emotions and intentions.

**closure.** The sense that something is finished or completed. The last scene of a video script should convey closure.

**communication.** The process by which information goes from a source to a destination.

**complex TV studio.** A TV studio that uses multiple video and sound inputs. Switching between cameras and other video inputs is done using video switchers and/or an a/v digital mixer. Switching between microphones and other audio inputs is done using an audio mixer or an a/v digital mixer.

**composition.** Using a camera to frame a picture so the picture communicates something.

**condenser microphone.** Less rugged yet more expensive than a dynamic microphone; good for picking up a musical concert.

**connector.** Another term for a plug at the end of an audio or video cable. A connector can have a male or female connection.

# Glossary continued

**contrast ratio.** The ratio between the lightest and darkest parts of the TV picture; it should be no greater than 15:1. Otherwise, the subject of the picture may be difficult to see.

**control room.** The room adjacent to the TV studio floor, where the technology director directs TV show.

**control track.** A special signal that the edit controller adds to the videotape in the assemble editing process.

**crystal/ceramic microphone.** Microphone found on cassette recorders. It is unsatisfactory for video production because it has poor sound quality.

**cue.** (1) moving an audiocassette or videocassette to an exact spot on the tape so the desired material on that tape can be added to the rest of the TV production at the appropriate time; (2) signaling the talent to begin speaking at the appropriate time in a TV production.

**cue card operator.** Cue cards are typed using a 48-point font size and are printed out and taped together in the correct sequence on a large tin can. The tin can is placed next to the camera. The cue card operator rotates the tin can so the talent can see and read the right cue card at the right time.

**cut away.** A shot in a scene from a different perspective. For example at a concert, a shot of an audience member would be a cut away. The audience would still hear the concert music, but they would see the shot of the audience member listening to the concert.

**cut out.** A figure cut out of paper or cardboard with moveable arms, legs, or other parts. The cut out is placed over a background. Small incremental changes are made in the parts of the cut out as an animation sequence is shot. When the sequence is played back, the cut out seems to be moving.

**data projector.** Projects images from a VCR or computer onto a wall screen. By moving the data projector away from the wall screen, the image becomes larger. The data projector has a built in speaker so the sound of the videotape or computer presentation can be heard.

**decibels.** The loudness of sound expressed in numbers is called decibels.

**depth of field.** The focused area of a picture from front to back; the longer the depth of field, the more likelihood that the shot will be attractive and interesting.

**digital.** Information such as a sound or picture is stored by a computer device in combinations of digits or binary numbers, zeroes, and ones.

**digital camera.** A camera that digitizes the TV picture for still shots, motion shots, or animation.

**digital mixer.** A switcher with additional functions such as chroma key, fade, and still. A digital mixer works with a character generator to create titles that can be superimposed over a camera shot. Digital mixers often have four video inputs and one video output, and the picture is digitized when it enters the digital mixer.

**digital video.** This is a video image that does not have an analog video signal. Instead, the video signal comes from a binary form of computer bits. It can be added to a computer software presentation like PowerPoint.

**dimmer.** A device which controls the intensity of a light.

**display camera.** *See* **visual presenter.**

**dissolve.** A transition; the picture blends from one scene to another so that gradually more of the second scene is seen and less of the first scene is seen.

**dolly.** (1) a set of wheels a tripod and camera can be placed on allowing for easy movement; (2) a camera movement where the entire camera moves toward or away from a scene.

# Glossary continued

**DVD (digital versatile disc).** A CD-shaped piece of software that allows the user to play full-length movies on a computer's DVD drive.

**dynamic microphone.** A rugged and inexpensive microphone that is good for recording voices.

**edit controller.** A device which controls two VCRs, allowing more accurate editing.

**Eisenstein's Law.** A video and film production principle from the work of Russian film producer Sergei Eisenstein. The idea is that when two scenes follow one another, a third scene is created in the mind of the viewer. For example, if scene one is a close-up of a man gazing longingly and scene two is a medium shot of a beautiful woman, the viewer's mind will create an image of a man's romantic intentions.

**ENG camera.** Abbreviation for electronic news gathering camera, which is a type of camera used outside the TV studio for on-location shots. Today, in a typical school TV studio an ENG camera could also be a TV studio camera as long as it has a VIDEO OUT jack. In the 1970s and 1980s, different types of cameras were used for TV studio and on-location work, so then ENG would mean not for used in a studio multi camera set up.

**EP (Extended play).** The speed a VHS tape is recorded that has a poorer picture quality than SP speed. The advantage of EP is that three times as many minutes of TV programming can be fit on a videotape recorded at EP speed than one recorded at SP speed.

**establishing shot.** A long shot that establishes the scene. The establishing shot tells the audience where the action is taking place. Establishing shots are used at the beginning of a video production.

**exterior (EXT).** An abbreviation in scriptwriting for an exterior or outdoors shot. This abbreviation would appear in the visual section of the script.

**extreme close-up (ECU).** A camera shot in which the neck and face of a subject would be seen on camera.

**extreme long shot (ELS).** A camera shot in which the entire body of a subject would be seen on camera with plenty of room to spare between the top of the screen and the head and the bottom of the screen and the feet.

**eye level.** The correct position of the camera in terms of height when shooting takes place for most camera shots. It should be at the height of an average person's eyes when the person is standing. This makes the camera shot seem more real to the audience.

**feedback.** (1) when recording while a television receiver or monitor's volume is on, a distracting sound may be heard; to eliminate it, the sound must be turned down on the television receiver or monitor. (2) Feedback is also part of the communication process. It is the communication someone gives back to the person who previously sent the message.

**female.** A connector (plug) or jack that has a hole (receptacle) where the male prong from an audio or video connector will be inserted.

**FG (foreground).** An abbreviation in scriptwriting for the foreground area. This abbreviation would appear in the visual section of the script.

**fill lighting.** A type of lighting where a light source is used to soften the shadows created by the key light. It's on the opposite side of the talent from the key light at a 45° angle from the talent. Fill lighting uses a floodlight to soften the harsh lighting coming from the key light. Fill light is used in two- and three-point lighting.

**flat.** A background behind a talent in a newsroom or other TV production set. It is built with strips of lumber that make up a frame. Muslin cloth or canvas is attached to a frame. The flat is then painted.

# Glossary continued

**floodlight.** A soft, unfocused light source.

**floor director.** Checks with the talent to be sure their microphones are turned on. The floor director also checks the cue card scrolls to be sure they are accurate and makes sure the talent an pronounce all the words on the cue card scroll. The floor director helps the tech director and producer communicate to the talent, camera operators, lighting director, and cue card operators.

**floppy disk.** Often a 3 1/2" plastic disk that can be inserted into a computer; information can be saved and retrieved on these disks through the computer.

**florescent light.** An electric lighting source used in many buildings that creates a greenish tint when used in video production. It is the least desirable light source for video production.

**fluid head.** The top part of the tripod. Tripods of good quality have fluid heads. This means the tripod head is sealed with a thick, oily substance that makes smooth camera pans and tilts possible.

**font.** A style of lettering in computer graphics; usually in a computer word processing or presentation software program. Many font styles are available.

**font size.** Size of font in computer graphics; the higher the number, the larger the font.

**footage.** Videotaped scenes that have already been shot and that need to be edited into a video production.

**generation (editing).** In analog editing the first time a scene on a videotape is electronically copied in the editing process, it is called second generation. The next time that tape is electronically copied in the editing process, it is called third generation. By the time the third generation of editing takes place, the loss of picture quality is evident. With each new generation of editing, the video scene shows more deterioration of picture quality.

**gobo.** A prop in the foreground that gives the illusion of a specific location. Using a window frame as a gobo on a TV set gives the viewers the illusion that they are looking through a window into a house.

**graphic.** A picture or title in a video.

**handheld microphone.** A microphone that an announcer holds in the hand. A handheld microphone is good for use by an announcer on location, awkward for use in a multi microphone set up in a TV studio. For multi microphone use in a TV studio, lavaliere microphones are much more convenient.

**handheld shot.** A camera shot that is achieved without the help of a tripod. The correct approach for a handheld shot with a camcorder is to hold the camcorder on the shoulder with the side of the camcorder up against the cheekbone so the camera operator can watch the scene through the viewfinder.

**hard drive.** The place on a computer where information is stored.

**HDTV (high-definition television).** A system for a TV receiver or monitor allowing for twice as many lines of resolution on the TV screen as are currently used, making the TV picture much sharper.

**head end.** Receives television channels from a cable provider, and relays certain lower tier channels to classrooms. The head end also can relay programming originating in a school, such as a school TV news show, to the classrooms of that school.

**Hi 8 videos.** A type of videotape that does not lose picture quality when edited.

**hi-fi.** An audio track on a videotape that is additional to the regular audio track. On a video editor regular audio and hi-fi audio can be combined, resulting in audio with more volume.

# Glossary continued

**high angle shot.** A high camera angle that makes a subject seem smaller or weaker than in reality.

**high impedance microphone.** A microphone that has more electrical resistance than a low impedance microphone. The sound produced by a high impedance microphone is of less quality and volume than the sound produced by a low impedance microphone. Also, the cable for a high impedance microphone is usually shorter than the cable for a low impedance microphone.

**high level signals.** Audio signals carried by LINE or AUX cables, usually using RCA (phono) connectors. When the audio signal is copied in tape transferring, the type of signal is a high level signal.

**high-speed shutter.** A camera shutter that records faster than usual, capturing fast moving objects with high detail.

**hook.** The beginning part of a video script where the scriptwriter is attempting to capture the interest and attention of the audience.

**HyperStudio.** Multimedia presentation computer software. It is used mainly with Macintosh computers but is also available in the Windows format for use with IBM-compatible computers.

**imaging device.** The device in cameras that changes light into electrical signals.

**impedance.** The electrical resistance to microphones and microphone mixers; the lower the impedance, the higher the quality of the sound.

**incandescent light.** An electric light source coming from light bulbs that creates a reddish tint. This is a desirable light source for video production.

**in-school cable TV system.** A closed-circuit TV system that a school uses, which delivers a cable TV signal to each classroom; specific channels going to classrooms are selected at the head end.

**INT (interior).** An abbreviation in scriptwriting for an interior or indoor scene that would appear in the visual section of the script.

**internal synchronization.** The capacity of a switcher to accept video inputs from two or more cameras, VCRs, or other video devices and select any one of these inputs for use in a video production. A switcher or a/v digital mixer in a TV studio must have internal synchronization.

**Intranet.** An online system in a school where the audio and video of a school TV news show could be digitized in a file in the Intranet server computer so that it could be accessed by the teachers in each classroom simply by clicking on the file on their computer.

**iris.** *See* **automatic iris.**

**jack.** A hole (receptacle) on a piece of video, audio, or computer equipment. The prong of a video or audio connector fits into the jack. The jack is also known as a port when used on a computer. The jack accepts visual or audio electronic information going from one video, audio or computer device to another via a cable.

**jump cut.** When two scenes are very similar, shot from the same angle, and edited together, a jump or jerk can be seen from one scene to the next. This is bad editing form.

**Kelvin Scale.** A scale for measuring light. The symbol for the Kelvin Scale is K. 3200 K is the ideal amount of light for shooting video shots.

**key lighting.** A type of lighting where a spotlight source faces the talent. The key light is placed 45° above and 45° to one side of the talent. The key light is used in one-, two-, and three-point lighting. Because it is a spot light source, it creates harsh shadows.

# Glossary continued

**lavaliere microphone.** A very small microphone that clips on to a talent, often used in television studios.

**lens.** The glass front on a camera that receives and focuses light.

**lens aperture.** *See* **aperture.**

**lighting director.** Turns on the TV lights before each show and adjusts the lights to ensure that the talent is well lit.

**LINE IN.** The jack on a video device, audio device, or computer that accepts a sound source coming from a CD player, cassette player, VCR or audio mixer.

**long shot (LS).** A camera shot of a scene from a distance, not close-up. If the shot is of a human subject, the entire body would be seen. There would be little room from the top of the screen to the head and from the bottom of the screen to the feet.

**low.** A low camera angle makes a subject appear to be greater or larger than in reality.

**lower tier channels.** On in-school cable TV systems, these channels are often provided. Examples of lower tier channels are NBC and CBS.

**low impedance microphone.** A microphone that has less electrical resistance than a high impedance microphone. The sound produced by a low impedance microphone is of better quality and more volume than the sound produced by a high impedance microphone. Also, the cable for a low impedance microphone is usually longer than the cable for a high impedance microphone.

**low-level signals.** Used by microphones. The signal from a microphone running into a piece of video or audio equipment is a low level signal. This signal is carried on a microphone cable.

**macro.** A feature on a camera lens that allows for an extreme close-up shot of text or a picture from a book or other print source. Macro can also be used to magnify a very small object such as a ring or paper clip.

**male.** A connector or plug that has one or more prongs.

**medium close-up (MCU).** A camera shot that shows the entire head of a human subject and cuts off the human body at the chest.

**medium shot (MS).** A camera shot that shows the entire head of a human subject and cuts off the human body at the waist.

**MIC input.** The input jack on a video device, audio device, or computer that accepts a microphone.

**microphone cable.** The cable used for microphones. A low-level signal runs on a microphone cable.

**microphone jack.** A jack on a computer, VCR, camera, or mixer that accepts a microphone connector, mini plugs (1/8"), phone plugs (1/4"), or XLR plugs.

**mini plug.** A connector coming from an electronic device, also known as a 1/8" connector. Mini plugs are used with microphones, head sets, or LINE IN or LINE OUT cables.

**mosaic.** An effect that can be created using the a/v digital mixer. A person's face in a mosaic can be made unidentifiable. The mosaic effect is often used on crime TV shows where the true identity of a person needs to be hidden. The mosaic effect actually looks like a picture made out of mosaic tiles.

**multimedia.** Computer software and hardware used for presentations that makes use of text, audio, still, and motion images.

# Glossary continued

**natural lighting.** A light source that flatters skin tones.

**neutral density filter.** A piece of glass that screws on over the lens of a camcorder. It is used for outdoor shooting on bright sunny days. It filters out some of the sunlight so the colors in the videotape will be captured more accurately. Reds will look redder, blues more blue.

**non-linear.** A type of video editing in which scenes do not need to be edited in a certain order. Digital video editors are described as non-linear.

**NTSC (National Television System Committee).** NTSC is the video signal used in televisions, VCRs, and videotapes in the United States, Japan, and Canada.

**objective angle.** Used in a dramatic work. The shot is of the actor looking at the other actors, not the camera.

**oblique angle.** An off-balanced camera angle that creates a shot that is neither parallel or perpendicular to the horizon; often seen in modern productions, such as on MTV.

**omnidirectional microphone.** Absorbs sound from all sides.

**on location.** Anywhere other than a television studio where video production work involving a talent and a production crew takes place.

**over modulation.** A volume level for a microphone or other sound receiver that is too loud, causing a distortion of the sound.

**pan.** The horizontal movement of a camera that happens when the camera pivots on a shoulder or tripod.

**PAL (phase alteration line).** The video signal used in televisions, VCRs, and videotapes in many countries, especially in Europe.

**palmcorder.** A camcorder using a VHS-C, 8-mm, or High 8 format. A palmcorder can be held in the camera operator's hand while shooting. The palmcorder is smaller and lighter than a regular camcorder.

**parallel action.** A scene in which two views are seen, creating suspense. For example, the audience may see someone racing down a hall, and a bomb counter ticking away; the camera shots go back and forth until the scene resolves.

**parallel port.** A jack in a PC in which certain peripheral devices can be inserted, such as a printer, scanner, or video in device.

**pedestal.** The movement of the camera, usually on the tripod, where the position of the entire camera moves up or down. The pedestal knob on the tripod allows for the camera's up or down movement.

**peripheral device.** A device located outside of a computer, such as a printer, monitor, or scanner; these devices are connected by a cable.

**phone plug.** A connector coming from a microphone, head phone, or audio LINE IN or LINE OUT cable; also known as a 1/4" plug.

**phono (RCA) cable.** A cable used with audio and video equipment. The male plug on this cable has a metal post and flanges.

**picture area.** The part of the TV screen where the subject should be placed. It would not be near the edges of the TV screen. Some TVs will cut off what is on the edge of the TV camera's screen.

**pixel.** The digital equivalent of the light and dark dots on a photograph. These make up lines of resolution on a television or computer screen; the more lines of resolution, the sharper the video or computer image.

# Glossary continued

**plug.** The end of the cable that fits into a jack on a piece of video, audio, or computer equipment.

**point.** The size of type in computer text. For example, 28-point type is bigger than 24-point type.

**port.** A jack allowing for input or output of a signal. It is located on a computer; See also **jack**.

**PowerPoint.** Computer software for making presentations. It is used mainly with the Windows operating system on IBM-compatible computers but is also used with Macintosh computers.

**pressure-zone microphone.** Omnidirectional microphone placed in the center of a room; used to record a conversation between people.

**producer.** Oversees all aspects of the daily news show. The producer checks to be sure all the equipment is working and turned on and makes sure that each person is present and ready to perform their duties. If announcer or a camera operator fails to show up for a show, the producer needs to quickly find someone else to do that job.

**production crew.** Camera operator, tech director, audio director, and all the other people involved in producing the video production except the talent.

**RAM (random access memory)** Memory built into a computer.

**RCA cable.** *See* **phono (RCA)**.

**receptacle.** *See* **jack**.

**reflector.** A reflector is a large piece of white poster board, approximately 24" by 36." The reflector is used to reflect light back on to the subject's face. Some people like to wrap aluminum foil, dull side out, on the poster board for even more reflection. By adjusting the angle at which the reflector adjusts light from the light source, the shadows on the subject's face can be softened.

**resolution.** The ability of the TV monitor, TV receiver, or computer monitor to show fine detail on the screen; the finer the detail that can be shown, the greater the resolution.

**RF cable.** The cable connecting the RF connector to the RF jack on a TV receiver or VCR.

**RF connector.** Handles a signal that contains both audio and video coming from a specific television channel.

**RF jack.** A jack on a television or VCR that receives an RF signal from an RF connector.

**RF signal.** Radio frequency. This refers to the frequency of a signal that will supply sound and picture for a TV receiver.

**RF splitter.** A device that sends the RF signal to multiple RF jacks so a TV program coming from one source can be seen on more than one TV receiver.

**ROM (read only memory).** Read only memory built into a computer.

**rule of thirds.** A principle of picture composition. The idea is that the centers of interest in the picture are at the intersection of horizontal and vertical lines one third of the distance from the top, bottom, and sides of the TV screen. One use of this principle is in the placement of a human subject's eyes in a close-up shot. The eyes of the subject are often seen on a horizontal line one third of the distance from the top of the screen.

**scrim.** A metal screen placed in front of the light source that softens or shapes the light.

**sequential color and memory (SECAM).** A type of video signal used in many places outside of the U.S.

**segue.** A video production term to describe a transition from one scene to another.

# Glossary continued

**sequencing.** An element of scriptwriting emphasizing that the steps in a process or story should be shown in their proper order or sequence in the TV script.

**SFX (sound effects).** An abbreviation in scriptwriting for use of sound effects in a scene that appears in the audio section of a script.

**shotgun microphone.** A unidirectional microphone similar to a zoom microphone. It is used to pick sound in areas you can't go to. For example, you would use a shotgun mike to pick up the sounds a quarterback makes when calling out signals in a football game.

**simple TV studio.** A TV studio using one camera and one microphone.

**SLP (slow play).** A speed at which VHS tape is recorded. The disadvantage of SLP is that picture quality is worse when recording at SLP than at SP. Its advantage is that twice as much TV programming can be recorded on a VHS tape on the SLP speed than at the SP speed.

**snow.** What you see when you play back a videotape where nothing has been recorded. It looks like a snowstorm.

**SP (standard play).** The speed a VHS tape is recorded at that allows for the best recording quality. All video production work should be done at the SP speed.

**split screen.** An effect that can be created on the a/v digital mixer. On a split screen, the screen is divided into two parts. Part of the screen is coming from one camera. The rest of the screen is coming from a different camera.

**spotlight.** A hard, focused and direct light source.

**streaming.** The technology by which both the audio and video of a school TV news show can be digitized and distributed to all the computers in the school on an Intranet. This may be the way school TV news show will be delivered to classrooms in the future.

**strobe.** An effect that can be created by an a/v digital mixer. Some cameras can also render the strobe effect. The strobe effect breaks down an action shot of the camera into a series of still shots, each lasting about a second. This is a very eye catching effect and often works well with rhythmic music.

**subjective angle.** In this type of camera shot, the talent looks at the audience directly. A news reporter delivers the news at a subjective angle.

**superimpose.** A function on an a/v digital mixer in which you can see the image from one camera input clearly in the TV picture you are recording. At the same time you also see something else clearly in the picture such as a title graphic. It is as if one picture is laid on the other so both can be seen at once.

**surge protector.** A device that video, audio, and computer equipment plugs into. If a power surge or other problem with the AC electrical line occurs, the surge protector will protect your video, audio and computer equipment.

**S-VHS.** A videotape built in the same shape as a VHS videotape, allowing a somewhat higher TV picture quality.

**S VIDEO cable.** A cable that carries a video signal of higher quality than the video LINE cable. In the S Video cable, the video signal is separated into distinct elements.

**S VIDEO IN.** A jack in a computer that accepts a video signal from another device, such as a VCR 3or television monitor; handles a video signal of better quality than that of a phono (RCA) cable.

**S VIDEO OUT.** A jack on a computer, VCR, camera etc., where a video source is being produced from; handles a video signal of better quality than the signal coming through a phono (RCA) cable.

# Glossary continued

**switcher.** A device that allows the technical director to select between video inputs from television cameras, VCRs, and computers while doing a video production; the input that the operator selects is sent to the recorder VCR; switchers often have four video inputs and one video output.

**talent.** An announcer, actor, anchorperson.

**tech director.** Runs the a/v digital mixer or camera switcher, communicates with the camera operators from the control room over the head set system or with hand signals, coordinates videotaped and live segments of the show, records the entire program each day.

**tilt.** The vertical movement of camera pivoting on a shoulder or a tripod.

**transition.** A video scene that links two adjoining scenes; a digital video editor, computer video editing software program or an a/v digital mixer can render such scenes in the editing process. Examples of these scenes are fades and dissolves.

**tripod.** A mounting device for a camera that has three legs. The purpose of the tripod is to help the camera operator to achieve a steady camera shot.

**truck.** A camera movement usually done on a tripod with a dolly where the camera moves parallel to the scene it is shooting.

**TV monitor.** A television that picks up video and audio LINE inputs and may also pick up S VIDEO inputs.

**TV receiver.** A television that picks up TV channels via an RF signal coming from a VCR, an antenna, or a closed circuit or cable TV system.

**unidirectional microphone.** Picks up sound only from the front of the microphone.

**upper tier channels.** On in-school cable TV systems, these channels such as HBO are not provided due to excessive cost or adult content.

**VHS-C.** Abbreviation for video home system-compact.

**video card.** A device is inserted into the computer. It has video and audio inputs and outputs. It makes it possible to add NTSC video and audio signals to a computer presentation. It also allows the video and audio signal from a computer presentation to be converted to the NTSC video format so the presentation can be video recorded for playback on a TV/VCR.

**VIDEO IN.** The jack in a computer, VCR, camera, and TV monitor that accepts a video signal from another device.

**video insert.** The counterpart of audio dub; adding a new video image to go with existing sound. The old video image is erased.

**VIDEO LINE cable.** This cable carries a video signal from LINE outputs to LINE inputs on video and computer equipment. This type of cable carries a composite signal. There is no separation between the various elements of the video signal. The quality of the signal coming on a video LINE cable is inferior to the quality of the signal coming on an S VIDEO cable.

**VIDEO OUT.** The jack on a computer, VCR, camera, etc. where the video source is coming from.

**video projector.** Projects the image from a videotape onto a wall screen. By moving the projector back, the video image becomes larger. The video projector has a built in speaker or speaker attachment so the sound on the videotape can be heard.

**videotape camera operators.** Use the camcorder to record a videotape feature producer (announcer) doing a feature story. In most cases, these videotape features are interviews with students, teachers, or people in the community.

# Glossary continued

**videotape feature producers.** A typical news show is part live and part on videotape. The videotaped segments feature announcers that are often not the regular anchors. Some announcers do better when they can produce their segment on videotape. They have more time to practice and can tape their segment over again if they make mistakes.

**visual literacy.** The ability to understand visual messages and to create and send visual messages.

**visual presenter.** Also known as a display camera. This device is a TV camera mounted on a copy stand. It shoots downward into an area where an 8 1/2" x 11" piece of paper or book easily fits. This camera can zoom in or out to get a shot of the entire 8 1/2" x 11" page or any section of it. Excellent focus is maintained.

**voice-over (VO).** The talent's voice is heard but the talent is not seen in the picture. Voice-over can be achieved by an audio dub or by having the talent talk into the microphone while the camcorder operator videotapes with the talent out of the picture.

**VU meter.** Volume unit on an audio mixer.

**white balance.** To adjust the camera's color response to existing light; to do so hold a pure white piece of paper in front of the camera and press the white balance button; some cameras have different light settings, so be sure to use the correct one.

**wireless/RF microphone.** A microphone with no cable connected to it. It allows the talent freedom of movement. Problems with wireless/RF microphones are lengthy set up time and sound problems caused by fluorescent lights and high voltage electric systems.

**XLR cable.** A cable used to carry sound. It may run a high or low level audio signal.

**XLR (Cannon) jack.** A type of jack for audio inputs and outputs used only on certain audio mixers of better quality sound (low impedance); the jack may be either male (three prongs) or female (three holes).

**XLR (Cannon) plug.** A type of connector used only for microphone cable connectors, audio cable connectors, and audio mixer inputs and outputs of better quality sound (low impedance); the connector may be either male (three prongs) or female (three holes).

**zip disk.** A 3 1/2" disk that can be inserted into a computer. A great deal of text, sound, graphics, motion video, and/or still video can be saved and retrieved onto a zip disk. A zip disk is thicker than a floppy disk and can store either 100 or 500 MB of information. It requires a separate zip drive to operate on a computer.

**zoom in.** To make the lens appear to move closer to a subject.

**zoom microphone.** Absorbs sound from thirty feet away.

**zoom out.** To make the lens appear to be moving away from a subject.

# Index

acoustics 102
analog signal 58, 74-80
analog video editor 77
anchor desk 104
animation (video) 175-179
    drawings, cut outs and claymation 176, 177
    software 175
aspect ratio 16
audio dub 74, 77
audio equipment
    audio mixer 71
    a/v digital mixer 66-70
    high impedance microphone 97
    lavaliere microphone 100
    low impedance microphone 97
a/v (audio visual) digital mixer 66-70

backdrops 102, 103
backlight light function 41
battery, camcorder 35
BNC cable 29, 30
book talks (video), student-produced 159-162
bounce light 50
buying video production equipment 197-202

camcorder 34
    battery 35
    handheld 35
    iris 53
    lending policy 144
    palmcorder 44
    shutdown procedures 42
    S-VHS camcorder 44
Camera
    angles 11-12
    basic shots 13-15
    cutaway 16
    depth of field 13, 38-40
    ENG (electronic news gathering) 34
    illusion of reality 18
    iris 53
    lighting 18, 49-55
    movement 11, 17
    shooting at eye level 11
character generator 67
chroma key 66, 67, 103
closed circuit TV 87
communication theory
    communication 3
    feedback 4
    visual literacy 5

computers and video 57-64
    digital video editing (with computer) 83
contrast ratio 53
control room 98
copyright permission 183-186
    face-to-face instruction 185
    guidelines 184
    media festivals and cable TV 187, 188
    music and sound effects 184, 185
    other permission 186
    visual materials 185
cutaways 16

data or video projector 89, 90
depth of field 13, 38-40
digital 45
digital camera 45-47
digital video editing (with computer) 83
digital video editor (Casablanca) 81
digital video signal 58, 80-84
display function, camcorder 41
dolly 37
DVD 46

editing (video) 73-84
    audio dub 74, 77
    analog signal 58, 74-80
    digital video editing (with computer) 83
    digital video editor (Casablanca) 81
    edit controller 79, 80
    parallel action 17
    video insert 74, 77
Eisenstein's Law 17
ENG (electronic news gathering) camera 34
erasing videotapes, 41

floodlight 51-52
florescent light 51-52
funding 193-196

grants 193-196

HDTV 46
headsets 102
high-speed shutter 38

illusion of reality 18
incandescent light 51
instructional design 116, 117
    P.I.E. model 117
instructional value of video production 118, 119, 149-154

# Index continued

interview, shooting 36-37, 133
    positioning the interviewer and interviewee 37
intranet 105

Kelvin Scale 51

labeling tapes 41
lavaliere microphone 100
lettering style 10
lighting 49-55
    barn doors 51
    bounce light 50
    ontrast ratio 53
    dimmers 51
    floodlight 51-52
    florescent light 51
    incandescent light 51
    iris 53
    Kelvin Scale 51
    kits and lamps 50
    one-point key light 51
    reflector 50, 53
    shooting outdoors 53-55
    spotlight 51
    three-point key, fill and back light 52
    two-point key and fill light 52
    types of light 51-52

macro lens function 38, 99
media festivals 187-189
microphones
    high impedance 97
    lavaliere microphone 100
    low impedance 97
motion, camera 17

NTSC (National Television System Committee) 58

orientation video (library media center) 155-157

PAL (Phase Alteration Line) 58
palmcorder 44
plugs, jacks and cables, audio and video 27-31
    BNC 29, 30
    mini (1/8") 29, 30
    phone (1/4") 29, 30
    RCA (phono) 28-30
    RF (radio frequency) 28-30
    S-Video 28-30
    XLR or Cannon 28-30

presentation (video) 85-90
    closed circuit TV 87
    data or video projector 89, 90
    RF splitter 86
    trouble shooting 109-112
    TV receiver/monitor 88
purchasing video production equipment 197-202

reflector 50, 53
research skills (computer/video projects) 163-173
    learning outcomes 164
    partnerships with teachers 163
    group job assignments 166-171
    group structure 164
RF (radio frequency) cable 28-30
RF splitter 86
rule of thirds, 8,9

script sheet 18-20
scriptwriting
    aspect ratio 16
    Eisenstein's Law 17
    motion, camera 17
    rule of thirds 8-9
    script sheet, 18-20
    sequencing scenes 17
    storyboarding 23-24
    SWEET Method 21
    writing a script 8, 18-22
SECAM (Sequential Color and Memory) 58
sequencing scenes 17
shooting outdoors 53-55
special effects
    chroma key 66, 67
    dissolve 67
    fade 67
    mosaic 67
    split screen 67
    still 67
    strobe 67
    superimpose 67
    transition 81
    wipe 67
storyboarding 23-24
streaming technology 105
S-VHS camcorder 44
S-Video cable 28-30
SWEET Method, scriptwriting 21
switchers and mixers 66-71
    audio mixer 71
    a/v digital mixer 66-71
    character generator 67

# Index continued

talent 129-133
training students 125-128
transitions 15
tripod 36
    dolly 37
    pan 36
    tilt 38
    truck 37
trouble shooting (video production) 109-112
truck 37
TV news show (organizing) 135-147
    audience 135
    camcorder lending policy 144
    classroom hook up 143
    family permission to show students on TV 186
    instructional value 149-154
    scheduling 136, 137
    teacher partnerships 137
    video production club 136
    TV studio job descriptions 138-143
TV receiver/monitor 88
TV studio (school TV news show) 93-105
    acoustics 102
    anchor desk 104
    backdrops 102, 103
    control room 98
    headsets 102
    lavaliere microphone 100
    visual presenter 99

video (computer) card 57-64
videotape tabs, pulling 41
    visual design 8-18
VHS (video home system) videotapes 35
    EP, extended play speed 35
    SLP, slow play speed 35
    SP, standard play speed 35
    VHS-C (video home system, compact) 34
video equipment
    analog video editor 77
    a/v (audio visual) digital mixer 66-70
    camera 33-47
    character generator 67
    data or video projector 89, 90
    digital video editor (Casablanca) 81
    edit controller 79, 80
    input/output computer device 58
    plugs and jacks 28-31
    TV receiver/monitor 88
    visual presenter 99

video input/output computer device 58
video insert 74, 77
video production
    careers 191
    contests 187-189
    hall of fame 191, 192
visual design 8-18
    arrows 11
    basic camera shots 13-15
    camera angles 11-12
    camera movement 11
    cutaways 16
    depth of field 13, 38-40
    Eisenstein's Law 17
    elements, balance 10
    illusion of reality 18
    images, clearly visible 8
    lettering style 10
    lighting use 18
    motion 17
    parallel action 17
    rule of thirds 8-9
    sequencing 17
    shooting at eye level 11
    transitions 15
    visuals, complex 10
    visuals, consistent 11
    voice-over 16
visual presenter 99
voice-over 16

white balance 38

XLR (Cannon) cable or plug 28-30

zoom in 36
zoom out 36

www.ingramcontent.com/pod-product-compliance
Lightning Source LLC
Chambersburg PA
CBHW080410300426
44113CB00015B/2458